PAUL RENNER

DA

Christopher Burke

Paul Renner

the art of typography

Princeton Architectural Press
New York

Published by
Princeton Architectural Press
37 East Seventh Street
New York, NY 10003

Published concurrently in the United
Kingdom by Hyphen Press, London

Designed and typeset by the author using
QuarkXPress 3.31

Typefaces: FF Celeste, Celeste Footnote,
Bitstream Futura

Printed and bound in the Netherlands under
the direction of Drukkerij Rosbeek, Nuth

Library of Congress Cataloging-in-Publication
Data for this title available from the publisher

ISBN 1-56898-158-9

For a free catalog of books published by
Princeton Architectural Press, call toll free
1.800.722.6657 or visit www.papress.com

for my parents

Contents

Acknowledgements

This book has grown from postgraduate research done at
the Department of Typography & Graphic Communication,
University of Reading, England. My research was made
possible by financial support from the British Academy,
the University of Reading, and the Ernest Hoch Award of
the Department of Typography & Graphic Communication,
University of Reading.

I wish to thank those colleagues at the University of
Reading who helped me, either by useful discussion or
by reading drafts of my PhD thesis: in particular, Michael
Twyman, Gerard Unger, Ken Garland, Ole Lund, Markus
Rathgeb, Margaret M. Smith, and Paul Stiff.

I would also like to thank the following people (in no
particular order) for their assistance:
James Mosley, Nigel Roche and the staff at the St Bride Print-
ing Library, The staff of the National Art Library and the
British Library, David Knott and the staff at Reading Univer-
sity Library, Sylvia Langemann (Bayerische Akademie der
Schönen Künste), Walter Baum (the last artistic adviser to
the Bauer typefoundry), Paul Barnes, Jeremy Aynsley, Axel
Bertram, Hans Peter Willberg, Klimis Mastoridis, Giovanni
Lussu, Karel van der Waarde, Richard Hollis, Hans Dieter
Reichert, John L. Flood, Claus Gerhardt, Susanne Arnold,
Robert Harling, Fred Bauman (Library of Congress, Washing-
ton D.C.), Dr Phil. Korn (Bayerisches Hauptstaatsarchiv), Phil
Baines, John Dreyfus, Eckehart SchumacherGebler, Hermann
Staub (Börsenverein des Deutschen Buchhandels e.V.), Nicholas
Biddulph, Walter Tracy, Hermann Zapf, Gertraude Benöhr,
Max Caflisch, Nicholas Smith (Cambridge University Library),
Erik Spiekermann, N. Kaut (Gutenberg-Museum, Mainz), Ruari
McLean, Wolfgang A. Hartmann (Fundición Tipográfica Bauer,
S.A., Barcelona), Prof. Dr H. Wysling (Thomas-Mann-Archiv,
Zurich), Jost Hochuli, Yvonne Schwemer-Scheddin, Christian
Scheffler and the staff at the Klingspor-Museum (Offenbach),
Dr Claus Pese (Germanisches Nationalmuseum, Nuremberg),
Alan Shelley, Andrew Boag, Renate Flagmeier (Werkbund-
Archiv, Berlin), Antoinette Cherbuliez (Deutscher Werkbund
Bayern), Lawrence Wallis, Mathieu Lommen (Amsterdam
University Library), Andrew Cross, and Patricia Córdoba.

I owe special thanks to:
Lilo Tschichold-Link, Philipp & Renate Luidl, Walter Wilkes, Christine Renner, Bert A. Haushofer, and Martin & Renate Haushofer.

Gustav Stresow gave generous and expert advice that set me on the right track from the very beginning. His article on Futura (which he allowed me to read in typescript) and his comments on early drafts of chapters in this book have been essential to my work.

Finally, special thanks to Robin Kinross, who supported my work long before he became the editor and publisher of this book.

However, any errors that may remain are entirely the responsibility of the present author.

Translations, captions and references

All translations from German are by myself, unless otherwise indicated.

When the subject of an illustration is not credited, it is by Paul Renner. When a piece of writing is not credited in a footnote reference, it is by Paul Renner. References to Renner's writings are followed by a date-code in brackets, which refers to an entry in the list of Renner's published writings, given on pp. 207–13.

When a book is referred to, but not listed in the bibliography, its details are given in full on its first appearance in a footnote.

Type terminology

In this book 'gothic' is used to denote generically all styles
of 'broken script', which have sometimes been grouped under
the term 'blackletter'. 'Gothic' is not used here in the American
sense to mean sanserif. When discussing sanserif in a particularly German context, I have found it useful occasionally to
adopt the German term 'Grotesk', and I have anglicized it by
using it without an initial capital.

It may be helpful here to describe briefly the main styles
of gothic script & type that are referred to in this book.

Textura

Schrift/Schmuck und Bilder für kirchliche und weltliche   Liturgisch

Formal, northern European script adapted in the first printing types around the middle of the fifteenth century. Heavy,
narrow and spiky. All formerly curved elements are broken.
Stroke terminations are conventionally diamond-shaped.

Rotunda

Listeners seldom hear good of themselves   Wallau

Rounder, less pointed form originating from southern
Europe. More affinities with roman type.

Schwabacher

Da nichts war dañ schlachen vnd rauffen   Alte Schwabacher

Type style developed from vernacular bastarda script in
Germany *c*.1470–80. Wider and less broken than textura or
fraktur. Generally superseded by fraktur around the middle
of the sixteenth century, but revived in the late nineteenth
century.

Fraktur

Werbewoche der deutschen Bäder und Luftkurorte   Neue Luthersche Fraktur

Type style developed *c*.1513–22 from the formal Chancery
hand used in the court of Emperor Maximilian at Nuremberg.
Narrow and pointed, sometimes with curly flourishes, especially in the majuscules. The curves of minuscule o and d are
broken on one side and round on the other.

Preface

Many studies of the work of individual designers or artists
have the implicit goal of wanting to establish that individual's
reputation within a canon of exemplary work. I cannot deny
that this desire formed part of my original interest in Paul
Renner: I was hooked by the fact that he designed Futura, a
typeface which became a central feature of graphic design's
modernist heyday in the late 1920s and early 1930s, and
which is still widely used today. What kind of man, and what
kind of ideas, lay behind such an enduring creation? Before
embarking on my study of Renner, I had seen a copy of his
1922 book *Typografie als Kunst*, which was set in a gothic
type, in a staunchly traditional style. To my English eyes,
unschooled in the subtleties of gothic letterforms, this object
(figures 16–18) seemed to be cloaked in the mysteries of
German culture; it could not have been more different from
the simple, accessible and seemingly international appeal
of Futura. The surface qualities of these two indexes of Paul
Renner's design work seemed to speak from different cultures, and I was persuaded that I would find some contrasts,
or at least development, in his work. As I began my research
into Renner's typography, I became less interested in purely
visual matters, and more interested in the views that he
expressed in his prolific writings about the nature of modernity in design.

I will attempt to position Renner as a designer in his time
and place. I will concentrate as much on his words about
designing as on the artefacts of his design work. Although his
stated views or intentions may not always accord with his
practice, his words are valuable in themselves as attempts to
reflect on his profession and to interact with contemporary
discourses.

It would be wrong to assess Paul Renner's thoughts and
deeds as if weighing him up against an ideal modernist of
the Weimar period. Yet a notion of such an impossibly super-
human figure rested at the back of my mind as a yardstick
while researching Renner's work. What would this fictional
modernist designer be like? He would be a man (almost certainly); German, Russian, or from somewhere else in eastern
Europe; around thirty years old; trained as a fine artist, but

disdainful of bourgeois notions of art; a social democrat if
not a communist; a free thinker, who rejects the class distinctions and religious doctrine of the old order, and is excited by
the prospects of a new secular, technological world; he lives
and works in a modern metropolis; he goes to the movies
and listens to jazz, as well as being an avid reader. Measuring
Paul Renner against this fanciful figure, significant differences immediately become apparent: at the inception of the
Weimar Republic in 1919, Renner was already forty years
old; he thought of himself as unpolitical, and was rather sceptical about the value of technological innovations, including
moving pictures.

I want to dig deeper behind the myths of modernism
to discover some of the facts about individuals that are not
easily assimilated by such myths. One of my intentions is
to enrich the orthodox idea of modernist typography that
can be gained from existing historical accounts. Central to
this orthodoxy are certain individual designers (including
Jan Tschichold, Herbert Bayer and El Lissitzky), and a small
amount of work done at the Dessau Bauhaus, which has ✓
acquired a disproportionate aura of importance due to the
mythology that now surrounds that institution. G.W. Ovink
commented that New Typography 'was prompted by the
Bauhaus but particularly developed by the Meisterschule für
Deutschlands Buchdrucker' (Master School for Germany's
Printers, where Tschichold taught under the directorship of
Renner).[1] The Meisterschule is rarely mentioned in histories
of graphic design, and the ideas in Renner's books on typography have never been seriously discussed. Implicit in the
following study of Renner is the assertion that, in addition
to his successful typeface Futura, he made a significant contribution to modern typography through his writings and his
educational work in Munich.

This book is arranged chronologically: each chapter briefly
introduces general trends of the given period, followed by a
consideration of Renner's work in that period. Chapters four
and five present two phases of Renner's story in magnified
detail: the designing of his seminal typeface, Futura, and his
arrest by the Nazis.

A guiding interest has been my curiosity about the relative
differences between the terms 'modernism', 'modern', and
'modernity'. I have been careful in my use of the term 'modern-

1 G.W. Ovink, *Festrede* [for Georg
Trump] (Munich: Typographische
Gesellschaft München, 1982) p.16.

ism': I do not use it in the sense developed by American art historians (notably Clement Greenberg) after the Second World War – modernism as a self-reflexive, artistic practice. This notion of modernism from the second half of the twentieth century seems to have been applied retrospectively to movements in art and design from the first half of the century. Designers who worked between the wars in Germany did not talk of 'modernism'; there were many other '-isms' around, but the disciples of those movements did not consider themselves as members of an undifferentiated group of 'modernists'. Twentieth-century modernism is a post-mortem phenomenon, an inevitably selective historical construction, extrapolated from the statements made by its young gods of the 1920s. Perhaps the first implication that there was a coherent historical logic to modernism was made by Nikolaus Pevsner when he described the 'Modern Movement' in 1936.[2] I shall use the term 'modernism' not only in referring to the style that has become associated with inter-war design, but also to denote an ideological dimension: a belief in rational, scientific approaches to design (and life), which assume that humanity is inherently receptive to rationality. This overlaps with a notion of 'modernity' which stretches back to the Enlightenment.[3] I shall further attempt to disentangle these terminological strands in chapter seven.

2 Pevsner, *Pioneers of the modern movement* (1936); re-published as *Pioneers of modern design.*

3 The path of modernity in typography has been convincingly traced in Kinross, *Modern typography*, a book which has significantly influenced my thinking.

PAUL RENNER

1 Background

Paul Friedrich August Renner was born on 9 August 1878 in Wernigerode in the Harz region, a part of Saxony-Anhalt, which at that time fell within the kingdom of Prussia. (When filling out a *curriculum vitae* for a teaching post in 1925, he declared his nationality to be 'Prussian'.) His father was an evangelical theologian, who became court chaplain to the Earl of Stolberg in Wernigerode. Consequently, it is difficult to categorize Renner's class background; priesthood is a peculiarly classless occupation. However, his education places him amongst a cultured middle-class; he attended a *Gymnasium*, a secondary school where one studied the humanities. At the end of the nineteenth century the *Gymnasium* was a bastion of *Kultur*, a word which had more charge than its English equivalent. Fritz Stern has evocatively described this kind of institution in his influential study of Germanic intellectuals, *The politics of cultural despair*:

> Given its original impulse by Humboldt, the Gymnasium remained throughout a century of modernization the citadel of humanistic learning and of philosophical idealism. It was essentially a conservative force, controlled by anxious officials who feared that knowledge of social evils or politics would breed corruption and radicalism.[1]

Nine exacting years of studying Greek and Latin provided students with a ticket to higher education. Renner chose to study art after the *Gymnasium*, attending several academies, and finally completing his training in Munich in 1900. Stern has characterized a certain kind of German intellectual at the turn of the century, who was not part of any moneyed or landed aristocracy, yet maintained a sense of class superiority by virtue of the cultivated education received at *Gymnasium* and university. These institutions sought to prepare the 'universal man', not the 'public-minded citizen'.[2] This new breed of unpolitical, cultured intelligentsia was suspicious of industrialization and democratization (not to mention Marxism) as threats to culture. Indeed, they had nothing to trade on except their 'culture'. It is tempting to observe that Renner's decision to be a fine artist, an explorer of the spiritual dimension, was a natural course for him to take, given his background. Renner was aware of the intellectual stratum in German society later described by Stern, and that he was part of it, but, in the hopeful days of the Weimar era, he struggled to find a path forward from an empty idealism. Here is a pas-

1 Stern, *The politics of cultural despair*, pp. 270–1.
2 Stern, *The failure of illiberalism*, p. 8.

sage of remarkable and characteristic prescience from 1927, when Renner was fully engaged with modern typography:

> We children of the '80s received our first impressions from a fin-de-siècle atmosphere. We found ourselves placed into an artificial world that stood alongside the real one, yet had almost no relationship to it. The spiritual person [*geistige Mensch*] felt disgusted by all politics; machines, factories, economy, progress – these things he left to the Bourgeois. He lived as a bohemian in the cafés, as a hermit, or in esoteric circles. Yet, already before the turn of the century, a change was afoot in this disposition of retreat from the world. Whether Nietzsche was a symptom or a cause, I do not wish to examine here. The European intellect was permeated by a political activism, of a partly nationalistic, partly revolutionary colour. ... After the war and the revolution the intellectual then had to spring into the vacuum created by the decline of the old world. Meanwhile, however, the new sense of form [*Formgefühl*] had acquired a power, which demanded to be heeded in the construction of the new world.[3]

As one of the intellectuals he referred to here, Renner sought to influence culture by designing, writing and teaching. He wanted to use his aesthetic and intellectual skills to help in shaping the new life – in both its material and spiritual forms. The *Formgefühl* he spoke of was not a trivial modish thing, but an outward sign of the new social relationships that arose after the First World War. Instead of earning a living by easel painting, Renner spent most of his life in 'applied art', trying to bring high cultural standards to material objects for use – typefaces and books. On this matter, he preached to his students a recommendation from Goethe, whom he regarded as the prototypical modern person: 'we should direct our view outwards, away from ourselves, into the world, not into the distance, but onto those things that are near, within a hand's reach'.[4]

♦ Renner always read widely, and was acquainted with the works of the great figures in German philosophy and literature (Kant, Goethe, Schiller, Nietzsche). He made a thorough study of philosophy and its methods.[5] Moreover, from 1908 ♦ onwards, he wrote extensively about typography and design. This occupation with crafting the sense of words seems a natural accompaniment to a concern for their visual form. Heinz Haushofer, Renner's son-in-law, commented: 'A day when he did nothing, at least read nothing serious, was for him a day sadly lost.'[6]

3 'Die Schrift unserer Zeit' (1927g) p. 110.

4 Goethe summarized by Renner in 'Die erste Diplomverteilung an unserer Meisterschule' (1932a) p. 38.

5 Heinz Haushofer, 'Paul Renner: ein Eindruck' in Luidl & Lange (ed.), *Paul Renner*, p. 13. Between 1914 and 1919 Renner taught at the Münchner Lehrwerkstätten with Hans Cornelius, a philosopher and art historian. As a teacher of philosophy in the early 1920s, Cornelius was a formative influence on Max Horkheimer, who led the Frankfurt Institute for Social Research. In responding to a letter in which Renner had dubbed himself a 'philosophical dilettante', Cornelius commented that Renner did himself an injustice by referring to himself in this way. (Letter from Cornelius to Renner, 14 January 1943; Nachlaß Renner.)

6 Haushofer, 'Paul Renner: ein Eindruck', p. 13. Details of Renner's family background are mostly taken from this essay. Bert A. Haushofer (1932–), Renner's grandson, remembers that, during stays at his grandfather's house as a young boy, Renner could not bear to see him idle: if he was, Renner would make him do some kind of 'geistige Arbeit' (spiritual work), like pumping water. (Conversation with Bert A. Haushofer, 13 May 1992.)

Renner was one of five sons. According to other family members, his upbringing as the son of a priest left him with an enduringly strict Christian ethic, in thought and work. Renner himself reflected in later years on the legacy of his childhood:

> I grew up in an evangelical vicarage. In many respects this was fortunate; in many other respects, my children had it better than me, in that they were brought up by a Catholic mother, or at least had the support of this mother against my attempts at rearing them. For Protestantism considers all people as one single being burdened with original sin and therefore in pressing need of redemption. The consequence of this in bringing up children is that one takes their foolishness far too seriously and attempts to scrub their little souls clean far too severely; so the bloom of uninhibitedness and security is wholly destroyed. If, in addition, the mother dies early, as happened in our family, then there is a lack of all the natural, matriarchal openness and tolerance that could counteract the strict, impatient patriarchal disposition. It is no wonder that children who grow up like this often achieve an uncommon amount as adults. For their elasticity is subjected at an early stage to a hard test and, if they are not broken by this, they will retain a strong inner tension into their old age. They do not make it easy on themselves, nor on others.[7]

Indeed Renner displayed this inner tension throughout his working life: he always had a sense for balancing opposites. While his younger colleagues in typography were writing manifestos in the 1920s, Renner was treading more carefully, alluding to Eastern philosophy in his writings. Similarly he resisted the polarization of political ideologies in Weimar Germany, and tried to select the most reasonable elements from both right and left. Renner was a middle-German in southernmost Germany; a Protestant Prussian in predominantly Catholic Bavaria, a region in which many native inhabitants felt a firmly rooted antipathy towards Prussians. He cut an ascetic figure as the principal of the Meisterschule in Munich (which he led between 1926 and 1933), but rejoiced in the vigorous ambience of that city, which was a traditional centre for German art: 'the hundred-kilometre-high southern sky, the thin, sharp air, ... a cheerful, southern way of living completely in the here and now'.[8] He had first settled in Munich at the turn of the century as a young painter and remained in its locality for most of his life.[9]

7 'Aforismen' (1946a) pp. 173–4.

8 From a brief contribution to a survey of the virtues of Munich, in the typographic periodical, *Der Zwiebelfisch* (1926a) p. 38.

9 A story about Renner told by his former colleague Georg Trump suggests that Renner was sensitive to the different 'nationalities' within Germany. Renner was surprised one day to see Edith Tschichold wandering the corridors in the Meisterschule; he joked: 'What are you doing here – one Saxon is enough!' (The Saxon Renner was referring to was Jan Tschichold, husband of Edith. Story related by Philipp Luidl, in a letter to me, 26 June 1995.)

A tension between tradition and modernity was integral to two twentieth-century debates in German design. The first was the question of style in typography. German-speaking countries were unique in still using gothic letterforms during the first half of the twentieth century. Gothic type became enmeshed in nostalgic notions of German culture during the protracted conservative reaction that crystallized radically with Hitler's accession to power. The relative virtues of gothic and roman type in a German context were the subject of much discussion during this time, and Renner had strong views on this matter, which will be examined in chapter four.

The second and more widespread debate was the *Streit um die Technik* (the debate on technology), a slow-burning dispute between conservative and modernizing elements in German society. In this debate, 'craft' and 'the machine' were pitted against each other as abstract symbols of the conservative and modern viewpoints respectively. Renner and his fellow members of the Deutscher Werkbund (the principal organization seeking to reform German design) were fully engaged in the *Streit um die Technik*. Initially Renner tended towards the conservative side in this debate, but his thinking and activity markedly shifted in the mid 1920s towards a conscious concern with modernity. During this period Renner attempted to resolve a style that suited Germany in the 1920s, a locus of economic rationalization and revolutionary social change. By this time in central Europe, technology had begun to transform the media of entertainment and communication: cinema, public radio broadcasting, and sound recording were in their first phases of development; and Logie Baird would soon demonstrate the first television in 1926. It seemed that science had begun to conquer the darkest corners of life: Freud had even tried to make human sexuality into a subject of science. Albert Einstein, whilst positing a theory of the universe's instability, had become a household name for having tried to extend the domain of rationality beyond perception. The work of young designers of the 1920s seems to be permeated by these developments.[10] Renner too felt the progressive urges of his time: he observed that the discovery of the powered press, the railway, and electric news transmission had encouraged the creation of 'a public forum for our political-social life unforeseen in any utopian novel; not a public sphere operating from eye to eye, or mouth to

10 As some index of this, Einstein was a member of the organization called 'Friends of the Bauhaus'.

PAUL RENNER

ear, but in a spiritual dimension overspilling every temporal and spatial barrier'.[11] However, Renner was reluctant to jettison all the old values of the humanist culture in which he had grown up.

11 *Kulturbolschewismus?* (1932) p. 43.

2 **Rejuvenation** 1900–24

The beginnings of cultural rejuvenation

Since the unification of the German *Länder* under Bismarck
in 1871, Germany had been undergoing intense and radical
industrialization, within a much shorter span of time than
Britain had. The Industrial Revolution in Britain had begun
a century earlier: William Morris's craft revivalism at the end
of the nineteenth century was therefore a reaction to a well-
established, industrial-capitalist culture. During the period
from 1870 to 1900 Germany's social structure was completely
transformed. Large numbers of the rural population surged
towards the newly-industrialized cities; only fifty years before,
Germany's disparate regions had depended mostly on agricul-
ture and were under the rule of local monarchs or aristocrats.
Rapid technological advances fed the development of mechanized industries, and the consequent surge in production was
accompanied by an intensification in division of labour.

In Germany, as in Britain, the industrial way of life encouraged among a cultural elite a perception of 'art' as the spiritual
realm, where all the fine values and feelings excluded by
everyday labour resided. This notion of 'fine art' (*bildende
Kunst*) fuelled the development of the art academies in the
nineteenth century. These academies took a decorative view
of art, in which 'design' simply meant draftsmanship. Walter
Gropius, the founder of the Bauhaus, later reflected on the
situation that existed before the First World War: 'The artist
was a man "remote from the world", at once too impractical
and too unfamiliar with technical requirements to be able
to assimilate his conceptions of form to the process of manufacture.'[1] Artists were partially re-integrated into production
before the First World War by 'applying' art to mass-produced
goods.

The German Werkbund

The Deutscher Werkbund was founded in 1907 by a group of
politicians, artists and industrialists in order to foster 'quality'
in production. Paul Renner became a member in 1910, and
was actively involved in the organization's running debates
on the place of art in society, and on the relative merits of
handcraft and machine production. Part of the impetus for
the Werkbund stemmed from a craving among intellectuals

1 Gropius, *The new architecture and
the Bauhaus*, p. 3.

for *Kultur* – a culture unique to Germany, which would convey its strength to the world.

Germany's unresolved 1848 revolutions had given way later in the century to Bismarck's militaristic regime, which preserved the power of land-owning families and expressed itself with bullish, national pride. Germany's status as an emerging world-power was limited by its lack of colonies and consequent lack of mineral resources. Conservative elements of society (including the Werkbund) held the new form of urban life and the demands of big business to be responsible for a general drop in the quality of work, goods, and, by extension, life in general. It is no surprise that one of the driving forces behind the foundation of the Werkbund, the architect Hermann Muthesius, had studied the influence of the Arts and Crafts movement in Britain while serving as architectural attaché to the German Embassy in London from 1896 to 1903. However, what distinguished the Werkbund from the Arts and Crafts movement was its alliance with industry and organized politics. The Werkbund sought to develop a prestigious export industry, fuelled by the collaboration of artists and industrialists. Friedrich Naumann, leader of the short-lived National Social Party (1896–1903), and the holder of a seat in the Reichstag in 1907, helped to develop the structure of the Werkbund, along with his cohorts, Karl Schmidt, a carpenter-turned-entrepreneur from Dresden, and the industrialist Peter Bruckmann. The Werkbund, then, was a peculiar experiment, in that art and design were seen as the means to achieve economic and political goals.

Muthesius believed that the necessary reforms would only be made possible by appealing to the bourgeoisie, by convincing them that 'taste' was necessary. 'Quality' became a catchword for the Werkbund and, in its essential vagueness, was symptomatic of the organization's dilemma: whether to concentrate on the visual style of objects, or on methods of work. The elusiveness of 'quality' as a goal concealed a reluctance to advocate a certain style, but also implied a deeper desire to improve the quality of life. 'Quality', here, can be interpreted as the mystical quality of German-ness that had been lost somewhere in the transition to the twentieth century. It followed naturally that the Werkbund soon became embroiled in a debate about the role of the worker in production, particularly during and immediately after the First World War.

PAUL RENNER

Germany's lingering craft tradition became a recurrent motif in this debate. The guild system of craft production had survived in Germany until the middle of the nineteenth century, although, by this time, a factory system of production had largely usurped its market. By 1850, the system of master craftsmen and apprentices had ceased to exist in its old form, and craft guilds no longer sold goods directly to the public; people had begun to shop in department stores. Journeymen were forced into factory jobs, although the remaining proprietors of craft businesses maintained their middle-class status: indeed a large proportion of the *Kleinbürger* (lower-middle-class) who participated in the 1848 uprisings in Germany were artisans. They became one of the most conservative and reactionary forces in Germany, often displaying their discontent with the rising industrialism of Bismarck's Germany.[2]

The Werkbund intellectuals inherited this critical view of Imperial Germany, without the affiliation to a craft tradition. They saw the answer to the call for good design in the independent artist.

The German cult of the book

Books were part of the applied artist's repertoire. Artists such as Henry van de Velde, Melchior Lechter and Otto Eckmann brought into books the sinewy, organic lines of *Jugendstil* (the Central European variety of Art Nouveau). These artists were concerned primarily with illustration and ornament, not with the details of text composition. The decorative aspect of designing books became known as *Buchkunst* (book-art), as distinct from trade work featuring no intervention by a named artist.

Several journals dealing with the arts were founded in the 1890s: *Pan* (1895–1900), *Die Insel* (1899–1902) and *Jugend* (1896–1940). In their subject matter and in their vaguely classicist typography, these publications exemplified a desire to reclaim an elusive set of values, which had somehow been eroded by the march of modernization. The rallying call for such thinking was the name of Friedrich Nietzsche, who epitomized what Fritz Stern has called 'cultural despair'.[3] Nietzsche diagnosed an over-intellectual decadence in late nineteenth-century Germany, to which his answer was a retreat into wilful individualism. Many disparate groups looked to Nietzsche

2 Holborn, *A history of modern Germany*, pp. 5–17.

3 Stern, in *The politics of cultural despair* (p. 283), commented: 'There was no academic exegesis of Nietzsche in pre-war Germany; everybody had his own sense of "what Nietzsche really meant".'

for spiritual leadership, not least those *Buchkünstler* (book-artists) intent on reviving books with 'art'.[4]

In late nineteenth-century Germany, mechanization had taken hold of the production of books for widespread publication, and had helped to create a thriving newspaper industry. Voices from the more exclusive areas of publishing in the early twentieth century expressed a desire for books of material quality, in order to maintain a literary culture that was disappearing fast. This was more than being a 'book lover' – it verged on a worship of the book for its object qualities instead of its literary content. Hans Loubier, a prolific writer on the book trade, argued for the potential of beautiful books in educating the public's taste. He invoked the image of a lone figure sitting quietly with a book at the end of the day, providing solace from the 'combative politics' of the newspaper and enabling the reader (or owner) to forget, for a few hours, the 'horrible present'.[5]

The revival of quality in book design that accompanied German bibliophilia around the First World War was a minority initiative. An introductory editorial in the first issue of the bibliophile journal, *Die Bücherstube,* proclaimed that 'The plan for this publication arose in the circle of several serious friends of the book, who were in the habit of gathering in a bookshop [*Bücherstube*] to talk about books and related matters'.[6] In the pages of this periodical, books were mostly noted for their illustrations, which were the most obvious evidence of an artist's involvement.

Yet there was a stronger utilitarian tendency within the bibliophile culture of Germany than there was in England. Germany had its private presses, although there were not so many of them. Carl Ernst Poeschel and Walter Tiemann's Janus Presse only produced sporadic output in between its owners' respective trades – business and teaching; F.H. Ehmcke's Rupprecht Presse also did not produce many books, as Ehmcke was busy teaching and designing typefaces & books commercially; Rudolf Koch and Rudolf Gerstung's Rudolfinische Drucke used the autonomy of a private press to produce some hand-lettered books. The Ernst Ludwig Presse in Darmstadt, run by the Kleukens brothers, was truly independent and unfettered by economic constraints, due to its ducal patronage. The most renowned German private press, Willi Wiegand's Bremer Presse, was also a peculiar case. In addition to produc-

4 Throughout its five-year run, *Pan* contained several articles on Nietzsche. Jhg 5, Heft 2 (1899/1900) contained an essay by Elizabeth Nietzsche, the philosopher's sister, who was largely responsible for popularizing (and distorting) her brother's thinking after his death.

5 Hans Loubier, 'Die Berechtigung des schönen Buches in der Gegenwart', *Die Bücherstube* (Jhg 1, 1920) p. 144.

6 *Die Bücherstube* (Jhg 1, 1920) p. 1. There was a bookshop called Die Bücherstube in Munich run by Horst Stobbe, who was a sometime editor of the periodical. *Stube* is untranslatable, literally meaning a room, but having the colloquial connotation of *Bierstube*, equivalent to an English public house.

ing luxurious, yet austere, limited editions, the Bremer Presse produced a series of cheap books printed on a powered press, which benefited from the experience gained in its handpress editions. Both kinds of Bremer-Presse book featured type cut especially for the Presse by Louis Hoell at the Bauer type-foundry.[7]

Rather than constituting an escape from a well-established industrial culture, as in England, private presses in Germany seemed to exist more harmoniously with industry and provided an interchange of ideas and personnel. This is perhaps to be expected, given that the novelty of industrial production was such a defining aspect of the early years of Germany's twentieth century. In 1911, Paul Renner himself discussed the setting up of a private press with Emil Preetorius, a Munich illustrator, and Kurt Wolff, later the publisher of Kafka and expressionist writers. But this came to nothing.[8]

Renner's entry into Buchkunst

In Winter 1897 Renner enrolled at the Berlin Academy of Fine Arts, transferring to the academy at Karlsruhe in late 1898. He transferred again in November 1899 to the art academy in Munich to complete his training in fine art. From 1900 he made a living as a painter in Munich, also contributing some landscape vignettes to the Munich-based satirical magazine, *Simplizissimus*. After marrying in 1904 and spending a year travelling in Italy with his wife Annie, Renner settled in Schleißheim, Munich. From 1906, as a twenty-seven-year-old student, he spent a year at the Debschitz Schule in Munich, a pioneering school of applied art founded in 1902 by Wilhelm von Debschitz and Hermann Obrist. Here students learned in workshops to design for manufacture. One of the specialized areas of study was *Graphik* – a subject area described as 'drawing, illustration, graphic art for printing [*Druckgraphik*], book-decoration and typography'.[9]

Having completed his study, Renner continued to make a living as a fine artist: he first exhibited a painting in 1907 at Munich's Glaspalast, which, until it burned down in 1931, housed the most important annual exhibition of art in southern Germany. Renner was inspired at this time by the speeches at the inaugural meeting of the Deutscher Werkbund.[10] Fritz Schumacher's keynote speech at this meeting, held in Munich in October 1907, set out the enduring principles of the Werk-

7 See Burke, 'Luxury and austerity: Willy Wiegand and the Bremer Presse', *Typography papers* (2, 1997) pp. 105–28.

8 'Münchener Typographie' (1920b) p. 116.

9 Wingler (ed.), *Kunstschulreform*, p. 77; see also Beate Ziegert, 'The Debschitz School, Munich: 1902–1914', *Design issues* (vol. 3, no. 1) pp. 28–42.

10 Renner, 'Interview mit Paul Renner', p. 7.

1 Poster for an exhibition of Georg-Müller-Verlag books at a Munich bookshop. Probably before 1917. (Credited to Renner in *Gebrauchsgraphik*, Jhg 3, Heft 1, 1926.)

2 Handwritten title page for Georg Müller Verlag's 1908 catalogue. 205 × 148 mm.

bund, which Renner strongly supported for the rest of his life: Schumacher stressed the need to reconcile art and mass production, and to reawaken the creative interest of the worker in order to achieve quality, both in life and work.[11]

Renner's activity in the field of book-art was exactly the kind of applied art that the Werkbund proposed. Also, as a married man with one child (Luise, born 1906), Renner may have welcomed the prospect of earning some extra money to supplement his income as a painter. He was taken to meet the publisher Georg Müller by a mutual acquaintance in late autumn 1907. Müller gave Renner a strip of cardboard corresponding to the spine of a new book, and asked him to make a design for it, without any further explanation. Soon, Renner was inundated with commissions from Müller.[12]

Georg Müller pursued a catholic publishing programme: although he issued the mandatory German classics (Goethe, Schiller, Hölderlin), his list also included a series called *Perlen der romanischen Prosa* (pearls of prose in the Romance languages), which included French, Italian and Spanish literature (figure 3). Georg Müller Verlag also issued a periodical called *Die Münchner Blätter* (Munich Bulletin), which included texts by D'Annunzio, Rimbaud and Baudelaire.[13] As Renner was concerned to find typefaces appropriate to texts, this programme gave him more reason to use roman typefaces (as opposed to gothic) than if he had been working for other publishers.

Gothic type (of the fraktur variety) was standard for German books of literature in the first decades of the twentieth century, and to many it was an unquestionable part of German culture. In 1920, the printing trade periodical *Archiv für Buchgewerbe und Gebrauchsgraphik* asked the opinions of type- & book-artists about the prospect of phasing out fraktur, in order to get the 'aesthetic' view of this matter.[14] Among those questioned (in addition to Renner) were the type designers, F.H. Ehmcke and Rudolf Koch, who both dismissed the suggestion as an attack on tradition. Renner did not consider the gothic/roman dilemma as an either/or choice

11 See the quotation from Schumacher's speech in Deutscher Werkbund, *Die Zwanziger Jahre des Deutschen Werkbunds*, p. 9.

12 'Erinnerungen aus meiner Georg-Müller-Zeit' (1939b) pp. [1–2].

13 *Nachricht vom Georg Müller Verlag an seine Freunde und Leser* (catalogue, 1920).

14 'Der Künstler zur Rechtschreibungsreform' (1920a) pp. 97–104. This question formed part of a threefold questionnaire concerning suggestions made by the

Bund der Deutschen Schrift (Association of German script): to restrict capitals to proper nouns and sentence beginnings; to adopt phonetic spelling; and to phase out fraktur (see chapter four for discussion of the orthographic issues).

3 Title page from an edition in the Georg-Müller-Verlag series 'Pearls of prose in the Romance languages'. 1910. 245 × 180 mm.

4 Title page for a German translation of Boccaccio. 1912–13. 201 × 124 mm.

at this stage. However, he did complain that the capital letter-forms in fraktur were simply decorative monstrosities. Renner was the only respondent in this survey to discuss roman and fraktur as if they both deserved attention; this is echoed by an equal use of both type-styles in his typographic design before 1920.

As Müller steadily increased his output of books, Renner's work for the publisher began to occupy all of his time. His studio, which he had rented for painting, filled up with designs and proof-sheets. Müller never had time for calm discussion during the week, so Renner often visited him on Sundays. In 1913, the 287 new editions and new titles issued by Georg Müller Verlag were handled at the publishing end by Müller and Renner alone. Renner found that checking with Müller before every decision became impractical, so he had to take responsibility himself: he decided that 'it was no longer possible without my own telephone', and he had one installed.[15] His first long-distance call was to the book-binding firm of Hübel & Denck in Leipzig, of which Müller was a major client.

15 'Erinnerungen aus meiner Georg-Müller-Zeit' (1939b) p. 2.

5 Hand-produced bindings for Georg-Müller-Verlag books.

6 Signets for R. Piper & Co.

16 'Vom Georg-Müller-Buch bis zur Futura und Meisterschule' (1939d) p. 1.

Renner worked for several German publishers in addition to Georg Müller between 1907 and 1917, including R. Piper & Co. (figure 6) and Delphin Verlag, but Müller became protective of Renner's skills, and eventually made him sign an exclusive contract with Georg Müller Verlag in 1917, shortly before the publisher's death.[16]

A fashion for bibliophile collecting thrived before the First World War in Germany, epitomized by the leather- or half-leather-bound editions of a single author's collected works. It is significant that Müller initially viewed Renner's involvement in terms of decorating the leather binding of a book (and the spine in particular). Renner used a repertoire of light decorative lines on a darker ground for designing such bindings. In his early years of designing books, he considered hand-crafted leather bindings, made for luxury editions of between ten and a hundred copies, as the ideal (figure 5). Later he came to pragmatically accept the 'publisher's binding' as the necessary standard (see below: p. 34 and figure 13).

The German culture of the beautiful book culminated in the *Internationale Ausstellung für Buchgewerbe und Graphik* (Bugra) held in Leipzig just before the outbreak of war in

PAUL RENNER

1914. A selection of Georg Müller Verlag books was exhibited there and Renner was awarded the grand prize for his work.[17]

'Book architecture'

Renner was not satisfied with merely designing bindings: he was a bookish man and felt a responsibility towards the visual form of words. He became responsible for controlling the typographic layout of all Müller's books, the very task that many book-artists did not address.[18] Renner also illustrated some books (figures 7–8), but he regarded this as a separate activity. He argued that the artistic value of an illustration is not the concern of the typographer, who must harmonize the 'decorative' value of the illustration with the typographic elements. In his view, this was best achieved by printing the illustrations together with the type in letterpress, using wood- or metal-engravings (or electrotype versions of them). Renner concurred with the principles of harmonious form espoused by Emery Walker and William Morris in the 1880s and 1890s: a basic tenet of Morris's private-press work was to print type and illustrations together by the same technique, thereby achieving a likeness of graphic effect.[19] Renner's opinion about reprographic processes was as puritanical as that of Morris in requiring that the integrity of handcraft was maintained. Renner rejected the photographic reduction of a drawing or woodcut, as this distorted the *Handschrift* (visible trace of the hand) of the artist, creating an effect of false contrast. In his view, only those who could draw specifically for this process, like Aubrey Beardsley, produced satisfactory work.[20]

7 Illustration for *Die fünfundsiebzig italienischen Künstlernovellen der Renaissance* (Georg Müller). 1911.

8 Lithograph for Matteo Bandello, *Novellen* (Georg Müller). 1920.

17 See *Internationale Ausstellung für Buchgewerbe und Graphik Leipzig 1914*, Amtlicher Katalog, p. 317; Renner's winning of the grand prize is mentioned in *Typographische Mitteilungen* (Heft 1, 1915) p. 11.

18 The tasks of a book-artist were ill-defined. Leitmeier, in 'Das deutsche illustrierte Buch unserer Zeit' (p. 131), gave a definition in 1927: 'With the term *Buchkünstler* we define here only the artists who supervise the printing [*Drucklegung*], who choose the type, who design the title page, the initials, the borders, vignettes, and the binding; they prepare everything that we usually call book-decoration [*Buchschmuck*], but do not furnish the book with self-contained pictures. These latter we will call illustrators.' Leitmeier named as book-artists: E.R. Weiss, Walter Tiemann, Rudolf Koch, F.H. Ehmcke, Melchior Lechter, Anna Simons, the Kleukens brothers, Paul Renner, and F.H. Ernst Schneidler. He stated that the categories sometimes overlapped and indeed named Renner in his list of illustrators too. The task of combining text and pictures, he asserted, was that of the *Typograph* (typographer).

19 This principle can be traced back to Emery Walker's influential lecture of 1888. See Dreyfus, 'A reconstruction of the lecture given by Emery Walker...', p. 47.

20 *Typografie als Kunst* (1922a) pp. 89–91. Renner's earliest article on typography – 'Paul Renner über Buchausstattung' (1908) – bore the puritanical traces of the Arts and Crafts movement, explicitly citing Ruskin as an influence.

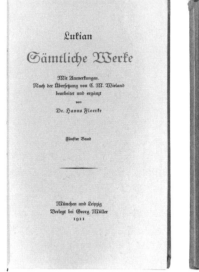

9 (above) Title page for the collected writings of Lucian, in Georg Müller Verlag's series 'Classics of antiquity'. 1911. 218 × 136 mm. All type black except for title in red.

10 (above right) Pages from the book in figure 9.

11 Detail of p.198 from book illustrated above (same-size). Shows use of letterspacing for the character names in drama setting with gothic type, which traditionally has no italic, or small capitals. The typeface is Unger-Fraktur.

For Renner, an illustration was a 'foreign body of fatal danger to the existence of the book' and only the most compact use of typographic elements could preserve the unity of the whole.[21] Already in 1912, it became clear that he regarded the unity of the double-page spread as the overriding, governing principle of book design. In his view, the impression of a double-page spread was dictated by the form of its smallest units, the individual letters, as it had been in handwritten books. He commented that book design had often been likened to architecture, and he seemed to agree, adding that typesetting must be regular in texture, like a well-constructed brick wall.[22] In these matters, Renner's attachment to the ideas of the British private-press movement was clear: indeed he cited as models 'all good books of the fifteenth century and those of the famous English presses', which were praiseworthy for their 'regular, tight typesetting'.[23] In 1912, he summarized his general principles (which seem implicitly to deal with roman typography):

> Regular, tight typesetting (with narrow word-spaces), without spaces after full-points that are larger than those between words; where possible avoidance of letter-spaced words (except perhaps

21 'Das moderne Holzschnittbuch' (1924d) p.239.
22 'Die Kunst im Buchgewerbe' (1912) p.158. Compare Emery Walker and William Morris, 'Printing', p.125, where the metaphor of tightly interleaved bricks is used explicitly.

23 'Die Kunst im Buchgewerbe' (1912) p.158. Strangely, Renner commented that there is a disparity between the aesthetic unity of the page set with narrow wordspaces and the requirements of legibility, which he seemed to imply needs wider spacing.

PAUL RENNER

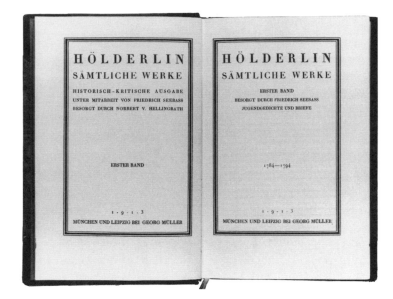

in capital setting); puritanical simplicity: these are, in brief, the demands according to our conception. ... The art of printing is a public-spirited affair;[24] proud resignation, as expressed in modern English hand-press printing, is a better clothing than carefree self-centredness that seeks to make itself seem precious.[25]

The restraint that Renner recognized in English private-press printing accorded with his own preference for structural severity. He was frustrated by the search for novelty in many contemporary, artist-designed books:

... an avid search for originality is conducted at the edges of the still permissible, of the still possible, instead of a search for the perfectly beautiful, which is never tiresome: because only that which we consider as absolutely perfect and valid for all time – the wholly original expression of our time and personality – is that which will always change with us and our times, without us having to bother about it.[26]

Renner seems to have undertaken a personal study of classic typography, which informed even his earliest writings on book design. Given that his task was to supervise the typography and 'architecture' for each of Georg Müller Verlag's books, Renner's ability to select the best aspects of tradition in typography must have saved him precious time.[27] Indeed Renner later commented that the sober style of the books that he designed was partly a result of his wanting to finish them quickly in order to concentrate equally on painting.[28] Yet Renner's historical knowledge is evident in the care with

12 (above left) Title-page opening of Hölderlin, *Sämtliche Werke* (Georg Müller / Propyläen Verlag). 1913–23. 219 × 142 mm. All type black, box-rules blue.

13 (above) Spines of two volumes from Hölderlin's collected works. Gold blocking on blue leather (publisher's binding). Note that the ornament and lettering on the spine has been subtly redrawn to cater for volumes of different thickness.

24 *'Die Buchdruckerkunst ist ein bürgerliche Angelegenheit'. Buchdruck* is also the specific term for letterpress, as opposed to *Steindruck* or *Flachdruck* (lithography), and *Gravur* (intaglio).
25 'Die Kunst im Buchgewerbe' (1912) p. 162.
26 'Zur Kultur des Buches: II' (1910c) p. 291.
27 Referring to his Georg-Müller work, Renner said: 'I myself, for a period of time from 1908 to 1914 and then after 1918, did the typographic design [*Anordnung*] for thousands of books.' 'Münchener Typographie' (1920b) p. 115.
28 'Vom Georg-Müller-Buch ...' (1939d) p. 7.

which he chose certain typefaces, ornaments and decorative materials in order to suggest the period of a text: for instance, he might choose a neo-classical roman or gothic typeface for a text from the late eighteenth century (see figures 9–15). Renner was seriously engaged with the minutiae of book typography; his attention to detail is clear in his typographic rules, formulated in 1917 (see pp. 40–2 below).

From minority interest to mass production

Renner, like many others, seemed aware of the pressures of the new industrial era in Germany, and the growing mass of city dwellers whose book-needs had to be catered for cheaply. His initial indignation at the cheapening of such standards turned to resigned attempts at reform. He sought mainly to improve the quality of cheaper books by concentrating on the *Verlegereinband* (publisher's binding).

> Can hand- and machine-work really be so different?... I saw clearly posed before me the central problem of the new age and grasped it here where I first encountered it. To counter the damning of the machine, I made a critical examination of all work processes producing the bound book and compared at each stage the advantages and disadvantages of hand- and machine-work.[29]

Renner saw the causes of the persistent weaknesses in mass-produced binding as too much haste, and a skimping on the quality of materials, which must have been a particular temptation in the lean years after the First World War. A practical approach to balancing the relative merits of hand- and machine-work marked Renner's willingness to reconcile the two, whereas the hand and the machine became totems of opposing sides in the German debate on craft versus technology during the 1920s (see pp. 36–7 below).

Renner disliked the vain aspiration to monumentality in book design. He felt that the production of luxurious books before the First World War was an insular activity; it had no beneficial effect on the majority of books. In his view, luxury book production should 'begin from the premise of not producing curiosities, but ideal types that unite the highest achievement and most complete beauty'. This trial operation should serve 'the improvement and ennoblement of models for use [*Gebrauchstypen*]'.[30] This search for a level of quality suitable for mass production reflected a key concept of the German Werkbund before the First World War: *Sachlichkeit*,

29 'Erinnerungen aus meiner Georg-Müller-Zeit' (1939b) p. 3.
30 'Zur Kultur des Buches: II' (1910c) p. 291.

PAUL RENNER

— 127 —

Söhne der Begeisterungen!
Kost' und jauchze Trunkenheit.   80

Schaar, zu künem Ziel' erkoren!
Still' und mächtig' Priestertum!
Lieblinge! von euch beschworen,
Blüht im Kreise güldner Horen,
Wo ihr wallt, Elysium; —
O! so lindert, ihr Geweihten!
Der gedrükten Brüder Last!
Seid der Tyrannei verhasst!
Kostet eurer Seeligkeiten!
Darbet, wo der Schmeichler prasst!   90

14 Detail of Hölderlin's *Sämtliche Werke*, vol. 1 (Georg Müller). 1913. This shows the effect that Renner desired for poetry setting: the right-hand edge of the type area is defined by the show-through of type from the other side of the paper, preserving the symmetrical layout. The typeface, originating in the typefoundry of Pierre Didot *c.*1819 (identified by small g) was rediscovered by German typographers early in the twentieth century.

15 Pages from Hölderlin's *Sämtliche Werke*, vol. 1 (Georg Müller). 1913. 219 × 142 mm. Notes and commentary on the main text.

a term that is usually translated as 'objectivity', but which also has connotations of plainness and practicality.[31]

Renner was already aware of the knowledge about reading that had been gained in psychological experiments around the turn of the twentieth century.[32] This openness to the potential value of scientific information about reading could also be regarded as an aspect of Werkbund *Sachlichkeit*: a search for plain and functional forms. The kind of functionalist thinking that became a central aspect of modernism after the First World War was nascent in this pre-war Werkbund tendency towards stripped-down form – functionality being equated with simplicity in appearance. Along with designers such as Peter Behrens and Hermann Muthesius, Renner began to express this tendency:

> The position of printing among the fine arts is not so simple. Immediately we perceive that its products also serve a practical purpose: that of being read. If they are not suitable for this, they have no more right to exist than a chair that one cannot sit on, or a telephone, gramophone or telegraph that does not work.[33]

Renner as a Werkbund figure

Renner's main contribution to the *Streit um die Technik* (debate on technology) was an essay of 1921, 'Künstler und Gewerbe' (The artist and the trade), published in the Werkbund's newsletter. Renner longed for the days of old when 'Every capable craftsman was an artist: every artist a craftsman'. He blamed division of labour for the spiritual wretchedness resulting from work in modern production. But he rejected Marxism, signalling a reluctance to regard economic matters as the defining aspect of life; like many of his German contemporaries, he yearned for a spiritual rejuvenation:

> The artist wants to go to the worker and say: your struggle so far has only been for material welfare, for clocking-off time; fight now for the working day itself, for humane work! Because mindless, unwillingly-executed work remains money-slavery even in a socialized business, even in socialist states. How fast the eight hours would pass if your work had a value to which you were spiritually connected.[34]

Renner's own preference was for William Morris's brand of socialism, and in his essay Renner acknowledged the inspiration of Morris and the British Arts and Crafts Movement.

31 John Willett, in the title of his book *The new sobriety*, has offered an alternative translation for *Sachlichkeit*, and also discusses the problem of translating the term (p. 112). Frank Whitford, in *Bauhaus* (London: Thames & Hudson, 1984) p. 121, has commented that the German term also implies 'matter-of-factness and directness'. See also Frederike Huygen's thoughtful essay 'Some terms defined' in Huygen (ed.), *1928*, pp. 42–63. (See also p. 124 below.)

32 In 'Zur Kultur des Buches: ii' (1910c) p. 291, Renner disputed the contention that the legibility of type increases in direct proportion to its size. He stated that there were only three principal text sizes to be recommended: Borgis, Korpus, and Cicero (9, 10, and 12 point). '... the eye glides over the lines, in which it does not fixate every word; instead it perceives smaller words included in so-called indirect vision. For this reason it must fixate at two points in particularly long words, in order to take in the word-shape. It is clear that larger type-sizes greatly increase the number of those words which demand two or more fixation points, which not only delays reading a great deal, but is also extraordinarily tiring for the eye.' (Renner had perhaps read August Kirschmann's article, 'Über die Erkennbarkeit geometrischer Figuren und Schriftzeichen im indirekten Sehen', *Archiv für die Gesamte Psychologie* [13, 1908] pp. 352–88.)

33 'Buchgewerbe und bildende Kunst' (1913) p. 70.

34 *Typografie als Kunst* (1922a) p. 21.

PAUL RENNER

In the debate on technology, a generic notion of 'the machine' became a central motif in the struggle between traditionalism and modernism. The debate peaked in the Weimar era with the publication of a great many books and pamphlets on the matter. The culture-shock of industrialization in Germany was still a very recent national memory. Certainly, in the printing industry, craft work seemed to survive longer than in Britain or America. Hans Schmoller remarked that 'The practice of setting books by hand survived somewhat longer in Germany than in this country [Britain], and it was not uncommon, even in the twenties, to produce large books without the use of composing-machines'.[35]

An early sign of the potential fervour of the debate on technology was the controversy at the 1914 Werkbund conference in Cologne. Here, Hermann Muthesius had proposed a policy of standardization in design work that some of the artists at the conference found threatening. Muthesius was suggesting the establishment of certain design 'types', but the rebel artists, led by Henry van de Velde (and including Walter Gropius) feared a mechanizing influence on their work and a restriction of their artistic individuality.[36] It is likely that Renner attended this debate (his book design work was exhibited at the conference). He commented on the issue in 1921:

> Werkbund members once argued seriously as to whether it is best to strive for original, individual achievement, or for the establishment of norms, types – a good average. The phrasing of the question was distorted, like the answers that were given. Here, one can differentiate, but there is nothing on which to make a decision; there is no either/or. When it comes to art, only a unique and self-determined [selbständige] achievement of the highest order matters.[37]

Renner resisted a polarization of views in this issue: he stressed the need for mechanical tools to be mastered with artistic sense. Yet his position in the *Streit um die Technik* in the early 1920s shared the conservative ideal of a utopia from the past in which art and labour were a quotidian unity. Renner's view, contained in his essay 'Künstler und Gewerbe', was directly addressed by Adolf Behne, an architect and Werkbund member, who expressed a modernist view of the issue. Behne argued for an acceptance of the new social relationships set up by developments in technology and rejected the illusion of a 'beautiful, good and simple past'.[38]

35 H.P. Schmoller, 'Carl Ernst Poeschel' in *Signature* (New series no.11, 1950) p. 23.

36 See Heskett's account of the debate in *German design 1870–1918*, pp. 135–6; and the extracts from the debate on pp. 5–11 in 'Documents', a unit of Benton et al, *History of Architecture and design 1890–1939*.

37 'Die beiden Ziele' (1924b) p. 372.

38 Adolf Behne, 'Kunst, Handwerk, Technik', *Die neue Rundschau* (Jhg 33 der *Freien Bühne*, Heft 10, Oktober 1922) pp. 1022–33. See also Ludwig Hilbersheimer, 'Handwerk und Industrie', *Bauhaus* (Jhg 3, Nr 2, 1929) pp. 21–4.

Organizations dedicated to the preservation of craft practice periodically gained influence within the Werkbund.[39] Some craft groups, feeling that traditional methods were inviolable, sought to promote the guild system at the expense of educating designers in schools, which had become a basic tenet of Werkbund policy.[40] Educating potential designers and exhibiting 'quality' work were proposed by the Werkbund as measures to effect a transformation in taste. Renner concurred with the Werkbund idea of the artist as part of a clerisy charged with leading a reform in the quality of life. He saw the figure of the *Kunstgewerbler*[41] as inadequate for the task: 'Mostly he was a somewhat self-conscious painter who preferred the secure income of the *Kunstgewerbler* to the unsure one of his own job.'[42] (Ironically, the bare bones of his description precisely fitted Renner himself.)

As a believer in the necessity of education for reform in the field of design, Renner participated in two educational projects before the First World War. In 1911, aged 33 and at the height of his activity for Munich publishers, he set up the Münchner Schule für Illustration und Buchgewerbe (Munich School for Illustration and Book Production) with his colleague Emil Preetorius. Preetorius was an illustrator and theatre designer, who formed a strong working friendship with Thomas Mann. Renner later stated that the aim of the school was to foster 'a new generation to carry out the tasks of the Munich publishers, whom we could no longer satisfy on our own'.[43] The school was privately funded by students' fees (45 Mark per month) and occupied space in a new building erected in Munich to house the successful printing firm, M. Müller und Sohn (no relation to Georg Müller). Renner was on good terms with this firm, which printed much of the work for Georg Müller Verlag. The technical apparatus of the firm was therefore at the disposal of the students at allotted times.

A contemporary announcement in a trade periodical mentioned that such a school had not existed in Munich before, despite the existence of similar establishments in Leipzig, Berlin, Düsseldorf and Darmstadt. It was also stressed that this new school would be innovative in its close links to commercial practice, achieved by its situation in the printing house and through the personalities of its leaders, who were well respected practitioners. The morning's teaching was

39 Campbell, *The German Werkbund* (1978) pp. 157–70.

40 Campbell, *The German Werkbund* (1978) pp. 44–5, mentions the influence of the Munich educator Georg Kerchensteiner, who inspired Hermann Muthesius's reform of Prussian Arts and Crafts schools. Kerchensteiner believed in the ethical value of manual training, and later, as a municipal official in Munich, he set up the system of trade schools, including the printing school which Renner took over in 1926. (See p. 56 below.)

41 *Kunstgewerbe* is most often translated as 'Arts and Crafts', but it is not directly equivalent. Renner used the term in the early 1920s as if it was a direct equivalent, but later he came to use it in a pejorative sense, with the connotation of superficial decoration (much the same as the connotation 'Arts and Crafts' has in Britain today). In Germany today *Kunstgewerbe* is the term applied to *völkische* tourist memorabilia. Posener, *Anfänge des Funktionalismus*, p. 14, commented that, in contrast to the Arts and Crafts movement, 'what one understood, and still understands in Germany by the word *Kunstgewerbe* hardly ever laid claim to be an important agency in the reform of life as a whole ...'. I shall use the original German term in translations.

42 *Typografie als Kunst* (1922a) pp. 15–16.

43 'Erinnerungen aus meiner Georg-Müller-Zeit' (1939b) p. 3.

PAUL RENNER

supervised by Preetorius, and it covered all applications of illustration. The announcement implied that the morning's work was more intuitive and freer than the more 'didactic' and 'methodological' teaching by Paul Renner in the afternoon. Renner taught what was described as 'artistic writing', and his approach was informed by the methods of two well-known teachers in the reform of writing: the Austrian, Rudolf von Larisch, and Edward Johnston, who led the historically-based revival of formal writing in Britain.[44] Renner later described his teaching at the Münchner Schule für Illustration und Buchgewerbe as the *Schriftklasse* (writing class).[45] The fact that he regarded writing as fundamental to an understanding of book typography aligned his views once more with the British school of thought stemming from Walker and Morris.

Renner's second teaching experience of this period developed directly from the first: the Münchner Schule für Illustration und Buchgewerbe merged with the state-subsidized Debschitz Schule shortly before the First World War. Renner had attended this school as a student in 1906, when it had a notable reputation. He commented later that he was 'pressed into' taking over the Debschitz school when its co-founder Wilhelm von Debschitz left in July 1914.[46] After the merger it was renamed Münchner Lehrwerkstätten (Munich teaching workshops), which cannot have helped to maintain its reputation. Renner co-directed the school, initially with Preetorius and Hans Cornelius, the philosopher and art historian. Renner gave up his post at the school after the expiry of his five-year contract: he no longer had time for his own work and he felt that the municipal and state subsidies for the school were not sufficient. The war economy cannot have helped such matters. Indeed Renner's teaching was interrupted by the First World War: between January 1915 and Autumn 1917 he was only able to teach in Munich on Saturdays, as he was serving as an Oberleutnant in charge of a recruiting depot in Landsberg am Lech (about forty kilometres west of Munich).[47]

The emergence of the designer

Renner's early years in book design led him into some conflict with the conservative printing industry. Renner felt that his fine-art training in the realm of the spirit gave him values unsullied by commercial expedient. As an outsider in the

44 Larisch, whose approach centred on fostering the individual's style, had published manuals on lettering since 1904, and Johnston's seminal manual, *Writing & illuminating, & lettering*, which reflects his emphasis on historical study, had been translated into German by his pupil Anna Simons in 1910.

45 Typescript entitled 'Lebenslauf' prepared by Renner for his application to the Frankfurter Kunstschule, 1925. (Stadtarchiv FFM, Mag.-Akt 1753/1: item 47f.)

46 'Lebenslauf' (Stadtarchiv FFM, Mag.-Akt 1753/1: item 47f).

47 Renner also served briefly as an Information Commander at the Front. ('Lebenslauf'. Stadtarchiv FFM, Mag.-Akt 1753/1: item 47f.)

printing trade seriously engaged with typographic details, he personified the emergence of a new role in the production of books: the professional typographer – an individual with aesthetic insight who dictated the form of a book. Renner commented in 1910 that every detail had to be specified in order for the printer to achieve 'a fairly tasteful book'. He continued: 'The ideal book artist is the highest authority in all disputes over aesthetic matters; he has to give the aesthetic directives and should not have his competence disputed by the director of a printing house who is involved in the production of a book.'[48] Renner made it his business to learn about composition, printing and binding – to become familiar with the conventions and limitations of these crafts – in order to know what could be achieved and how to specify it.

It is impossible to know how Renner operated in his capacity as a book-artist, although it is fair to assume that he became a well-known figure among the printing houses, compositors and publishers of Munich, building up a rapport with many of them. Having been formed by the conservative educational institutions of the nineteenth century, Renner would surely have been able to navigate the channels of book production in a polite and amiable way. He commented later that 'my influence on the printing houses was not restricted to typographic layout [*Anordnung*], I also decided for the most part the typefaces that they acquired'.[49] He had a particular liking for the stock of classic types held at the Enschedé typefoundry in Holland, and he encouraged their use among German printers.

Renner's early work as a book typographer culminated in his typographic rules, first published in 1917. (This was the year of Georg Müller's death; after this Renner became less active in book design.) He later claimed that his military service had provided partial inspiration for his effort towards formulating rules. During his service in the First World War it was his responsibility to train hundreds of field-artillery men, and, in order to explain the 'laws of gunnery' to them, he drew diagrams that were mimeographed and distributed:

> Furthermore, the style of military rules pleased me: ever since the days of Caesar and Napoleon, the language of soldiers has been clear and concise. Since for years I had been giving printers and publishers considered rules in my correspondence to prevent repeated mistakes, it followed logically that I would set out my

48 'Zur Kultur des Buches: 1' (1910b) p. 243.
49 'Erinnerungen aus meiner Georg-Müller-Zeit' (1939b) p. 4.

rules in the style of such service regulations. I published them without foreword or commentary in the trade press and gave free permission for reproduction.[50]

The drive towards standardization in Germany did owe a lot to the war effort, especially in the field of engineering. A German standards organization, the Normenausschuss der Deutschen Industrie, was formed in 1917 to establish standards for measurement and production in war-time industry. However, Renner's rules were not standards for industrial components; indeed, he was protective of the book-artist's freedom in the light of Wilhelm Ostwald's *Weltformat*, a precursor of the DIN paper-size standards.[51]

Renner's rules were a serious attempt to suggest standard approaches to the details of book design that tended to be overlooked by printers. He addressed the technical processes of composition and printing, with an emphasis on aesthetic and linguistic detail. In a preface he suggested that familiarity with his rules could enable publishers to 'give every book a pleasant design [*Ausstattung*] without the costly collaboration of a book-artist'.[52] Yet Renner's exclusive concentration on continuous text setting, as found in novels, betrayed the limits of his interest and activity. He did not address any more complex areas of composition, such as tabular or mathematical setting. In elaborating his typographic rules for his first book, *Typografie als Kunst* (Typography as art, 1922; figures 16–18), Renner described them as 'only an attempt to communicate my personal creative experience', not to 'deny the learned compositor (or the person responsible for giving order to the typesetting) the responsibility he has for typographic work'.[53] Renner's rules caused a minor controversy in the trade; he was chastized for presuming to tell professionals their business. In 1939, he reflected on this episode:

> It all passed the artists by, because it dealt with matters only pertaining to specialists. ... In principle, the specialists were right: typography is a matter for compositors and not graphic designers [*Graphiker*]; it is like this again today. So why did publishers call the painters away from their work? The best book-artists of the generation that is now over seventy years old, were all, like me, originally painters; that the state of the book industry is better now than thirty-five years ago is no coincidence, rather the result of a collective effort, to which we all contributed.[54]

50 'Vom Georg-Muller-Buch ...' (1939d) pp. 1–2. Renner's military inspiration for his rules was perhaps in keeping with the Werkbund's brand of 'Prussian socialism' – militarism was a defining characteristic of the Prussian state. The freedom to reproduce Renner's rules was taken up by the printing house Brügel & Sohn in *Typographische Regeln und Beispiele nach Angaben Paul Renners* (Ansbach: Brügel & Sohn, n.d.).

51 *Typografie als Kunst* (1922a) pp. 153–4.

52 'Typographische Regeln' (1917) p. 265.

53 *Typografie als Kunst* (1922a) pp. 61–2.

54 'Vom Georg-Müller-Buch ...' (1939d) p. 2.

16 & 17 Spine and cover of *Typografie als Kunst* (Georg Müller). 1922. 205 × 128 mm. Spine: yellow on black leather; cover: black on green board. Note the mixture of roman and gothic letterforms.

An artist such as Renner – although his rules derived from the established conventions – was the object of resentment among printers and compositors who considered their own approaches to be quite sufficient. As he admitted, guidelines of the same kind were available in printing handbooks, but these were mostly written by printers whose aesthetic views were much less critical than his.[55] If Renner's rules had been entirely superficial, concerned only with ornamental book-art, they would probably not have caused such a stir: the source of the controversy lay in his presumption to dictate details that were regarded as secrets of the 'black art'. There was not yet a place for the typographer, an outsider to the printing trade whose expert judgement demanded respect from compositors and printers. Renner elaborated on the matter in 1922:

> As I gave permission to reprint, they [the rules] were distributed to the compositors in many leaflets. This brought me thanks and recognition, but also severe enemies. Specialist teachers and the managers of printing houses were indignant that an 'artist' ventured to discuss typographic questions!
>
> Typography, you 'professionals', is technology *and* art![56]

55 For example, see August Müller, *Lehrbuch der Buchdruckerkunst* (9th edn. Leipzig: Verlagsbuchhandlung J.J. Weber, 1913). An English-language equivalent of the genre is Theodore Low de Vinne's series of manuals *The practice of typography* (New York: Century, 1900–4).

56 *Typografie als Kunst* (1922a) p. 63. As Renner mentioned, his efforts were welcomed by some and he began to give lectures due to his newly-acquired notoriety. His lecture at the Stuttgarter Graphischen Klub (Stuttgart Graphic Club) prompted trainees and printers there to formulate some rules for typographic spacing with Renner's collaboration. They were published by the Fachschule für das Buchgewerbe in 1921, and became known as the 'Stuttgart rules'. (*Typografie als Kunst* [1922a] p. 69.)

18 Pages from *Typografie als Kunst.* 1922. Part of the chapter containing Renner's typographic rules.

In these attitudes, Renner was a typical Werkbund figure: the Werkbund realized that the artist-craftsman could no longer satisfy the needs of modern production and it was groping for the idea of the industrial designer, although the term for this concept did not exist at that time.

The tension between artist and tradesman came to a head in Renner's case with an argument in print in 1920. He wrote an essay surveying the recent history of Munich typography, which caused a bitter response from the editors of *Typographische Mitteilungen* (Typographic News; henceforth referred to as *TM*). Renner's essay was a laudatory ramble through recent high-points in the revival of aesthetically-conscious printing, which was largely based in Munich.[57] Although he concentrated on sober examples of book design in accordance with his taste, he presented a kind of narrative, peopled by colourful characters who did influential things – most of them book-artists. He considered the *Jugendstil* efforts of Peter Behrens and Otto Eckmann as without influence; for him the era began with the founding of the periodical *Die Insel* in 1899. Renner applauded the writer Otto Julius Bierbaum, a collaborator

57 'Münchener Typographie' (1920b).

on *Die Insel*, for having brought the hidden treasures of the Enschedé typefoundry to light. He described F. H. Ehmcke as the only other person in Munich, apart from Renner himself, 'who took serious pains with typography'.[58] Carl Ernst Poeschel, Anna Simons and the Bremer Presse were all singled out for praise, along with notable books that they had produced. Renner's case seemed to rest on a notion of Munich spirit – a fiery individualism springing from Schwabing, the northern district of Munich, which was traditionally the artists' quarter. According to Renner, the young graphic designers [*Gebrauchsgraphiker*] who arrived after the First World War were not interested in real typography; the wilful book-artists were his protagonists ('amateurs' and 'bohemians' he proudly called them) and he proclaimed: 'Not in the drawing rooms of the hereditary bourgeoisie, not in the rhythmically-droning rooms of the printing houses, rather in the ateliers and attic studios of Schwabing are to be found the strengths that have made Munich a centre of the book trade.'[59]

These sentiments of a proud artist, and especially this last comment, angered one of the writers at *TM*. Just a few months after the publication of Renner's article, an anonymous editorial in *TM* replied to him.[60] This periodical, founded in 1903, was published by the Bildungsverband der Deutschen Buchdrucker (Educational Association of the German Printing Trade Union). It was aimed at workers such as trade compositors, and heavily emphasized matters of training and education. Many detailed issues of compositional practice were covered in its pages, such as the niceties of letterspacing, the question of roman or gothic, and orthographic issues.[61]

The *TM* writer described Renner's account as a 'stroll through the sunny peaks' of Munich typography, 'resounding with praise and triumphant song for the acts of his friends'. The writer went on to suggest that an accurate picture should take account of the co-operation between artists and the capable members of the Munich printing trade, instead of denigrating the latter for the sake of the former. *TM* chastized Renner for being ignorant of the educational work initiated by German printing workers themselves:

Hat off, Mr Renner, to such working men! – and hat off, Mr Renner, to such progressively-minded communities as have been set up by the Munich compositors in the interest of trade members! Go and take a look at the way the Typographische Gesell-

58 'Münchener Typographie' (1920b) p. 116.

59 'Münchener Typographie' (1920b) p. 112.

60 'Künstlerkritik am Typographen', *Typographische Mitteilungen* (Jhg 17, Heft 11, November 1920) pp. 169–70. The retort to Renner is unsigned but may well have been written by Bruno Dressler, who had trained as a compositor and was 'Herausgeber und verantwortlicher Schriftleiter' (editor-in-chief) of *TM*.

61 *Typographische Mitteilungen* had a large circulation for a trade paper: by 1925 it had reached 22000. See Evans, *Modern typography on the continent*, p. 30.

PAUL RENNER

schaft München operates, and at the other local groups of the Bildungsverband der Deutschen Buchdrucker, so that in future you speak the truth about Germany's capable compositors and printers. As a god-gifted artist you can then, Mr Renner, also hold lecture courses and arrange exhibitions – the German printing apprentices are always thankful to those who assist in the promotion of the professional class [Berufsklasse].[62]

The views Renner expressed in his 'Munich typography' essay accorded with those of other leading Werkbund intellectuals, such as Hermann Muthesius and Friedrich Naumann, in suggesting an oligarchic process of reform, led by a select few, filtering down to general practice. The views of the *TM* editorship were the opposite: quality work was to be achieved from the bottom up, by collaboration amongst the workers.

Latent in this feud were social issues peculiar to Germany in the years immediately after the First World War. Renner yearned for a bygone age of spiritual well-being, to be regained by a collective act of will – a view characteristic of those on the conservative side of social debates. *TM*'s belief in the power of a unified work-force was clearly a sign of the workers' socialism that was still strong in the wake of Germany's 1918–19 revolutions. The 'success' of Russia's revolution must also have been a distant source of inspiration for those on the political left. Although the Weimar constitution had been adopted by the National Assembly in July 1919, the future was still uncertain. The Weimar government was in a kind of limbo. In this atmosphere, radicals from both sides saw the possibility for cultural transformation, leading to an intense ideological debate during the 1920s.

The argument between Renner and the author of the *TM* article touched on issues concerning the German character. During and immediately after the First World War, the nature of German-ness was an important issue for writers and thinkers. The thoughts of Nietzsche, along with Julius Langbehn's (initially anonymous) Germanic tract, *Rembrandt als Erzieher* (1890), inspired a strain of neo-conservatism, which was carried on into the 1920s by writers such as Arthur Moeller van den Bruck and Oswald Spengler. An early champion of the new conservatives was Thomas Mann. He considered his 1918 book, *Betrachtungen eines Unpolitischen* (Reflections of a non-political man), as his 'war effort', although his standpoint was suffused with irony.[63] He acknowledged

62 'Künstlerkritik am Typographen', p. 170.
63 Mann himself later called this book 'a last great retreat action, fought not without gallantry, of a romantic bourgeoisie in face of the triumphant new'. Mann quoted by Nigel Hamilton in *The brothers Mann* (London: Secker & Warburg, 1978) p. 191.

Nietzsche's contribution as the rejection of intellect and affirmation of 'life', and himself rejected the liberal ideas of the eighteenth century as alien to the German soul: 'democratic enlightenment' was 'psychologically anti-German'.[64]

Bavaria had a history of asserting its cultural difference from the north-German states. Renner characterized Munich as the artistic centre of Germany, the place where 'culture' resided, in comparison to the industrialized 'civilization' of Berlin. He called Munich one of Germany's 'spiritual poles: Berlin's opposite pole'.[65] Munich was certainly a conservative heartland, which ironically endured the longest experiment in socialist revolution among the German states during 1918 and 1919. On 7 November 1918, independent socialists led by Kurt Eisner seized power in Munich with minimal gunfire and no bloodshed. This victory was due to the determination of a small group of individuals, as there was no mass movement in Bavaria to consolidate the revolution. Bavaria's industrial modernization had been slow and the majority of the working population were still living in rural communities. The events in Munich probably did not touch the lives of most Bavarians. Eisner's regime fell back on the old civil-service structure, and after his assassination in February 1919 (a month after the assassination of Berlin's Spartacist revolutionaries), a short-lived Soviet republic was set up. This was bloodily suppressed in May 1919 by the Freikorps, a lawless, right-wing army that was ostensibly employed by the Social Democrat government in Weimar. Bavaria's counter-revolution was the bloodiest in the whole of Germany.[66]

Yet, whilst Munich was ever-present in Renner's intellectual orientation, he did not live there between 1919 and 1924. In 1919 he moved with his family to Hödingen overlooking Lake Constance (about 185 kilometres south-west of Munich), where he retired briefly from book design to take up painting again. He also spent a lengthy period in Stuttgart as adviser to the Deutsche Verlagsanstalt (DVA; German Publishing Association), a position that he was prompted to accept by Germany's descent into economic ruin. Many members of the middle-class became impoverished during the astronomic inflation of the early 1920s, by losing their savings or having sources of work dry up. They were thus 'proletarianized' by the changing times: their dreams of escape from hardship were driven by personal needs, as well as social conscience. It is difficult to

64 Thomas Mann, *Reflections of a non-political man*. Translated by Walter D. Morris (New York: Frederick Ungar 1983; first published as *Betrachtungen eines Unpolitischen*. Berlin: S. Fischer, 1918) p. 18.

65 'Münchener Typographie' (1920b) p. 112.

66 See Allan Mitchell, *Revolution in Bavaria 1918–1919* (Princeton: Princeton University Press, 1965).

PAUL RENNER

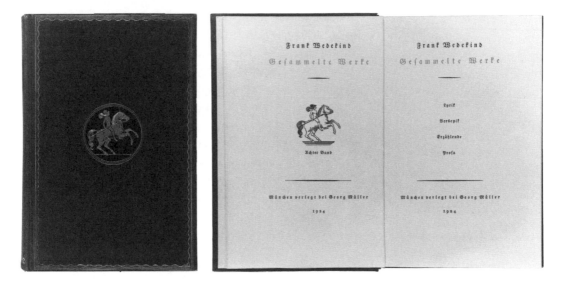

know the exact state of Renner's finances at this time. In the
early 1920s, he was married with three children, and his work
for Georg Müller Verlag had by his own choice almost dwin-
dled to nothing. After Müller's death in 1917, his publishing
house fell under the control of the ultra-conservative newspaper empire of August Scherl, and was given a new right-
wing direction. Renner obviously disapproved, commenting
later that Müller's successors were 'typical beneficiaries of the
war, revolution, and period of inflation'.[67] He no longer felt tied
to Georg Müller Verlag and spent the last of his family inheritance on buying his house in Hödingen. He made occasional
trips to Munich to take care of lingering book-design work.[68]
He recalled later that, by summer 1922, 'inflation was becoming ever more worrying', and this prompted him to accept
the invitation from the DVA in Stuttgart to design its large editions of classic literature. This position may have been offered
to him as a result of his earlier collaboration with Stuttgart
printers in formulating the 'Stuttgart rules' for composition.
He did not move his family to Stuttgart because there was a
lack of accommodation, but he remained in this post until the
end of 1923. It seems that Renner took the job reluctantly; his
reason for leaving it was that 'this publishing house, which
concentrated on cheap mass-production, offered too little
satisfying work.'[69] Having survived the period of inflation,
he returned to Lake Constance in 1924 to concentrate again
on painting.

67 'Vom Georg-Müller-Buch…'
(1939d) p. 1.
68 'Vom Georg-Müller-Buch…'
(1939d) p. 1.
69 'Lebenslauf' (Stadtarchiv FFM,
Mag.-Akt 1753/1: item 47f).

Renner began to work more regularly for Georg Müller Verlag again in April 1924, after his return from Stuttgart. His two eldest children left to enter higher education, and Renner found a studio flat in Pasing, Munich. Georg Müller Verlag was under new ownership and Renner helped to plan a new programme of classic literature (figures 19–21).[70] But this effort was short-lived, and the ruinous state of the German economy caught up with Georg Müller Verlag: it was finally taken over by the staunchly neo-conservative Deutsche Hanseatische Verlagsanstalt (German Hanseatic Publishing Association). Renner obviously liked the idea of continuing the affluent pre-war ways, but was finally forced to realize that things had changed irreversibly.

70 'Vom Georg-Müller-Buch ...' (1939d) p. 4.

21 Binding (spine and cover) for E. G. Kolbenheyer, *Das dritte Reich des Paracelsus* (Georg Müller). 1925 (third in a series, of which the first was published in 1918). Pen-made letterforms. Red and black printed on coarse, oatmeal-coloured cloth.

3 **Renewal** 1924–32

From 1924 Renner began to move in educational circles that brought him into contact with younger designers who were more involved in the new styles of design. Yet it would be too simplistic to see an uncomplicated change in Renner from conservative to progressive around this time; many of his opinions remained constant throughout his life. He consistently struggled to resist the dogma of any '-ism'.

Socially-engaged design

Renner's views in the Werkbund debate of the early 1920s concerning the relationship of manufacture to culture centred on the spiritually healing value of creative labour. On setting up the Bauhaus in 1919, Walter Gropius's views had been similar: he craved a 'spiritual revolution' to be achieved largely by the return of artists to craft work.[1] It is likely that Renner would have followed press coverage of the Bauhaus from early in its existence. Gropius made public statements from the inception of the Bauhaus, and the press backlash had begun almost immediately: it was declared a 'Spartacist', 'Bolshevist' institution that attracted too many foreigners. By 1923, after many staff changes, the Bauhaus found its enduring identity with Gropius's idea of 'Art and technology – a new unity', which permeated the Bauhaus's first major exhibition in that year. Craft skills now became the means of making prototypes for machine production, and the school's students began to design objects for mass production and sale. It is significant that the 1923 exhibition coincided with the high-point of inflation; the guiding spirit of this second Bauhaus phase seems to have been the realization that new ways of life were emerging in the new urban centres – ways of life which required a correspondingly new kind of design. The need for housing in Germany at this time went beyond aesthetics. Pre-fabrication and serial production were a necessary means to an end in the work of Gropius and other architects associated with the building societies in Berlin and Frankfurt.

Germany's recovery from its massive economic problems was due partly to financial aid from the USA, but Germany also imported certain American strategies of industrial practice. Frederick Taylor's books on 'scientific management' were translated into German soon after 1910 and his principles were quickly assimilated by German industry, which was

1 See Lane, *Architecture and politics...*, pp. 141–3. Peter Gay, in *Art and act* (p. 130), takes seriously Gropius's intention to set up an 'unpolitical' community at the Bauhaus. What politics there was in Gropius's speeches and writings is regarded by Gay as 'politics for the unpolitical', a description that could equally apply to Renner's views, and also significantly echoes the title of Thomas Mann's *Reflections of a non-political man*.

already organized along military lines. Henry Ford's autobiography was translated into German in 1923 and, as Judith Merkle has explained, this translation lent Ford's ghost-written prose an 'aura of social concern', which fostered his reputation in Germany as a 'quasi-socialist industrialist'.[2] The process of industrial rationalization began in earnest after the stabilization of currency in 1924, the year in which the Ford company of Germany turned out its first car at the Cologne factory. Indeed, the first application of the term 'rationalization' to industrial and economic matters occurred at this time in Germany: *Rationalisierung* consequently became a fashionable concept embracing any kind of systematic endeavour. This pervasive idea surely influenced the approaches and aesthetic preferences of those designers who developed the 'modern' style, with its associations of economy and efficiency.

The New Typography

Renner had assisted in reviving the bibliophile culture that he had known before the First World War with his work on luxurious editions for Georg Müller Verlag in 1924. However, the wealth of the book-buying middle class had been eroded by war and inflation. New modes of urban life emerged during the 1920s, in which leisure time became increasingly filled with sport, recorded music and movies, instead of books. Certainly the trend in book production was towards cheaper, mass-produced editions. This movement is perhaps best exemplified by the book societies begun in the 1920s, which were mostly linked to left-wing political organizations. The two most successful societies were the Büchergilde Gutenberg and the Bücherkreis. Both were formed in 1924: the Büchergilde Gutenberg was founded by Bruno Dressler of the Bildungsverband der Deutschen Buchdrucker, and the Bücherkreis was linked to the SPD (Social Democratic Party). Dressler recruited designers like Jan Tschichold, Georg Trump and Wilhelm Lesemann (a teacher at the Bielefeld School of Arts and Crafts) to design Büchergilde books. They designed editions that combined type and photographic illustration in a fluent unity for the first time. Tschichold also designed books and publicity for the Bücherkreis in the early 1930s. The Büchergilde had 5 000 members in 1925, a figure which had grown to 68 000 by 1929. For a monthly contribution of one Mark, members received four books per year.[3]

2 Judith Merkle, *Management and ideology* (Berkeley: University of California Press, 1980) p. 194. The term 'Americanization' was actually used in discussions of culture in mid-1920s Germany; see Kaes et al (ed.), *The Weimar Republic sourcebook,* p. 401. The term was also used by one of the Bauhaus theorists, Josef Albers, with regard to typography; see Albers, 'Zur Ökonomie der Schriftform', *Offset: Buch und Werbekunst* (Heft 7, 1926) p. 395.

3 See Walter Plata, 'Büchergilde Gutenberg' in *Typographica* (15) pp. 16–23. For a wider discussion of the book clubs of this era, see Bühnemann & Friedrich, 'Zur Geschichte der Buchgemeinschaften der Arbeiterbewegung in der Weimarer Republik'.

PAUL RENNER

22 Jacket (spine, front and back) for Georg Krause, *Bali* (Georg Müller). 1926. 285 × 225 mm. (Design credited to Renner in *Die Form*, Jhg 4, Heft 21, 1929.)

By 1927 the production of books in the prestige areas of the trade was dwindling, provoking many publishers to speak of a 'book crisis' [*Bücherkrise*]. A note of concern was sounded in the bibliophile periodical, *Der Zwiebelfisch*: 'Hopefully we will not entirely forget how to read in the tempo of our present existence.'[4] The total number of new editions and new titles published in Germany in 1927 was 31026, a figure which had hardly risen since 1908. 16.3 per cent of the total was 'Schöne Literatur' (*belles lettres*), and 0.55 per cent was classical literature. Those publishers specializing in literature published fewer titles than the publishers of children's books and schoolbooks. The most successful of the literary publishers in 1927 was the DVA, which, as already described, had employed Paul Renner to rationalize production of its mass-produced classics (see p. 47 above).[5]

The New Typography of the 1920s and 1930s was not hampered much by the book crisis, because it defined itself mostly outside the field of book production. The new breed of artist-typographers, who had progressed into graphic design from painting, set a new agenda for typography, both in their writings and in the kind of work they did. Examples of this new breed were Kurt Schwitters, Willi Baumeister and Walter Dexel, who were all initially fine artists. All wrote about the principles of New Typography, with a common stress on *sachliche* clarity, and, in Schwitters's case, Dadaistic innovation.[6] Publicity material and advertising posters were the staple tasks of these artists, although their work did occasionally encompass books and business stationery. Outside the confines of traditional book typography, they could use photography and the forms of New Typography to create dynamic, painterly compositions related to abstract art. Many leading

4 Quoted by Paul Raabe in 'Das Buch in der zwanziger Jahren: Aspekte einer Forschungsaufgabe' in Raabe (ed.), *Das Buch in den zwanziger Jahren*, p. 31.

5 Figures for 1927 from Raabe, 'Das Buch in den zwanziger Jahren ...', p. 18. Figure for 1908 from *Börsenblatt ...* (Jhg 78, Nr 3, 4 January 1911). Renner himself admitted in 'Das Luxus-Buch und unsre Zeit' (1932c) that 'the luxury book seems initially to be so superfluous in such a time of material need', but he saw prestigious publications as having a 'doubled' role in setting the pace for the average production.

6 See the articles by these three reprinted in Fleischmann (ed.), *Bauhaus: Drucksachen Typografie Reklame* – Schwitters, 'Thesen über Typographie' (1924) p. 328; Baumeister, 'Neue Typographie' (1926) p. 339; Dexel, 'Was ist neue Typographie' (1927/8) pp. 340–1.

practitioners of New Typography were members of the Ring neuer Werbegestalter (Ring of new advertising designers), the international organization instigated and led by Schwitters from 1928, which served to publicize its members work with the aim of generating further business. The Ring organized 22 exhibitions throughout Europe between 1928 and 1931. Among its members (in addition to those named above) were Max Burchartz, Jan Tschichold, Georg Trump and Piet Zwart. (Renner never joined.)

Although the phrase 'New Typography' was first used by László Moholy-Nagy in the catalogue of the seminal Bauhaus exhibition of 1923,[7] the principal theoretician of the New Typography was Jan Tschichold, who was inspired by that exhibition. Tschichold did most to elaborate the principles of the new movement in his book *Die neue Typographie* (The new typography, 1928), but he first elucidated these principles in 'Elementare Typographie', a special issue of *Typographische Mitteilungen* that he edited in 1925. This was the first compendium of New Typography, featuring work by El Lissitzky, Schwitters & others, and it also included a thoughtful article by its young compiler, in which Tschichold defined a persuasive credo for functionalist typography.[8]

Renner confronts modernity

The Frankfurter Kunstschule

In 1925 the director of the Frankfurter Kunstschule (Frankfurt School of Art), Renner's friend Fritz Wichert, asked him if he was prepared to take over a preliminary class in typography. Courses at this school were structured in three levels: preliminary class, design class and workshops.[9] Renner accepted and, after two months as a guest lecturer, he was appointed as a full-time member of staff in July 1925 to reorganize all levels of study in the typography department.[10]

Fritz Wichert had been appointed as principal of the Frankfurter Kunstschule in 1923 and had remodelled the school's curriculum along the lines of the Bauhaus. In 1925 he appointed the painter Max Beckmann to the staff, and in 1926, Adolf Meyer, the architect who had collaborated with Walter Gropius on certain seminal pre-war buildings. Under Wichert's leadership, the school and its staff collaborated with the Frankfurt city planner, Ernst May, in an enlightened pro-

7 László Moholy-Nagy, 'Die neue Typographie,' (1923) in Fleischmann (ed.), *Bauhaus: Drucksachen Typografie Reklame*, pp. 14–16.

8 Tschichold, 'Elementare Typographie', pp. 191–214. See the translation of Tschichold's principles of 'Elemental typography' by Kinross, *Modern typography* (1992) pp. 87–9.

9 Wingler (ed.), *Kunstschulreform*, p. 142.

10 Letter of 15 July 1925 from Ernst May on behalf of the Deputation für Wissenschaft, Kunst und Volksbildung to the Magistrats-Personaldezernenten. (Stadtarchiv FFM, Mag.-Akt 1753/1: item 47b.) There were already typographical technicians among the staff: Philipp Albinus was the technical instructor for typesetting. Albinus wrote a booklet on 'fundamentals of the New Typography': *Grundsätzliches zur neuen Typographie* (Berlin: Verlag des Bildungsverbandes der Deutschen Buchdrucker, 1929), which is rather slight and superficial.

PAUL RENNER

gramme of civic design during the late 1920s. May, an architect, was appointed as city planner in 1925, and he drew up a ten-year plan for urban housing to be executed in co-operation with building societies. John Willett has claimed that 'Frankfurt emerged as the first twentieth-century city'.[11]

Renner was only present at the very beginning of this programme – indeed he left in early 1926 before any of the major building developments were completed. His only task seems to have been the redrawing of Futura (then work in progress) as a model alphabet for public signing.[12] Yet he was stimulated by the milieu of socially-driven design in the new 'functionalist' style. In particular, he seems to have had a fruitful relationship with his colleague at the Kunstschule, Ferdinand Kramer, an architect and furniture designer. Kramer, who had studied briefly at the Bauhaus, designed unit furniture for sale to tenants through a non-profit-making municipal firm and also held a post in the standardization department of Ernst May's City Building Office. Renner wrote an appreciative article on Kramer's design in the Werkbund periodical, *Die Form*, describing it as 'free from all historicism' and 'no less free of the dogmatic formalism that characterizes false modernity'.[13]

The movement towards cheap, rationalized housing for accommodating workers in overcrowded cities culminated in the international exhibition 'Die Wohnung für das Existenzminimum' (Housing for basic living) held in Frankfurt in 1929. This concept seems to have made some impression on Renner, who perhaps only realized the extent of such a problem after moving from Munich to Frankfurt, which had experienced a rapid growth in its population of industrial workers.

Return to Munich

Renner enjoyed his time at the Frankfurter Kunstschule, where there was a 'refreshing intellectual atmosphere' in which he and his colleagues made a 'two-pronged attack' against 'historicism and the romantic denial of machines, and against the materialism of art's enemies'.[14] In autumn of 1925 the post of Oberstudiendirektor (Principal) at the Munich printing Gewerbeschule (Trade School) was advertised. Despite pleas from some Munich printers, Renner did not apply for the post, as he was satisfied with his Frankfurt position. Although there were two hundred other applicants for the Munich post, Renner was personally invited to take control of the Gewerbe-

11 Willett, *The new sobriety*, p. 125. Willett discusses 'The New Frankfurt' in some detail. See also Heinz Hirdina (ed.), *Neues Bauen, Neues Gestalten: Das neue Frankfurt/Die neue Stadt* (Berlin: Elefanten Press, 1984) for extensive excerpts of the periodical associated with the Frankfurt programme.

12 'Vom Georg-Müller-Buch…' (1939d) p. 7.

13 'Zu den Arbeiten von Ferdinand Kramer' (1927j) p. 320. Some writers have also hinted at a collaboration between Kramer and Renner on the design of Futura (see pp. 89–90 below).

14 'Vom Georg-Müller-Buch…' (1939d) p. 7.

schule (which came to be known as the Graphische Berufs-schule) by Hans Baier, the Munich Oberstadtschuldirektor (Municipal Educational Director). Baier persuaded him to return, and Renner took up his new post in Munich at Easter 1926.[15]

Munich has never become a modern, industrial city in the same sense as Berlin or Frankfurt. In the 1920s, it was still a very conservative city, and it was the base from which the Nazis were slowly gaining support. None of the Munich news-papers was owned by the National Socialists, but they never-theless fell into line with the kind of nationalism purveyed in the Nazi-owned Berlin paper, *Völkischer Beobachter*. For instance, during the 1924 controversy over the expulsion of the Bauhaus from Weimar, the Munich press was united against the school.

On 29 November 1926 Renner took part in a public gathering in Munich's Tonhalle (oratorium), which can be seen as a refutation of the nostalgic Germanism fostered by Hitler and his propagandists. The event, entitled 'Kampf um München als Kulturzentrum' (Struggle for Munich as a cultural centre) took place in front of a packed audience. Renner's fellow speakers were Thomas Mann, Heinrich Mann, Leo Weismantel, Willi Geiger and Walter Courvoisier. Renner had met Thomas Mann, another adopted citizen of Munich, in December 1918: their point of introduction was that Renner had served with Mann's brother Viktor in the First World War.[16]

In 1926, Thomas Mann was fresh from success with his novel *Der Zauberberg* (The magic mountain) and was a well-known public commentator on political events. His older brother Heinrich was also a successful novelist and this Munich gathering signified their reconciliation after a public, filial dispute. Thomas Mann's conservative Germanist tract of 1918, *Reflections of a non-political man*, was written partly in response to comments made by Heinrich Mann in favour of liberal, Western culture. In this bizarre feud, Thomas Mann had set himself against such 'civilization' with his invocation of the powerful German 'life force' (see pp. 45–6 above). However, in the early 1920s Thomas Mann perceived that the Nazis were vulgarizing his ideas, and he turned to support the Weimar Republic in speeches and essays. Those who voiced this kind of resigned acquiescence to the new regime became

15 'Vom Georg-Müller-Buch...' (1939d) p. 11. Hans Baier was the successor to Georg Kerchensteiner, an educational theorist who, as a privy councillor, had reformed the Munich system of trade schools. Kerchensteiner refuted the tra-ditional notion in German education that a 'cultivated' individual could only be formed by an esoteric curriculum. Instead he advocated a combination of practical work and theoretical study within the framework of vocational training. Kerchensteiner thus sought to break class barriers in German educa-tion, arguing that a cultivated individual was simply one who was 'thoughtfully involved' in any sphere of activity. Kerchensteiner was a respected figure among academics, and the Munich trade schools soon gained a national reputation. See Fritz K. Ringer, *The decline of the German mandarins: the German academic community, 1890–1933* (Hanover and London: University Press of New England, 1969) p. 271. Renner admired Kerchensteiner's work and shared his belief in the fruit-ful alliance of theory and practice. Renner had expressed this principle in his speech at the inaugural meeting of the Arbeitsgemeinschaft für buch-gewerbliche Fortbildung (Working Party for Education in the Book Trade) in 1924, which Kerchensteiner had attended.

16 Thomas Mann, *Diaries 1918–1939* (London: André Deutsch, 1983) p. 26.

known as *Vernunftrepublikaner* (rational republicans, a term coined by a contemporary historian, Friedrich Meinecke).[17] The *Vernunftrepublikaner* had allegiances to the old order, yet came to realize that the Republic was the best chance for some kind of continuity, considering the extreme positions of some other factions. Renner – then in his late forties – was almost the same age as Mann, and his views at this time also indicate a shift away from his earlier conservatism towards a forward-looking stance.

Renner's inclusion as a speaker among such distinguished company must indicate a certain status in literary and intellectual circles in Munich. His fellow speakers were all respected Munich academics or intellectuals. One can imagine the event being planned at a soirée in one of the participant's houses in Schwabing, which had a thriving social life.[18]

Mann's speech at the Tonhalle repeated his standard ironic view of the polarities in German society: he set Munich in opposition to Berlin, claiming that the southern town had always been 'democratic' in contrast to Berlin's 'feudal-militaristic' nature.[19] Renner's speech, however, was a plea for a radical change of approach to developing Munich as a city, which would force it into the new era.[20] He lamented the fact that Munich, known as a 'city of art', was lagging behind the new movement in design. He blamed Munich's lethargy on its proximity to the southern home of humanism and on its still largely rural situation in Bavaria: 'Here is the real cultural problem of Bavaria. The European culture of today is not a rural one, but an urban one.' Renner called for architectural modernization. There was no use in waiting for a royal patron to set this process in motion, as in the pre-War days – no use in waiting for a 'dictator': the initiative had to come from government – 'The German Republic stands on firm ground', he declared.[21] The New Architecture, as a return to basics from the stagnant classical tradition, embodied for Renner 'a new feeling for unity of content and form' in which 'our time has found its creative virtue'.[22] Munich was still so conservative that neon signs were prohibited in the city. The Münchner Bund, the Munich division of the Werkbund, campaigned for neon to be permitted. Renner was notable in this regional Werkbund group for his progressive views, in contrast to the largely craft-oriented contingent.[23]

17 See Peter Gay, *Weimar culture*, pp. 24–7, and Ringer, *The decline of the German mandarins*, p. 203.

18 In a letter of 26 June 1934 to a Herr Kiefer, Thomas Mann wrote from his exile in Zurich that he did not have Renner's address, which he regretted 'as we were on very friendly terms in Munich'. (Thomas-Mann-Archiv, Zurich.)

19 Mann, 'München als Kultur-zentrum' in *Politische Schriften und Reden* (Frankfurt: Fischer Bücherei, 1968; vol.2) pp. 159–64.

20 Renner's speech was printed with those of the other participants in *Kampf um München als Kulturzentrum* (Munich: Richard Pflaum, 1926).

21 'Kampf um München ...' (1926d) p. 54. The term 'dictator' may be an oblique reference to Hitler, or at least to the mythical *Führer* longed for in the neo-conservative tracts by the likes of Oswald Spengler.

22 'Kampf um München ...' (1926d) p. 52.

23 'Interview mit Hans Eckstein in Lochahm bei München am 28.9.1978' in Deutscher Werkbund, *Die Zwanziger Jahre ...*, p. 161.

Renner later recalled the loud bursts of applause that punctuated his speech at the Tonhalle gathering.[24] Thomas Mann described the event as a '"cultural-political rally" – six speeches against the Munich reaction, to frenetic applause. It was an explosion'.[25] The gathering was a topic of conversation for many weeks afterwards, although the press chose to ignore it, and Renner believed that he was unofficially banned in the newspapers after this event.[26] Hans Baier, who had chosen Renner as principal of Munich's Graphische Berufsschule, called him for a meeting at the Town Hall the day after the rally. Renner recalled later:

> This otherwise so calm and peaceful man paced up and down his room heavily like a bear in a cage. Then he stood still in front of my chair and said: 'Herr *Oberstudiendirektor*, I thought you were more sensible than that!' I considered for a moment and then said: 'Herr *Oberstadtschuldirektor*, there are moments in the life of an individual and of a people, when one should not be sensible. If I had to do my speech over again tonight, I would only say the same thing.' I saw in Baier's eyes that he understood and that I had won a friend.[27]

The development of the Munich Meisterschule

With the help of Hans Baier, who was sympathetic to his friend's controversial ideas, Renner began to build up a new staff and curriculum at the Munich Graphische Berufsschule. The school was housed in a building along with several other trade schools in Munich's Pranckhstraße (where a printing-trade school still exists today). Around the turn of 1926 Renner contacted the young Jan Tschichold, then living in Berlin, with a view to suggesting him for the post that Renner had left vacant at the Frankfurter Kunstschule. Tschichold is reputed to have eagerly studied Renner's 1922 book *Typografie als Kunst*,[28] and Renner would certainly have known the special October 1925 issue of *Typographische Mitteilungen*, 'Elementare Typographie', which Tschichold had edited. No doubt they discovered common ground and, as a result of their correspondence, Renner invited Tschichold to join his staff in Munich. He took up a position teaching 'the art of typography and calligraphy' in June 1926. Tschichold later commented vaguely that Renner – who was already busy designing the typeface Futura – hoped that Tschichold would help to foster Renner's ideas for the school.[29]

24 'Aus meinem Leben' (1939a) p. 8.
25 Mann in Hans Bürgin and Hans Otto-Mayer, *Thomas Mann: eine Chronik seines Lebens* (Berlin: S. Fischer Verlag, 1965) p. 77.
26 The *Münchner Zeitung*, for instance, was opposed to the efforts of Ernst May in Frankfurt, which Renner had praised in his speech.
27 'Aus meinem Leben' (1939a) p. 9.
28 McLean, *Jan Tschichold: typographer*, p. 35.
29 Tschichold's anonymous autobiographical essay 'Jan Tschichold: praeceptor typographiae' in Tschichold, *Leben und Werk ...*, p. 20.

PAUL RENNER

Renner's initial contact with Tschichold was also spurred by accusations made in the periodicals *Zeitschrift für Deutschlands Buchdrucker* and *Schweizer Graphische Mitteilungen* that both men were 'Bolshevists'. Renner was chastized for his publicly expressed view that a new style in typography and architecture must replace the prevailing historicism.[30] Tschichold's interest in Russia was evident: he had changed his given name Johannes to Iwan in 1923 in his enthusiasm for Russian art and design. When Tschichold took up his position in Munich, Renner requested that he change his name from Iwan, fearing opposition from the conservative Munich officials if they suspected Tschichold of having Russian links. Tschichold then adopted the name Jan.[31] Renner was not discouraged by these Russian connections, and he pushed Tschichold's appointment through the necessary authorities. It seems that Renner and Tschichold both took the accusation of 'Bolshevism' to be empty rhetoric; they could not know that the charge would be levelled at them again in early 1933 by the Nazis, with serious consequences.

Renner also became involved in negotiating the foundation of a national school, which would run parallel to the Graphische Berufsschule. In early 1926, he heard that funds had been made available by the Deutscher Buchdrucker-Verein (German Printers Association) to set up a school for the training of prospective printing-house managers.[32] Printing organizations in Leipzig and Berlin were bidding to be host to the school and Renner saw a chance to secure its establishment in Munich. In collaboration with the Verein Münchner Buchdruckerei Besitzer (Union of Munich Printing House Proprietors), Renner negotiated with the Deutscher Buchdrucker-Verein. The advantage of the Munich bid was that it had local governmental support of 50 000 marks, and the donation of free premises in the Pranckhstraße site, already occupied by the Berufsschule. Also, given the existing structure of Renner's Berufsschule, the staff and equipment was already in place to serve the new school.[33] Renner drafted an elegant booklet outlining the proposed curriculum for the new school: his plans centred on the combination of training in aesthetic issues and practical capability, to convince the students that 'there is a higher goal than the profitability of business'.[34]

30 Renner answered this charge with an unfocussed essay, 'Bildungskrise' (1926b).

31 Renner, 'Über moderne Typographie' (1948f). Edith Tschichold recalled: 'The "Iwan" disturbed the Munich school authorities, including Paul Renner, who were not at all well-disposed towards this typographical revolutionary, and they demanded time and again that he call himself by his "correct" name.' Quoted in Luidl (ed.), *J.T.*, p. 31. In his contribution to this book, Werner Doede quoted a letter from Tschichold of 5 July 1926, in which he said: 'now Jan instead of ivan, since munich! ivan is impossible here!' (p. 19; small letters in original). Robin Kinross discusses Tschichold's names in his introduction to Tschichold, *The new typography*, p. xvi. See also pp. 177–8 below.

32 These future printing-house managers were referred to by Renner and others as *Prinzipalssöhne* – the sons of existing printing-house managers.

33 Letter of 12 July 1926 from Verein Münchner Buchdruckereibesitzer to Ministerium für Unterricht und Kultus (Akt MWi1882, Bay HStA, München).

34 'Vom Georg-Müller-Buch...' (1939d) p. 12.

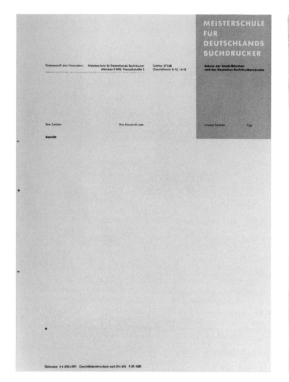

23 (left) Letterhead for the Meisterschule. 1928. A4. Designed at the school. Adheres to the DIN standard placements of information for use with window envelopes.

24 (right) Front page of journal *Graphische Berufsschule*. 1929. A4. Edited by Renner and produced at the Meisterschule. Shows the adoption of the DIN standard for periodicals in A4-format, with a line of bibliographical information consistently placed on each issue at the foot of the front page.

So, on 1 February 1927, the Meisterschule für Deutschlands Buchdrucker, Schule der Stadt München und des Deutschen Buchdrucker-Vereins (Master School for Germany's Printers, School of the City of Munich and the German Printers Association) was officially opened.[35] As its full title shows, it was jointly funded by the city of Munich and a professional body, which enabled provision of equipment as a worthwhile investment in the future of the printing industry. The two Munich schools were distinct from each other: the Berufs-schule trained apprentices for the trade, and the Meister-schule gave an all-round theoretical and practical education for those who were to run printing establishments. However, the staff and their approach to teaching seem to have served both schools alike. Workshop teaching was combined with lectures and demonstrations. Instruction at the Meisterschule encompassed typesetting, all reprographic and printing techniques, scientific business theory, book-keeping, legal theory,

35 In 'Vom Georg-Müller-Buch...' (1939d) Renner gives the opening date as 1 February 1926, which must be a misprint as Renner was still at the Frankfurter Kunstschule at this time. (Proven by a letter of 17 March 1926 from Fritz

Wichert on behalf of the Deputation für Wissenschaft, Kunst und Volksbildung to the Magistrats Personaldezernent (Stadtarchiv FFM, Mag.-Akt 1753/II: item 63).

PAUL RENNER

printing house organization, and colour theory.[36] The school also ran a varied program of lectures by visiting speakers: among them was Walter Gropius, who gave a lecture on 'Neues Bauen' (New Architecture) in 1931.[37] Renner maintained the practice of *Schriftschreiben* (formal writing/typographic sketching) at the heart of the curriculum, as it had been in his earliest educational work. He recognized that his insistence on the utility of skilled writing was perhaps not fashionable; compare, for instance, the reductive exercises in constructing letterforms from geometric parts carried out at the Bauhaus. Yet Renner believed that tactile engagement with creating letters through a self-contained activity of handcraft was still the most effective means of learning about the qualities of letterforms. Students came to understand letters from 'the inside out, so to speak'.[38] They were then able to draw a typographic layout in an accurate rendition of a particular type style, to judge its formal qualities, and then, based on the sketch, they could specify the correct measurements for others to carry out the typesetting and printing.[39]

By comparison with the enduring reputation of the Bauhaus, for example, the Munich Meisterschule hardly figures in conventional design history. This is undoubtedly due to its specialized nature as a school for the printing trade, but also because it was not associated with a stream of well-known pedagogues and designers who enjoyed a second wind of success in the United States (Walter Gropius, László Moholy-Nagy, Ludwig Mies van der Rohe, Herbert Bayer). The graphic design work of the Bauhaus has a reputation today for bold

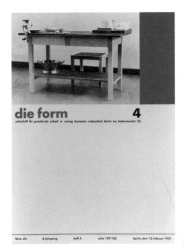

die form 4

25 Cover of *Die Form*. 1931. A4. Designed at the Meisterschule by Jan Tschichold and his students.

36 See the prospectus for the Meisterschule included in *Archiv für Buchgewerbe und Gebrauchsgraphik* (Jhg 69, Heft 8, 1932).

37 See the poster designed for the lecture by Jan Tschichold in his *Leben und Werk...*, figure 37. Renner was never professionally affiliated with the Bauhaus. He must have known Gropius from meetings of the Deutscher Werkbund, but the two men do not seem to have been close acquaintances. Renner was much friendlier with Ludwig Mies van der Rohe, who was director of the Bauhaus from 1930 until its closure in 1933. Renner certainly visited Mies at least once in Dessau: in a letter of 1 April 1931, Renner thanked Mies for the pleasant welcome he was given there (Nachlaß Renner). Also, Lilly Reich, Mies's partner, wrote to Renner on 21

September 1932 to ask him, 'perhaps indiscreetly', about the student fees for the Meisterschule; she explained that the Bauhaus was losing its state support and would have to be run on a private basis. The Nazis had taken control of the Dessau city parliament and they finally closed the Dessau Bauhaus on 30 September 1932. It then moved to a short-lived base in Berlin as a private school.

38 *Denkschrift über die Errichtung eines Buchdruckertechnikums in München* (1926c) pp. 7–8.

39 Renner summarized these issues in 'Wie müssen die Arbeitskräfte des Buchdruckgewerbes ausgebildet werden' (1930f) p. 753. See also Renner's justification of teaching *Schriftschreiben* in 'Warum geben wir an Kunstschulen immer noch Schreibunterricht?' (1929g) p. 52. The printing apprentices who were

students at the Berufsschule spent two of their nine hours of study per week drawing letterforms; in their fourth year this was replaced by workshop experience of the printing machinery. At the Meisterschule Renner taught *Schriftschreiben* for three hours per week in semester 1, and for two hours in semester 2. In both semesters 1 & 2, almost half of the week's forty hours of study was taken up by *Satz* (composition), taught jointly by Jan Tschichold and Josef Käufer. Tschichold was the teacher (*Studienrat*) and Käufer was the technical tutor (*Fachlehrer*). Renner also taught *Werbelehre* (advertising theory) in semester 4. (These curriculum details are in the prospectus supplement to *Archiv für Buchgewerbe und Gebrauchsgraphik* (Jhg 69, Heft 8, 1932).

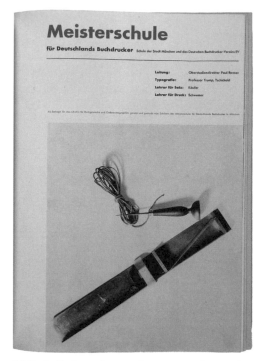

26 Periodical supplement featuring student work from the Meisterschule. *c*.1930. 320 × 232 mm.

27 Book advertisement. 1932. A4, on newsprint. Designed and typeset by students at the Meisterschule.

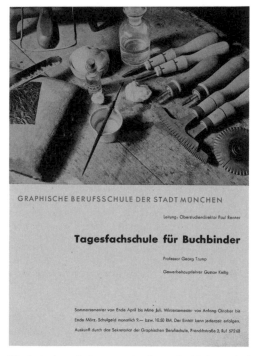

28 A student design exercise from the Meisterschule. *c*.1930. A4.

29 Publicity leaflet. 1929. A5. Designed and typeset by students at the Meisterschule.

PAUL RENNER

innovation, whereas, in truth, typography was a sideline at the school. The common perception today of Bauhaus typography – compositions with sanserif, red and black bars, and oversized page numbers – is largely formed by official and publicity documents designed for the school itself by the teachers Moholy-Nagy, Bayer and Joost Schmidt.[40] The New Typography was given impetus by the Bauhaus, but it was developed into an approach that was widely applicable at the Munich schools.

The Munich schools were not set up to train freelance designers; graduates took up positions in the trade, and in this sense, the Meisterschule gained a solid reputation, attracting students from all over Europe, in particular from Scandinavia and Switzerland. Although student work from the Munich Meisterschule clearly displays the strong influence and example of teachers like Jan Tschichold and Georg Trump, it also shows a flexible adaptation of modernist style to suit a variety of commercial printing tasks (figures 23–9). In contrast to the overt stylization of Bauhaus typography, the Munich New Typography was tempered by the structural principles that Renner and Tschichold elucidated in their writing about typography.

The Munich schools did not promote a doctrinaire adherence to New Typography. Renner felt that it did not offer the best solution to all problems, although the student work from the Meisterschule shows a general acceptance of asymmetric layout as the most adaptable basis for modern tasks of typography. In type-composition exercises students used roman, sanserif and gothic typefaces, and they were sometimes requested to set a title-page, for example, in both a contemporary style and the classical style of Bodoni (figures 30–1). Renner believed that a critical judgement of historical, typographic forms could only be made after mastering those forms. Someone who was truly 'modern', he believed, would not ignore the 'old and worthy' as 'unmodern'.[41] Renner's critical stance towards New Typography may have caused some tension between him and Jan Tschichold, who was the principal evangelist for New Typography during his Meisterschule period. This may partly explain a strong remark that he made about Renner: Tschichold asked Piet Zwart to send examples of work directly to him, rather than to Renner, and added: 'Renner still doesn't know who you are. And he is someone

30 & 31 Two title-page setting exercises executed by students at the Meisterschule. *c.*1929. Typefaces are Walbaum-Fraktur and Bodoni-Antiqua.

40 See the reconsideration by Robin Kinross of the Bauhaus's reputation for typography in 'Das Bauhaus im Kontext der neuen Typographie', in Brüning (ed.), *Das A und O des Bauhauses*, pp. 9–14.
41 'Modern, traditionell, modisch' (1932d) p. 66.

32 & 33 (above) 'Before' and 'after' versions of an advertisement, from a student exercise at the Meisterschule.

34 (above right) Standardized letterhead designed by students at the Meisterschule. *c.*1930. Detail of A4 sheet. This shows that gothic type was not fully excluded from typography at the Meisterschule under Renner and Tschichold. Here a gothic is mixed with Futura.

who has changed sides [*ein Überläufer*].'[42] Jan Tschichold's wife Edith recalled later that her husband enjoyed a collegial relationship with his fellow members of staff, but that Renner, who was much better paid than his subordinates, remained rather distant. She also suggested that Renner did not approve of Tschichold's ongoing links with Russian artists.[43]

Renner knew that Tschichold was not entirely happy at the school and that he was considering leaving. Tschichold had threatened to resign, and Renner knew that there were not many suitable replacements for him. This may be one reason for Renner having invited Georg Trump to teach in Munich. Trump was a successful book designer in the style of New Typography, with practical experience in typesetting and printing. He had built up a successful graphic design workshop at the Kunstgewerbe- und Handwerkschule (Arts and Crafts School) in Bielefeld, and Renner was impressed by some of the Bielefeld school's work shown at the 'Pressa' exhibition in 1928. Trump joined the staff at the Munich Meisterschule in 1929 and stayed until 1931, when he moved to the Berlin Kunstgewerbeschule. While he was in Munich, Trump's

42 Letter from Tschichold to Zwart, 14 December 1927, quoted by Kinross in his introduction to Tschichold, *The new typography*, p. xl, note 11.

43 'Interview mit Edith Tschichold in Berzona am 16.8.1979' in Deutscher Werkbund, *Die Zwanziger Jahre…*, pp. 185–6. Edith Tschichold recalled that Renner was only a guest once in the Tschichold house during their seven-year stay in Munich. There was some confusion surrounding Tschichold's appointment at the Meisterschule. Renner had evidently offered him the post of professor, but Renner had mis-understood the situation: Tschichold would only become a professor after a number of years. However, Renner later recalled the 'composure' with which Tschichold met this situation. In some correspondence from the mid 1940s (when the 1920s may admittedly have taken on a rosier glow in the correspondents' minds) the two men seem to have been on friendly terms: Renner even recalled that his wife Annie treasured Tschichold as the only truly gifted teacher at the Meisterschule. (Letter to Tschichold, 31 May 1946.)

innovative slab-serif typeface City was released by the Berthold typefoundry, and it soon became a useful tool for the New Typography.[44]

Other graphic designers who taught at the Munich Meisterschule were Hermann Virl and Eduard Ege. Renner's role was largely that of a figurehead: he had, after all, been cultivating a relationship with the Munich printing trade since before the First World War, and achieved some national notoriety in the process. He later described his position as an 'official', a role in which he felt uncomfortable.[45]

Theories of modern design

Renner's book *Mechanisierte Grafik* (Mechanized graphic design, 1931; figure 35) is often regarded as one of the few serious books on the New Typography, along with Tschichold's *Die neue Typographie*.[46] Renner's book is not a practical manual and it covers several media, including a brief discussion of motion pictures and photography. (These two subjects were integral to the writings of Moholy-Nagy, for example, and Renner may have felt duty-bound to address them.) In contrast to his younger contemporaries, Renner was quite conservative in his guarded acceptance of photographic technologies. Indeed, *Mechanisierte Grafik* is prefaced by a section dealing once more with the philosophical problems of industrialization and mechanization, which Renner still regarded as potential threats to the human spirit. The language in his writings was less apocalyptic than that of his younger contemporaries – such as Moholy-Nagy, Herbert Bayer and Jan Tschichold – and, unlike these theorists, he refrained from listing commandments of modern typography. In *Mechanisierte Grafik,* as well as in several articles he wrote between 1925 and 1932, Renner comprehensively expressed his thoughts on modern design in general, and modern typography in particular.

Renner's contact with the 'New Frankfurt' group of architects and designers spurred him to consider seriously the nature of the new design movement. His contact with Jan Tschichold must also have resulted in some exchange of ideas, although the two men seem never to have been very close. Tschichold's writings about New Typography shared an evangelical zeal with the programmatic writings of

35 Cover of *Mechanisierte Grafik.* 1931. 210 × 155 mm. Black on orange cloth.

44 See Trump, *Vita Activa*, p. 73.

45 'Aus meinem Leben' (1939a) p. 7.

46 Lang, in *Konstruktivismus in Buchkunst*, p. 167, describes Renner's book as an important document, although it was far less widely read than *Die neue Typographie* (1928). Tschichold's book was published by the Educational Association of the German Printing Trade Union and was made available in that trade network: its first edition of 5000 was sold out within three years. *Mechanisierte Grafik* was published by Hermann Reckendorf Verlag, the principal Werkbund publisher: it was published in a quantity of 3000, for which Renner received payment of 3000 Marks and ten per cent royalty. (Letter of 18 November 1930 from Reckendorf to Renner; Nachlaß Renner.) By September 1933 only 1387 copies had been sold, of which only 157 between October 1932 and December 1933. According to the original contract the Reckendorf Verlag was then permitted to pulp the remaining stock, due to these meagre sales. (Letter of 11 December 1933 from Reckendorf to Renner; Nachlaß Renner.)

Constructivism; Renner's views were more critical and distanced. Tschichold was only twenty-six years old in 1928, when his *Die neue Typographie* was published, whereas Renner was fifty, and as an artist trained in the classical tradition, he was more concerned to take a wider historical view of the new design, seeking to place it in relation to traditions of European style and thought.

Renner made a distinction, between what he called 'humanism' and 'materialism'.[47] In his view, the humanist tradition had reached its nadir in the nineteenth century, with a superficial regurgitation of styles 'from the junk cellar of the centuries'. Renner held the art academies partly to blame for this 'eclecticism'. These institutions collected original artefacts and reproductions of art in order to provide models for an education based on imitation. In Renner's view, these schools had 'estranged the artist from craft; he became a draftsman'.[48] From the ever-decreasing circles of historicism, Ruskin and Morris led the way back to what Renner called the 'craft motherland'.[49] However, he considered their example to have ended inevitably in a *cul-de-sac*: '... they did not break free from historical example in this flight into a romantic no man's land. On the contrary, the use of old tools in itself led them progressively back to the medieval forms'.[50] In this judgement Renner included the penmanship of Edward Johnston.

Renner felt that it was inappropriate to transplant the forms of handcraft on to machine-made products. Machine-produced forms do not carry the direct trace of the human hand and, therefore, Renner recommended that they be plain [*sachlich*] and make no pretence of being hand-crafted.[51] In writings of this time, he attempted to analyse how modern, unornamented form related to contemporary German culture:

> One could perhaps say that between the form-tradition still plundered by our eclectics (from which all historical styles of the last millennium have originated) and the New Architecture, there exists a relationship similar to that between an impoverished aristocratic mother and her only daughter, who earns her living herself in a public-sector [*bürgerlichen*] job, and is disowned by the mother, whose name she had long ago given up.[52]

Renner sensed that the society in which he grew up had changed, and, for better or worse, this change had to be accepted. He suggested that symmetrical order was an

47 Herbert Read, in *Art and industry* ([1934] 2nd edn; London: Faber & Faber, 1944) pp. 20–2, made a similar distinction between two kinds of design: that of the humanist tradition, and the 'practical' kind, which was related to abstract art only by its non-prescribed form.

48 'Vom Handwerk zur Großindustrie' (1925f) p. 28. Compare the similar statement by Gropius in *The new architecture and the Bauhaus*, pp. 41–3.

49 'Vom Handwerk zur Großindustrie' (1925f) p. 24.

50 *Mechanisierte Grafik* (1931d) p. 32.

51 'Warum geben wir an Kunstschulen immer noch Schreibunterricht?' (1929g) p. 51. Renner's preference for unpretentious forms in industrially-produced objects is very close to Eric Gill's view. Indeed, in a perceptive review of Gill's *An essay on typography*, Konrad F. Bauer noted the similarity of views expressed in Renner's book *Mechanisierte Grafik* (1931d). Although the difference in the style of the two men's design work might imply that they were opposed in their views, Bauer commented that this was not the case: they were both concerned with the fate of '"craftsmanship" in a mechanized world'. Bauer in *Zeitschrift für Bücherfreunde* (Jhg 36, Dritte Folge 1, Heft 3, March 1932) p. 66.

52 *Kulturbolschewismus?* (1932b) p. 47.

PAUL RENNER

antiquated custom: 'Today the middle seems to us too self-conscious, too emphasized, too final.'[53]

Yet he did not fully assent to a 'materialist' conception of design. He wrestled with the canonical axiom of functionalism defined in the 1860s by the exiled German architect Gottfried Semper: that form should be the result of *Gebrauchszweck, Rohstoff und Technik* – purpose, material and technology.[54] Renner described Semper's axiom as an attempt to 'explain our mysterious world as if it was a mechanical gearbox that set itself in motion a long time ago'.[55] Renner believed that the imagination of the artist or designer was bound to make some contribution to an object's form. He implied that Semper's 'materialist' conception of design was perhaps only fully accepted by the Constructivists in Soviet Russia, but he admitted that Semper's view had provided a necessary cleansing agent, a means of severing the stultified humanist tradition and returning to a consideration of purposeful design.[56]

Renner believed that a 'materialist' approach to design could result in what he called 'technological form'. He perceived this in buildings, bridges and vehicles constructed by modern engineers. He assumed that such people had no artistic pretensions and therefore they utilized the newest materials in a pure response to function. He considered engineers to have brought to life 'the style of our era' because they had soberly responded to the tasks at hand and not been tempted to 'attach the thin cladding motifs of tradition'.[57] Renner derived hope from these efforts for the re-introduction of 'art' to everyday life. In 1926, he stated: 'It is no longer possible to make a living from fine-art painting in a respectable, bourgeois manner. ... This is all very sad, of course. But this collapse poses us the task of searching for a new, wider and more solid basis for art.'[58] He envisaged a situation in which 'technology also means art'.[59] (Here he was returning to the Greek root of the word 'technology': *techne*, meaning 'art'.) Modernism of this kind, also espoused by Walter Gropius, was a curious mixture of looking backward and forward: the Arts and Crafts idea of leap-frogging the last few centuries back to a medieval ideal of non-elitist art was mixed with a pragmatic realization that this ideal could only be achieved with modern technology.

Renner recognized that the functionalist designers of his day praised the work of anonymous engineers, but he com-

53 *Mechanisierte Grafik* (1931d) pp. 85–6.

54 *Technik* is sometimes translated as technique. See Semper's original formulation of the idea in *Der Stil in den technischen und tektonischen Künsten, oder Praktische Aesthetik* ([1861–3] 2nd edn; München: Friedr. Bruckmann's Verlag, 1878) Band.1, p.7.

55 *Mechanisierte Grafik* (1931d) p.22. Renner set the Austrian art theorist Alois Riegl in opposition to Semper. This marked a distinct similarity to the ideas of Peter Behrens, Renner's fellow Werkbund member. See Behrens's essay 'Art and technology' from 1910 in Tilmann Buddensieg & Henning Rogge, *Industriekultur: Peter Behrens and the AEG* (Cambridge, Mass: MIT Press, 1984) pp. 212–19. All the motifs of inter-war modernism are already in evidence here, including the cult of the engineer.

56 'Futura: die Schrift unsrer Zeit' (1928a) pp. 1–2.

57 'Zu den Arbeiten von Ferdinand Kramer' (1927j) p. 322.

58 'Bildungskrise' (1926b) p. 130.

59 'Entbehrliche Künste, notwendige Kunst' (1925b) p. 246.

mented that the functionalist approach, once assimilated into artists' theories, no longer remained unconscious and untainted: instead it acquired the status of a conscious style. Any conscious, formal decision, even if it was the rejection of a notional style, signified to Renner a stylistic choice: he never believed that the forms of New Architecture or New Typography were determined purely by an imagined function:

> Certainly materialism plays an essential role in the development of the modern style. But this development is more mysterious than it appears at first sight. ...
>
> Furthermore, one cannot say that every individual form is ornament if it has no practical function, that it ceases to be ornament at the moment when it is demanded by practical purpose. Everything can have sense and meaning in different spheres of consideration. It is an error in the thinking of our era to leap from one area of thought to another by logical conclusions. Something can be purposeful and beautiful, but it is simply false to say that it is functional and *therefore* beautiful; or that it is unfunctional and therefore ugly. ...
>
> To really know the Modern is to realize that it is not hidden in the undesigned formlessness that is expected by the pure theory of artistic dogma.[60]

Renner felt that the essence of modern design lay in what he called the 'timeless' aspects of design. Despite his assertion that 'art is nothing more than logical design', he believed that a designer had to consciously apply standards of aesthetic quality in order to make an object an artistic success. In his view the 'time-bound' aspect of design was the response to the material and functional demands of any situation. This provided only raw material, 'technological form', which, in order to become good design, required the addition of a 'timeless' aesthetic quality. This belief in certain 'eternal rules of artistic design' marks Renner's views as less radical (and perhaps less romantic) than those modernists who could accept no inheritance from the past, only forms that they imagined to be directly derived from new technology.

To become acquainted with the 'eternal rules', Renner stated that 'we do not need the doubtful aesthetics of art-isms. ... [The eternal rules are] what Cézanne meant when he wrote to Émile Bernard: ..."everything in nature models itself on the sphere, cone and cylinder; it is necessary to learn to paint along these simple lines, then one can do what one wants".'[61]

60 *Kulturbolschewismus?* (1932b) pp. 49–57. Italic in original.
61 *Mechanisierte Grafik* (1931d) p. 34.

PAUL RENNER

The 'timeless' rules, then, were an underlying adherence to primary geometric shapes – the 'simplest and most contrasting forms'.

> It is a matter of basic concepts, categories, categorized seeing. The artistic worth of simplification does not lie in a mysterious magical power emanating from circle, triangle and square; instead the artist simply designs so that the consistent variation, the logical differentiation from these highest categories is apparent, because we only understand such forms.[62]

This concern with geometrical purity is a recurrent idea in twentieth-century modernist art and design, but it is not peculiar to this era. An obsession with geometrical construction permeated the architecture of the ancient world and the Renaissance. Renner had been applying a notion of primary geometry to an appreciation of Roman capital letters since his 1922 book *Typografie als Kunst*.[63] The clarity of this script, he claimed, derived directly from its basis in simple geometric shapes: 'Roman capitals are unsurpassable of their kind. They are a perfection removed from the course of time and appear to belong to every present.'[64] This statement declared an affinity with another of Gottfried Semper's fundamental ideas: the *Urform* (primordial/essential form). Renner posited Roman capitals as the *Urform* of script.

He demanded the integration of utility and beauty in the design of things for use: 'These things should be *sachlich*, usable, efficient, but they should also look good.'[65] He discerned a conscious 'artistic' element in even the most anonymous-seeming modern design. He was trying to derive some way forward from a point between 'humanism' and 'materialism'. He did not accept that form could be derived purely from technology; his advocacy of certain 'timeless' formal laws signified a belief that some solutions were better than others. He remarked that 'culture is not slow perseverance in some venerable, historical form, rather it is eternal renewal under the hierarchy of value'.[66]

Modern typography

Although Renner occasionally designed publicity material (figures 38–43), he remained principally a book designer. He considered, first of all, whether New Typography could be applied to book design. El Lissitzky and Moholy-Nagy both expected New Typography to cause an imminent revolution

62 *Mechanisierte Grafik* (1931d) p. 35. Renner's ideas here bear a striking similarity to those of Le Corbusier in *Towards a new architecture*, pp. 21–3. It is reasonable to assume that Renner had read Le Corbusier's text closely, as he quoted him admiringly on several occasions. For instance see 'Futura: die Schrift unsrer Zeit' (1928a). Le Corbusier also asserted that a functioning object was not inherently beautiful: it only became so by a conscious application of 'platonic grandeur' and 'mathematical order'. Renner had expressed this idea as early as 1910, in 'Zur Kultur des Buches: 1'. Renner's son, Otto, trained as an architect in Le Corbusier's studio, which delighted his father.

63 *Typografie als Kunst* (1922) p. 39. Renner also recalled that his honeymoon in Rome in 1904–5 was an aesthetic experience that defined his life.

64 *Mechanisierte Grafik* (1931d) p. 39. Renner does not qualify his statement by referring to a specific model of Roman capitals.

65 'Modern, traditionell, modisch' (1932d) pp. 71–3.

66 'Kampf um München ...' (1926d) p. 56.

36 & 37 Two entries by Renner for a competition to design the cover of the Werkbund periodical, *Die Form*. 1928. A4. The competition was won by Walter Dexel of Jena.

in the appearance of books. Lissitzky heralded the 'bioscopic book' and Moholy-Nagy also sought to bring the dynamics of film to the pages of a book. In *Die neue Typographie* (1928) Tschichold looked forward to the incorporation of bold typographic distinctions into books, as had been advocated by the Futurist Marinetti, and demonstrated by El Lissitzky in his design for an edition of Mayakovsky's poetry, *For the voice*.

Tschichold admitted however that New Typography was unlikely to revolutionize book design, because existing forms of the book were quite adequate. Paul Renner seems to have implicitly agreed, because the only part of a book that he sought to reform was the title page. He questioned the traditional centred title page, and this led him to question the whole notion of symmetrical typography:

> Nobody would deny that symmetry had become a rigid schema in the old typography, in which the sense and purpose of the printed object were all too often sacrificed. Just as the New Architecture does not seek to make every house a centre of ordered art that isolates itself from the landscape ... so the New Typography has reduced the isolation of individual typographic jobs. A page of classified advertisements, in which no item is centred, consequently loses some of its fragmentary nature and submits itself more easily to a unified total effect.
>
> Considered superficially, New Typography's aversion to symmetry has only one cause: the simple principle that, above all else, a design is to be condemned if it gives priority to beautiful form instead of the task at hand. Present-day applied art is permeated by the attempt to do without ostentation. Not every printed document can or should be made into a work of art. For the mass of printed matter, which must be designed without long deliberation,

38 Poster for exhibition of work from the Bavarian Trade Schools held in Zurich. 1928. 127 × 90 cm. Signed 'Renner' in bottom left-hand corner. The hand-drawn letterforms here prefigure Renner's later typeface Steile Futura (see figure 116).

39 & 40 Cover and pages of a publicity booklet entitled *Krauss ins Haus* (Krauss in the house), for a firm of bathtub manufacturers. 1930. 140 × 150 mm. A collection of poems are combined with drawings and photographs. Photographs by Hans Landgraf; drawings by F. P. Blum. The booklet was sewn with silver thread; the cover is embossed.

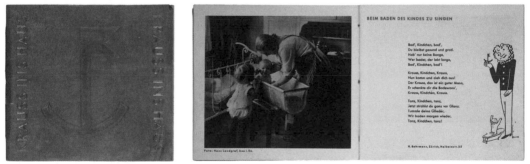

we seek a modest, natural attitude [*Haltung*] that may not satisfy the highest artistic criteria but at least meets practical and technical demands.[67]

Here Renner suggested that modesty (not monumentality) in form was appropriate in fulfilling modern society's workaday needs. Yet he was aware that a moral affirmation of asymmetry held the potential for dogma: New Typography proposed asymmetric order as 'a rebellion against symmetry'; 'Symmetry will again have a chance as soon as asymmetric design becomes so widespread, that it is not simply experi-

[67] *Mechanisierte Grafik* (1931d) pp. 83–4.

41 Cover of a publicity booklet entitled *Spaziergang durch eine Badewannenfabrik* (Tour through a bathtub factory) for the firm of Krauss. 1929. A4. Photographs by Albert Renger-Patzsch.

enced as a reaction to symmetry'.[68] But around 1930, the novelty of New Typography's 'style' seemed integral (at least to some of its theorists) to the functionalist philosophy used in its propagation. Renner himself listed certain visual features specific to the repertoire of New Typography:

> The New Typography adopts from abstract painting the artful construction of surfaces. The calming, abstract forms of those new typefaces that dispense with handwritten movement offer the typographer new shapes of tonal values that are very purely attuned. These types can be used in light, semi-bold, or in saturated black forms. They can be printed in black or in colour; one can link them with coloured, black or tinted [*gerasterten*] shapes; and so New Typography has at its disposal a palette of tonal richness that was not known in earlier times.[69]

Renner stressed here the contrast value of typefaces with systematically linked weights, like his own Futura. He also suggested that new typefaces like Futura provided a natural, formally-neutral environment for half-tone photographs (figure 43). He considered ornament to be out of place in New Typography; rules of all weights could be employed, but only if they could be 'accounted for and justified on purely functional grounds'.[70]

What distinguished Renner's view of modern typography from that of Tschichold was Renner's scepticism about the relation to abstract art. Tschichold's 1925 essay 'Die neue Gestaltung' (The new design) acknowledged the influence of Russian Constructivism and abstract painting on the form of New Typography, although he did take care to point out the difference between art and design.[71] As a painter himself, Renner saw abstract art as a threat to the new tasks of design. Constructivist sculpture seemed faintly ridiculous to him, taking 'free' art to its most absurd:

> Typography is related to free art as a graphic art, but it is at the same time tightly bound up with architecture as an applied art. Hence the New Typography is governed by ideas of modern painting as well as by the concepts that motivate the New Architecture. However, these two worlds of ideas stand in stark opposition to each other. Many opinion-makers of the New Typography only allow the importance of abstract painting. This is a play of pure form, quite a formalism. From here the so-called elemental typography adopted its red circles, its black bars and squares. These were a fashionable success, which shamed the typography more than it served it. Abstract painting is totally irrational; it is an

68 *Mechanisierte Grafik* (1931d) p. 84. In his article 'Gegen den Schematismus in der Typographie' (1933a), Renner described the practice of a formalist, which he characterized as someone who 'does not allow the final form of a document to arise from the given pre-conditions, and does not take into account everything that deserves consideration, rather forces the given text into a schema, either traditional or self-invented'.

69 *Mechanisierte Grafik* (1931d) pp. 82–3. All of these attributes of New Typography can also be found listed by Moholy-Nagy in 'Contemporary typography – aims, practice, criticism' (1924), in Passuth, *Moholy-Nagy*, p. 293.

70 *Mechanisierte Grafik* (1931d) pp. 92–3. Most of the features of New Typography listed by Renner seem to have been adopted from Tschichold's 1925 definition of 'Elemental typography', translated in Kinross, *Modern typography* (1992) p. 89.

71 Tschichold, 'Elementare Typographie', pp. 193–4.

PAUL RENNER

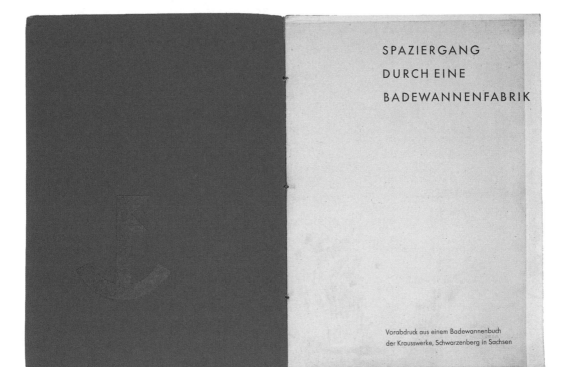

SPAZIERGANG

DURCH EINE

BADEWANNENFABRIK

Vorabdruck aus einem Badewannenbuch
der Krausswerke, Schwarzenberg in Sachsen

Es ist gut, daß Sie, lieber Leser, nicht dabeistehen. Es spritzt manchmal heftig, wenn die geformten Füße an die Wanne geschweißt werden. Ein kurzer Prozeß und ein tadelloser! Der elektrische Kurzschluß treibt so manchen Unfug, hier verrichtet er schnell gute Dienste.

Karl Louis Krauss führte die Feuerverzinkung der Badewannen mit geschweißten Verbindungen und angeschweißten Füßen im Jahre 1905 ein. Ein silberglänzendes Vermögen schwimmt in den riesigen Kesseln. In Glut und Glanz ist jede der schlichten Volkswannen geboren. Hat die Zinkhaut ihre Feuerprobe bestanden, hält sie Jahrzehnte.

42 & 43 Pages from *Spaziergang durch eine Badewannenfabrik*. 1929. A4. (Acetate inserted over title page.)

elevated spirituality, set free from any purpose. The fact that New Typography also recognizes itself in New Architecture often gets its protagonists into arguments with themselves.[72]

According to Renner, the only element of abstract art that might be of positive value to typography was the analytical process of ordering: 'the timeless factor of design' that 'one cannot learn in the drawing and painting classes of academies'. He rejected 'the content-free formalism that characterizes the beginnings of elemental typography'.[73] The geometric forms that Tschichold listed in 1925 as part of the repertoire of 'elemental typography' do not correspond to what Renner meant by the underlying 'geometric' basis of design. He did not mean geometric ornaments, such as were released by the Bauer typefoundry without his involvement as an accompaniment to Futura. The typefoundry, understandably, was trying to profit from the popularity of the new style of New Typography, which became very quickly commercialized by imitation, as its initiators feared. Herbert Bayer was already complaining in 1928 about the proliferation of a misunderstood 'Bauhaus style'. He stated: 'Superficial imitation, however, misunderstands, or overlooks the actual meaning, namely functional application of the elements.'[74]

Standardization

The adoption of standards in New Typography can be seen as part of a rationalized approach to design. Renner had shown an early desire to set out principles (although not exactly standards, or 'norms') for typography in his typographic rules of 1917. These rules were guidelines for quality in typesetting that he intended only as a starting point for compositors. The standards under discussion here are the Deutsche Industrie Normen (DIN), promoted by the Deutscher Normenausschuß (German Standards Committee), as it was called from 1926. This body was initially formed in 1917 to rationalize production for the war effort, but it also established standards for paper sizes (1922) and the disposition of elements in letterheads to accord with standardized stationery and envelopes (1924).

Perhaps the most ardent supporter of standardization in typography was Jan Tschichold, who included a chapter on the subject in his book *Die neue Typographie* (1928). Renner also subscribed wholeheartedly to the adoption of DIN standards for business documentation: in *Mechanisierte Grafik*

72 *Mechanisierte Grafik* (1931d) pp. 71–2.
73 *Mechanisierte Grafik* (1931d) p. 73.
74 Bayer, 'Typography and commercial art forms' (1928) in Wingler (ed.), *The Bauhaus*, p. 135.

PAUL RENNER

(1931), he discussed the standardized letterhead as if it was the most representative aspect of New Typography. He also regarded the business letterhead as the natural environment for asymmetric typography:

New Typography does not begin from any form, rather it considers first of all the function, the required result, the use of the letter and letterhead.

One does not need to think this through for oneself any longer, because the result of a fundamental consideration is available in DIN document 676. In fact everything is considered here: that the address is also usable in a window envelope, and that one can also read the name of the sender in the window; that the date, telephone number, telegram address, post-giro and bank details, as well as the sender's reference, are in a very specific location where every addressee receiving a comprehensively standardized letter will look for them and immediately find them. And, at the same time, every consideration is given to the comfortable service of the typewriter.

We have here in a concrete example the product of purpose, material and technology, not as a goal or end result, rather much more as the starting point for artistic consideration by every modern designer.[75]

Renner regarded the DIN standard as a safeguard against stupidity, but believed that an excellent design would have an added element of aesthetic sensibility.

He also proposed a standardization of information and its layout for the bibliographic details of a book. He argued that cataloguing a book would be made much easier if the information about publication was finally grouped in one place instead of being scattered between the title page and an assortment of other pages. He recommended that: 'The leading librarians should finally work out a standard prescription, in which all necessary or possible details of this kind would be allocated a specific hierarchy and position.' This prescription would provide the 'brief' [Bauaufgabe] – the limits within which the designer could then work. He wanted 'boundaries drawn around objects for use by architectonic design'.[76] This is a desire characteristic of Moderns in the 1920s: to have tasks analysed and clearly described, so that a rationalized solution could be found.

44 & 45 Letterheads for the Munich Municipal Authority, before (top) and after treatment by students at the Meisterschule. c.1930. Both A4. The re-designed version follows the DIN standard for window envelopes.

75 *Mechanisierte Grafik* (1931d) pp. 91–2.

76 'Modern, traditionell, modisch' (1932d) p. 78. Compare the guidelines in the British Standard publication, BS 4719: *Specification for the title leaves of a book* (1971).

4 Futura and the modern letter in Germany

The question of gothic versus roman

The debate concerning the importance of gothic letterforms in German culture, which had been present in learned circles for some centuries, became a political issue in the early twentieth century, not merely restricted to the pages of specialist journals. The first three decades of the century were a period of great political and economic change in Germany, which was redefining its role on the world stage; consequently, there was also a domestic struggle to define the German cultural identity, of which many believed 'Deutsche Schrift' to be an integral part.

Renner's position on this issue was consistently progressive: he openly called for the abolition of fraktur. In some respects, Futura can be seen to reflect his views on the appropriate style for letterforms designed in Germany – an alternative solution to the choice of gothic or roman.

Gothic letterforms have been promoted as inherently German at those times in history when the German national identity was under threat. The first period of such pride in gothic script was the Reformation, when, of course, Germany did not exist in its modern form as a nation state. Martin Luther's use of a gothic typeface for his vernacular bible of 1523 is perhaps the source of the persistent sense of identification with gothic letterforms in Germany.[1] In the sixteenth century, gothic typefaces were in use all over northern Europe for setting texts in vernacular languages, although roman type had gradually spread from Italy and found centres of innovative design in France and the Low Countries. In the first half of the seventeenth century gothic type fell into disuse in England, and in 1739 the Swedish Academy recommended the use of roman type for books. S.H. Steinberg commented that gothic had become a 'German provincialism' by the end of the eighteenth century, but fraktur remained in frequent use well into the nineteenth century in some Scandinavian countries.[2] Certainly, by the turn of the twentieth century, Germany was almost the last outpost of gothic. The tenacity of gothic in Germany also had political causes. Neo-classicism and the international success of modern-face, roman types in the late eighteenth century threatened the supremacy of gothic in Germany. In the spirit of the Enlightenment, German scientific books began to be printed in roman type. Cultural influence from France turned to military imperialism during

1 Luther's bible was initially typeset in a Schwabacher style of typeface, but, from 1534 on, in a fraktur. For a detailed discussion of the ideological dimension behind the use of gothic in Lutheran printing, see John L. Flood, 'Nationalistic currents in early German typography' in *The Library* (Sixth series, vol. xv, no.2, June 1993) pp.125–41.

2 Steinberg, *Five hundred years of printing*, p.126. See also Gustav Stresow, 'Nationale Druckschriften, ja oder nein?' in *Börsenblatt...* (Nr 26, 31 März 1994) p. A88. Jakob Grimm, in the preface to *Deutsches Wörterbuch* (column LIII), also stated that gothic type was still in everyday use in Sweden, Denmark and Finland.

the Napoleonic occupation of the German lands around the turn of the nineteenth century. During the consequent suppression of German culture, gothic script gained symbolic importance as a bulwark of German values.

Some German scholars in the nineteenth century voiced the opinion that gothic typefaces were damaging the international reputation of German books. A leading exponent of this view was Jakob Grimm, the Germanist and (along with his brother, Wilhelm) collector of traditional folk-tales. Grimm believed that the fraktur types generally used in his day were 'malformed and ugly', making German books seem 'barbaric' in comparison with those of other countries. He also remarked that learning both gothic and roman letterforms doubled the problems of schoolchildren, and that German printers had to bear the expense of stocking type of both roman and gothic styles.[3] The dictionary compiled by Grimm, and his works on grammar, were printed in roman (combined with a reformed spelling), a practice that had a long-lasting influence in German philological circles.[4]

Since the Reformation, the cultured elite in German-speaking countries had expressed views on the value of gothic script. For example, Georg Christoph Lichtenberg commented that, when he read a German book printed in roman, he felt as if he had to translate it first.[5] In a letter of 1882 to a German author, Otto von Bismarck emphatically stated that he took much longer to read a page set in roman type than he did to read the same page in gothic. To set the German language in 'Latin' letters, he continued, was as much of an anachronism as setting French or English in 'German' script.[6]

In the German printing trade of the early twentieth century, roman letterforms found some use in specialized applications, such as cartography, and roman type was used in the trade sections of some newspapers, in which international understanding was essential. Some book-artists also began to feel that the florid forms of the common fraktur typefaces were outmoded.[7] However, for most books, newspapers and official documentation, the fraktur variety of gothic type was standard (with roman reserved occasionally for setting foreign words). In 1928, fifty-seven per cent of books published in Germany were typeset in fraktur, a situation that had changed little for one hundred years.[8] Furthermore, schoolchildren still learned to write principally in a gothic cursive, although

3 Grimm, *Deutsches Wörterbuch*, columns LII–LIV.

4 For a detailed account of Grimm's views and his influence see John L. Flood, '"Es verstand sich fast von selbst, dasz die ungestalte und häszliche schrift … beseitigt bleiben muste.": Jacob Grimm's advocacy of roman type'. Yet, in his other role, as a revivalist of German fairy tales, Grimm had his works published in fraktur – they would certainly not have been so popular otherwise. See Kapr, *Fraktur: Form und Geschichte der gebrochenen Schriften*, pp. 64–6. See also David L. Paisey, 'Roman type for German text, a proponent in 1733' in *Gutenberg Jahrbuch* (1983) pp. 232–40.

5 Stresow, 'Nationale Druckschriften', p. A87.

6 Letter quoted in Plata, *Schätze der Typographie: gebrochene Schriften*, p. 15.

7 See comments by Peter Behrens in the preface to the type specimen of his simplified gothic typeface, Behrens-Schrift, in Burke, 'Peter Behrens and the German Letter', *Journal of design history* (vol. 5, no. 1, 1992) pp. 19–37.

8 Flood, '"Es verstand …": Jacob Grimm's advocacy of roman type', p. 303.

PAUL RENNER

generally they also learned to make *lateinische* (roman) letterforms.[9]

On 4 May 1911, a debate took place in the Reichstag in response to a petition from the Allgemeiner Verein für Altschrift (General Association for Antique Script [roman]). This body proposed that the forms of roman type be made standard for use in Germany, especially in handwriting. To this end, it demanded that the teaching of handwriting in schools should begin with roman forms, leaving the more difficult 'broken script' [*Bruchschrift*] until later school years. Opinions in the Reichstag discussion seemed to be split evenly on the issue: some delegates pleaded for gothic to be maintained as integral to the German character, whereas others (mostly liberals and Social Democrats) agreed with the petition, denying that Germany would be harmed by a more general adoption of roman letterforms. The debate ended in confusion, and the vote on the issue was deemed to be inconclusive.[10]

In 1917 the six largest German municipal academies agreed that schoolchildren should primarily be taught to write roman letterforms, but the First World War halted the progress of this initiative. When the Deutsche Akademie in Munich debated the issue in 1926, its members (teachers, typefounders, historians of the book, publishers, professors and public officials) voted almost unanimously against roman: only one voice, Adolf Sommerfeld, prevented a unanimous resolution in favour of gothic.[11]

Renner's views on gothic and roman

In some of Renner's first articles on the issue of the 'typeface of our time', which began to appear in 1925, when work on Futura was underway, he expressed doubts about the suitability of roman letters for the German language. He regarded the combination of capitals (derived from inscriptional forms) and minuscules (derived from cursive writing) as 'problematic' in roman, especially since the German language still used so many capitals. (This was a greater problem in gothic type, as Renner had already observed; see p. 29 above.) Roman type was the perfect garb for Latin, with its predominance of n, m and u shapes, and infrequent capitals, but for German it seemed to him 'a badly fitting loaned garment'.[12] He understood that round elements had been broken and condensed

9 Plata, 'The present status of Black Letter in German-speaking countries', p. 134. This remained the case until the Nazi ban on gothic in 1941.

10 See the account of the debate in Kapr, *Fraktur*, pp. 68–70. The typographer Hans Peter Willberg (born 1930) remembers that he first learnt to read and write 'German script' and later 'Latin script' at school. Willberg, 'Schrift und Typografie im Dritten Reich', p. 87.

11 'Fraktur eller antiqua' in *Norsk Boktrykk Kalender* (Utgitt AV. Den Typografiske Forening I Oslo, 1936).

12 'Revolution der Buchschrift' (1925e) p. 280.

in gothic script to save space; he felt that this feature matched the needs of the German language, which had many long compound words.[13] But he was in no doubt that fraktur, the principal form of 'German script', was decadent. He correctly dated the development of the fraktur style to the chancery of Emperor Maximilian I in the early sixteenth century. The scribe Vincenz Rockner has been credited with developing a decorative, cursive form of gothic script that was then adapted for printing type by the printer Hans Schönsperger and the punchcutter Hieronymous Andreæ. The first fraktur types were used in luxurious courtly printing, such as the book *Theuerdanck* of 1517. In terms of usability as a 'book-script', Renner felt that Rockner's florid style was inferior to the sober forms of gothic script developed by monastic scribes before the advent of printing. 'After Gutenberg', he commented, 'there is no art of writing, only calligraphy'.[14] Renner believed that the forms of fraktur had lost any root in function, because they derived from a luxury script, not from writing for everyday use. Fraktur was 'a self-satisfied, narrow, pointed chancery script; a hermaphrodite, a cross between gothic book-script and gothic cursive'.[15] But he admitted that 'one can, strictly speaking, no longer call a German script without these features "fraktur".'[16]

In the later 1920s, Renner argued that fraktur was not particularly German. This followed from his interpretation of the history of gothic or 'broken' script in general.[17] According to Renner, Roman capitals were the basis of all later western development in letterforms; minuscules had evolved from capital forms during a period of many centuries by progressive influence from the tools and speed of writing. The forms of small letters still present in roman type date back to the Carolingian Minuscule developed in the scriptorium of Charlemagne, or, as Renner called him 'Karl the Great'. Karl's empire (the first German Reich) was centred in what is now Germany, so Renner claimed that roman letterforms were indeed more German than gothic ones, which had originally developed in northern France, the cradle of gothic style in the arts. He remarked that gothic script, which was developed in the twelfth and thirteenth centuries, was written in most of Europe whilst Germany clung to the Carolingian forms.[18]

Renner formulated quite a complex idea of the 'family tree of script', in which the central trunk was the roman form. In

13 Noordzij, in 'Broken scripts and the classification of typefaces' (p. 228), denied that fraktur suited German text in particular; like most scripts derived from the Latin alphabet, he asserted, fraktur looks best used for Latin.

14 'Futura: die Schrift unsrer Zeit' (1928a) p. 3.

15 'Revolution der Buchschrift' (1925e) p. 280.

16 'Die Zukunft unserer Druckschrift' (1925g) p. 87. The DIN 16518 classification of typefaces implies that fraktur is defined by flourished elements. Noordzij, in 'Broken scripts...' (p. 239), disputed this idea, claiming that they are not integral to the style.

17 Renner sometimes used the word 'gotisch' to generically denote all gothic styles, but 'Gotisch' was also the name given by typefounders to the severe form of Textura, the formal gothic style of Gutenberg's first printing type. Of the term 'fraktur' Renner stated in *Die Kunst der Typographie* (1939) p. 242: 'Fraktur is actually the collective name for all typefaces of a gothic style as opposed to roman; today fraktur is mostly understood as a specific kind of gothic typeface that derives from the Theuerdanck-type and differentiates itself from gothic [Textura], rotunda and Schwabacher typefaces.'

18 *Mechanisierte Grafik* (1931d) p. 58.

his view, those stylistic developments that led to digression from roman were side-branches, which, by definition, could only progress further from the central development. Renner categorized gothic styles as such a side-branch, which could only lead to a 'blind alley of specialization'.[19] Fraktur was 'the last outrider of a side-branch that got ever further away from the "middle".'[20] (Renner did not illustrate his idea.)

An informed, opposite view to Renner's was offered by F. H. Ehmcke, a prolific type designer. Ehmcke had been a colleague of Renner's in the Bund Münchner Buchkünstler (Association of Munich Book-Artists), and he taught at the Munich Kunstgewerbeschule. Ehmcke's views were opposed to Renner's on the gothic/roman issue, although the two men seemed to have remained cordial acquaintances. Ehmcke's observations sometimes specifically countered Renner's version of the history of gothic. To include fraktur in the general history of gothic was misleading, in Ehmcke's view: he claimed that no other country had experienced the particular development in the gothic style between the sixteenth and eighteenth centuries that gave rise to the unique German form of fraktur. He contested that the Germans had made gothic their own, even if it was not exclusively German in the beginning.[21] He patriotically evoked the memory of the great period of German literature in the late eighteenth century: he implied that, because the great works of Goethe and Schiller had been printed in fraktur, this style of script was both modern and German.[22] This vague enlistment of the reputation of great Germans was a mark of the conservative faction in twentieth-century debates on German culture. Just as Nietzsche's name could be relied upon as a statement of position without clarification, Goethe and Schiller became sacred words denoting an unarguable level of culture. These two authors were actively involved in the printing of their works, but their preference for fraktur is not beyond question. Both had used Latin and gothic script in their handwriting, and Goethe preferred roman type, which he considered more appropriate for his learned reading audience.[23] Many of Goethe's works were printed in roman during his lifetime by Johann Friedrich Unger, a champion of roman type, who bought the sole rights to distribute Didot's roman in Germany in 1790.

19 *Mechanisierte Grafik* (1931d) p.38.
20 'Vom Stammbaum der Schrift' (1927i) p.86.
21 Ehmcke, 'Deutsche Schrift und ihre Entwicklung' (1933) in *Geordnetes und Gültiges*, pp.70–1.
22 Ehmcke, 'Zum Streit um die Fraktur' (1910) in *Persönliches und Sachliches*, pp.20–1.
23 Kapr, *Fraktur*, pp.64–6.

Renner believed that it was insulting to the great figures of German culture to ally them with the ostentatious forms of fraktur:

> All typical frakturs lack the simple humanity, the natural nobility of the roman forms. Furthermore, I am not one of those Germans who consider such petit-bourgeois elaborateness as an inborn quality of the German people that we should take care to preserve.[24]

Renner's rejection of gothic was more strident in his writings of the late 1920s and early 1930s: his Futura typeface was released in 1927 and he publicized it in his writings as a solution to the question of 'gothic or roman?' From 1925, the Bauhaus graphic designers also began to publish their views on the appropriate form of letters for the modern age, and Renner may have caught some of their epoch-making tone, although he distrusted many of their views. The Bauhaus letterform-theorists, Joost Schmidt and Herbert Bayer, were not ignorant of typographic history, but they shared a view that history was there only to be swept away in favour of sanserif, the only true typographical expression of the modern age.[25] Like them, Renner dismissed fraktur, but he only accepted sanserif as its replacement on the condition of further development.

Indeed Renner can be fairly said to have developed his advocacy of a sanserif form independently of the Bauhaus theorists.[26] He was keen to point out later that the final form of Futura had been substantially realized before the publication of Bayer's 'universal' alphabet in July 1926.[27] Already in January 1925, he was tentatively suggesting that 'roman itself is very capable of development', and that modern machine technology 'will probably create a new abstract roman *Typus*', the beginnings of which he saw in the 'unjustifiably so-called grotesk types'.[28] As the 1920s wore on, and Futura came on the market, Renner had articles published with titles like 'The typeface of our time', and 'On the script of the future', in which he began to advocate a new form of grotesk, supported by general theories about form in the mechanized era (see pp. 65–9 above). He attempted to promote Futura as a kind of 'typeface to end all typefaces' [my words], and, consequently, there was no more room for doubt in his writings about the need to be rid of fraktur. He compared it to a style of national dress, like *Lederhosen*, a left-over of a style from a previous era that could now only seem quaint.[29] (To express such a quaint-

24 'Die Zukunft unserer Druckschrift' (1925g) p. 86.

25 See Schmidt's article 'Schrift?' (1929) in Fleischmann (ed.), *Bauhaus: Drucksachen Typografie Reklame*, pp. 30–1.

26 In his book *Typografie als Kunst* (1922a) p. 53, Renner was already thinking his way towards the concept of a typeface that would express 'the specific and functional will-to-art' of the twentieth century. In some books that briefly mention Futura, it is lumped together with the Bauhaus alphabets: for example, Peter Karow, *Font technology* (Berlin-Heidelberg: Springer Verlag, 1994) p. 221, and Mike Mills, 'Universal type in its historical context' in Ellen Lupton and J. Abbott Miller (ed.), *The ABCs of ▲ ■ ●: the Bauhaus and design theory* (London: Thames and Hudson, 1993) p. 41. Yet Renner does not seem to have been in contact with people at the Bauhaus during the 1920s.

27 Letter to the Bauer typefoundry, 5 April 1940 .

28 'Neue Ziele des Schriftschaffens' (1925c) pp. 22–3.

29 'Type und Typographie' (1928e) p. 461

PAUL RENNER

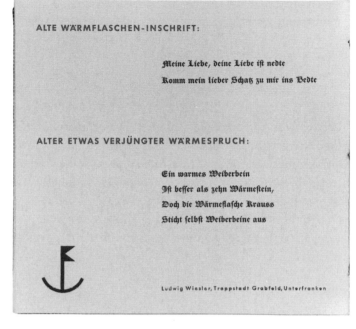

ALTE WÄRMFLASCHEN-INSCHRIFT:

Meine Liebe, deine Liebe ist nedte
Komm mein lieber Schatz zu mir ins Bedte

ALTER ETWAS VERJÜNGTER WÄRMESPRUCH:

Ein warmes Weiberbein
Ist besser als zehn Wärmestein,
Doch die Wärmeflasche Krauss
Sticht selbst Weiberbeine aus

Ludwig Wiesler, Trappstadt Grabfeld, Unterfranken

46 Page from publicity booklet *Krauss ins Haus.* 1930. 140 × 150 mm. Gothic type black, Futura red, anchor blue.

ness, he used fraktur in 1930 for a few lines of archaic verse in the design of a publicity booklet; figure 46.) Echoing Jakob Grimm, he turned the conventional nationalist viewpoint on its head and argued for an outward-looking policy; according to Renner, roman type was now the 'world letter' (he should have said European), and Germany had to bring itself up to date. He stated: 'In the national interest and in the interest of our wonderful German language we should finally renounce broken script.'[30] While he always criticized conventional, backward-looking notions of German culture, it is clear from his words that he never lost an element of national pride. But by 1931 he must have sensed that gothic script was becoming a part of Nazi propaganda, because he wrote in the *Frankfurter Zeitung*: 'Therefore all gothic typefaces will also disappear, even if they are dubbed German by a misguided nationalism.'[31]

'The typeface of our time can only be a roman.' So Renner stated in 1928, the year after Futura came on to the market. Yet he thought that 'classical' typefaces seemed old-fashioned in the era that produced the 'noble forms of cars and aeroplanes, of sail yachts and ocean liners, of machines and bridges'.[32] Renner's language here echoes the writing of Le Corbusier, with whom he shared a view that the basic forms of modern engineering had to be consciously elevated to the status of art by an artist:

30 'Gegen den Dogmatismus in der Kunst' (1928b) p. 314.
31 'Das Schöne Buch' (1931e) p. 4.
32 'Über die Schrift der Zukunft' (1928f) p. 190.

These demands of our current sense of form [*Formgefühl*] are best met by the image of grotesk types, the most recent stage in the organic development of script, untouched by the artist. These grotesk types are the 'nature' to which we must return; they mean the same to us as engineer-buildings do to modern architects. If we succeed in conquering this material, in becoming masters of this 'nature' as artists, then we will find the typeface of our time.[33]

Renner's answer to the question 'gothic or roman?' seemed to be a characteristically German yearning for a 'third way' – a revitalization of grotesk (sanserif), to make it some kind of elemental, universal form of roman. Thereby Renner certainly denied that gothic was essential to modern Germany: instead he sought to enter into the arena of international, contemporary style, carried along by the rhetoric of the Moderns of the late 1920s.

Futura

Renner made the first drawings for the typeface that became Futura in the summer of 1924. One day, Siegfried Buchenau, the founder of the bibliophile journal *Imprimatur*, brought Jakob Hegner to visit Renner in his Munich studio. Hegner, who ran a publishing and printing firm in Hellerau near Dresden, was an early champion of roman type in Germany for modern, literary publishing. He did not know that Renner was also an artist, and was pleasantly surprised to see his landscape paintings. Hegner was seeking a designer for a modern printing type, and he entreated Renner to work on this project. Hegner believed that only a painter could carry out his commission, as he feared that 'the famous masters of the art of script might approach the task with too much

33 'Die Schrift unserer Zeit' (1927g) p. 110. Also in this article Renner mentioned that grotesk had formerly been called *Steinschrift*, literally meaning 'stone-script'. In a useful discussion of terminology for sanserif letterforms, G. K. Schauer equated the term *Steinschrift* with *Lapidarschrift*, implying that it alluded to monumental inscriptional models ('Die Herkunft von Linearschriften' in *Börsenblatt*..., Frankfurter Ausgabe, Nr 22a, 19 March 1959, pp. 294–8). In another essay, Schauer also suggested a derivation of the term grotesk from *Grotte* (grotto), which implies that lettering in tombs and vaults served as models for serifless letterforms. (Schauer, 'Schrift und

Typographie' in Ernst L. Hauswedell & Christian Voigt [ed.], *Buchkunst und Literatur in Deutschland 1750 bis 1850*, Hamburg: Maximilian-Gesellschaft, 1977, p. 52.) Grotesk was probably a German modification of the term 'grotesque' used in British type specimens. James Mosley has provided a convincing account of epigraphic lineage for the British revival of sanserif letterforms in the late eighteenth century in his essay 'The nymph and the grot'. But Renner suggested that *Steinschrift* was a style that 'arose under the sponsorship of lithography', implying that the 'stone' in 'stone-script' referred to lithographic stone, as in the German term for lithography, *Steindruck* ('Die Schrift

unserer Zeit' [1927g] p. 109). Lettering drawn for lithography in the nineteenth century displayed an eclectic and inventive mixture of styles (including sanserif), which German typefounders made it their business to emulate by cutting imitations of many of the lithographed letterforms. It is likely that the epigraphic source of *Steinschrift* had been forgotten by the 1920s, when Renner was writing. In the comprehensive collection of German typefaces edited by Emil Wetzig, *Handbuch der Schriftarten*, issued just before the release of Futura, Erbar, and Kabel, most of the sanserif typefaces shown are called 'Grotesk'; a few are called 'Steinschrift', and one is called 'Lapidar'.

PAUL RENNER

aɑɑɑbbþbc
ddefgghij
klmɲooɔpp
qqrrſstuv
wxxyz
ʌɪɪʃɪɪʃɪck ß

ABCDEFG
HIJKLMN
OPQRST
UVWXYZ
1234567890
&-»!?*§(,,

47 (above) Drawings described as 'Paul Renner's first designs for Futura' in Megaw, '20th century sans serif types'. (80 per cent; the fault in ſ occurs in the original reproduction.)

prejudice'.[34] He had already commissioned designs for type-faces from two other painters, Lyonel Feininger and Karl Schmidt-Rottluff.[35] Hegner said that he was on the advisory committee of a Dresden typefounder, the Schriftgießerei AG (formerly Brüder Butter).[36] The day after Hegner's visit Renner drew several versions of the words 'Die Schrift unserer Zeit' (the typeface of our time), which he implied later were the words Hegner had used to him.[37] Buchenau and Hegner liked the version that later became Futura: Hegner especially liked the ſſ ligature (figure 47), which he compared to the shape of a horseshoe magnet. Renner quickly supplied the rest of the characters, sketched on blue graph paper, and sent them to Hegner. He heard nothing for some months, and requested the drawings back. Then he sent them to his former student, Heinrich Jost, the artistic adviser at the Bauer typefoundry in Frankfurt, who showed the design to the proprietor of the foundry, Georg Hartmann. Hartmann was enthusiastic and a lengthy collaboration on the design began with the immediate cutting of a trial size in winter 1924/5 (figure 48, overleaf).[38]

34 Hegner's view summarized by Renner in 'Aus der Geschichte der neuen deutschen Typografie' (Unpublished typescript of a lecture given at the Jahresversammlung des Graphischen Gewerbes [Annual Conference of the Graphic Trade] in Freiburg, 1947; Nachlaß Renner) p. 8.

35 'Aus der Geschichte der neuen deutschen Typografie' (1947; Nachlaß Renner) pp. 8–9. Feininger made illustrations for publications of the Bauhaus in its initial, expressionist phase; Schmidt-Rottluff made some lettering compositions in 1920, illustrated in Ehmcke, Schrift, pp. 56–7.

36 This foundry had produced an expressionist typeface designed by Georg von Mendelssohn in 1921, which Renner had described as an attempt to produce a contemporary roman. 'Neue Ziele des Schriftschaffens' (1925c) p. 24.

37 'Vom Georg-Müller-Buch ...' (1939d) p. 5.

38 'Aus der Geschichte der neuen deutschen Typografie' (1947; Nachlaß Renner) p. 8. Konrad F. Bauer, a prolific printing scholar and type designer, who collaborated with the Bauer typefoundry (although unrelated to the family that founded the business), commented in Imprimatur (Jhg 2, 1931) p. 68, that the first trial settings of Futura were made in 'Winter 1925', by which he must have meant 1924/5. A trial casting of Futura was illustrated by F. H. Ehmcke in an afterword to his book Schrift (figure 48), which was dated by Ehmcke: 9 July 1925. At this stage the typeface had already been christened; the name 'Futura' was given by Renner's colleague at the Frankfurter Kunstschule, Fritz Wichert.

48 (left) Trial cut of Futura illustrated in Ehmcke, *Schrift*. 1925. (57 per cent.)

> VON SCHREIBKUNST UND DRUCKSCHRIFT
> An der Spitze der europäischen Schriften ſtehen
> die römischen Versalien, aufgebaut aus Dreieck,
> Kreis und Geviert, den denkbar einfachſten und
> denkbar gegensätzlichſten Formen.

49 Invitation card typeset in a trial cut of Futura. 1925. The unconventional forms of small letters are all present, whereas the capitals are little different to those in the finally released typeface. Note that the German rules for the use of long ſ and short s are observed in line 6. First word and third line in red. (59 per cent.)

> EINLADUNG zum Vortrag
> des Herrn Paul Renner aus München:
> TOTE ODER LEBENDE SCHRIFT?
> am Freitag, den 3. Juli abends 8 Uhr
> im großen Saale des Löwenbräu
> Große Gallusſtraße 17
> Bildungsverband der deutschen
> Buchdrucker Ortsgruppe Frankfurt

Renner specifically dated his drawings and the trial cutting in a lecture of 1947, as he came to feel a little resentful that many similar types were released almost simultaneously with Futura in late 1927: for instance, Rudolf Koch's Kabel (Klingspor), Neuzeit-Grotesk and Elegant-Grotesk (both Stempel). Erbar-Grotesk (Ludwig & Mayer), which is very similar in its capital forms to Futura, was released in 1926, before Futura, although Renner claimed that it too relied heavily on his own design, which he had publicized early in 1925.[39] Renner claimed later that, ignorant of how long it took to produce a typeface, he 'unthinkingly' showed slides of the first trial proofs at lectures he gave during 1925, and 'told the whole world what had led me to this new type form'.[40]

39 In a letter to Karl H. Salzmann of 1944, Renner wrote: 'Erbar and Kabel stem from Futura, although they came on the market earlier. Futura was the type that, already in 1925, had to be applied to everything in Frankfurt am Main, by order of the City Planning Office. The imitations of Futura prove that I found the type to fit the style of that time.' Jakob Erbar claimed to have begun his sanserif in 1913/4: see Megaw, '20th Century Sans Serif types', p. 28; and Tracy, *Letters of credit*, pp. 92–3. Indeed, Erbar had been concerned with grotesk forms already in 1910, when he designed his Feder-Grotesk, a sanserif

with stroke contrast, for Ludwig and Mayer. Neumann, in 'Frankfurter Typografie' (p. 33), commented that Erbar could therefore have provided some inspiration for Futura, but the trial versions of Futura from 1925 (figures 48–9) show that the design was well underway before Erbar's release in 1926. Indeed, soon after Futura's release, Erbar was offered with alternative versions of sev-

eral capital letters (the splayed M, with pointed apexes for instance), to make it more similar to Futura, and in 1961, the same was done for the small letters.

40 'Vom Georg-Müller-Buch …' (1939d) p. 7. Renner also recalled that he showed initial versions of Futura in a 1925 lecture at the Kölner Werbeschule, where Jakob Erbar taught. (Letter to the Bauer typefoundry, 14 March 1940.)

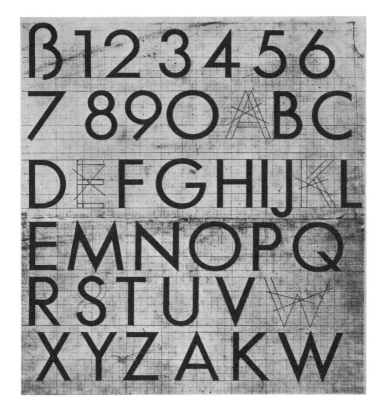

50 Design for geometric capitals, variously attributed to Paul Renner or Ferdinand Kramer. c.1925.

The trial cut of Futura was also used in invitations to these lectures (figure 49). Renner explained the lengthy genesis of Futura (from late 1924 to early 1928) as the result of his collaboration with Georg Hartmann at Bauer, whose standards of excellence matched Renner's own. The typeface could have been rushed, but Renner and Hartmann were not content until many trial versions had been rejected in the interests of achieving the subtle design features that gave the appearance of true geometric letterforms.

Some writers have commented that Renner was inspired to design Futura by the signing alphabet designed by his colleague at the Frankfurter Kunstschule, the architect Ferdinand Kramer. This suggestion was first made by Hans Peter Willberg in 1969, and has been repeated in several publications since.[41] Renner only began teaching in Frankfurt in May 1925 (when Futura was firmly in production), and it is not likely that he knew of Kramer before this. Renner stated in 1939 that soon after his arrival in Frankfurt, he was commissioned by the City Planning Office to re-draw his typeface (still work in progress) as a model for public signing in the city.[42] A sketch of

41 Willberg, *Schrift im Bauhaus/ Die Futura von Paul Renner*. See Spiekermann, 'Futura – a typeface of its time' for a more balanced view. An authoritative examination of the Kramer/Renner issue can be found in Stresow, 'Paul Renner und die Konzeption der Futura'. Stresow questions the accuracy of attributing partial credit for Futura to Kramer, with reference to Renner's autobiographical essays.

42 'Vom Georg-Müller-Buch …' (1939d) p. 7. See the photographs of lettering on Frankfurt buildings of these years in Lane, *Architecture and politics…*, pp. 100–1.

51 Shop fascia in Frankfurt am Main, with lettering similar to Futura capitals. Photographed c.1927.

some constructed capitals on graph paper, which are very similar to Futura capitals, has been variously reproduced and described as either a preliminary sketch for Futura by Renner, or as the so-called 'Kramer-Grotesk' developed by Ferdinand Kramer for signing in Frankfurt (figure 50).[43] Hans Peter Willberg asserted that Kramer used his design for the fascia of his family's hat shop in Frankfurt (figure 51). A photograph of this shop fascia was shown in the periodical *Das Neue Frankfurt* (along with other examples of a Futura-like set of capitals in use on buildings), but the design was credited to Paul Renner.[44]

It would be impossible now to ascertain the exact roles played by Renner and Kramer in the development of Futura. By his own account Renner had begun work on Futura before he reached Frankfurt.[45] Yet Renner and Kramer became good friends and were both impressed with each other's work. It seems likely that there was a free exchange of ideas between them.[46] The graph-paper sketch (figure 50) – if not executed by Kramer himself – could have been done by Renner for Kramer's purposes as an official of the City Planning Office. The sketch contains only capital letters, as is customary with architectural lettering, whereas Renner's initial sketches for Hegner of 1924 included small letters (hence Hegner's liking of the ſt ligature; figure 47). It was undoubtedly Renner's designs which were developed into printing type as Futura.

This is not to say that Renner must be considered the sole author of the typeface. The execution of Renner's ideas was overseen at the Bauer typefoundry in Frankfurt by Heinrich Jost, the company's artistic adviser. Jost had become a distinguished type designer and typographer himself: he designed a slab serif typeface released soon after Futura called Beton,

43 Renner is credited as the author of this sketch in: Bauer, *Wie eine Buchdruckschrift entsteht*, and in Karow, *Font technology*, p. 61. It is credited to Ferdinand Kramer in Willberg, *Schrift im Bauhaus/Die Futura von Paul Renner*; 'Hans Eckstein zum 80. Geburtstag unseres Ehrenmitglieds Ferdinand Kramer', *Form* (Jhg 81, Nr 1, 1978) p. 68; and in Kramer, *Ferdinand Kramer Werkkatalog 1923–1974*, figure 21.

44 'Neue Reklame in Frankfurt am Main' in *Das Neue Frankfurt* (Jhg 2, Heft 3, January 1927) p. 61.

45 A version of Renner's account of the events that led him to design Futura was also contained in his autobiographical fragment, 'Vom Georg-Müller-Buch...' (1939d), which appeared in *Imprimatur*. This periodical was edited by Siegfried Buchenau, one of the visitors present at the meeting that gave rise to the first designs. It seems unlikely that Buchenau would have allowed the inclusion of the story if he did not believe it to be true. Stresow, 'Paul Renner und die Konzeption der Futura', p. B44.

46 Arnold, *Entstehung und Werdegang der Futura*, p. 19.

PAUL RENNER

which exhibits the same sensitive moderation of constructed geometric forms (indeed it can be considered as Futura with slab serifs; figure 52). Bauer did not have a drawing office in the sense that the Monotype works in England did: Bauer typefaces were still produced in 1927 by a mixture of hand-punchcutting and pantographic processes.[47] In many of his articles about Futura, Renner's words imply that the typeface was produced using machine processes: he commented that 'the engineer collaborated' in Futura.[48] Renner may have been referring to the engineers at the Bauer typefoundry, yet his statement perhaps carries more rhetorical weight than factual accuracy. By 'the engineer' he was surely referring to the romantic, generic idea of the engineer, as invoked by Le Corbusier and Tschichold. But there is evidence that Futura was cut pantographically, rather than manually. Some copper patterns for pantographic matrix production still survive, showing rejected versions of some characters (figure 54, overleaf). The presence of several forms of the same letter on these copper patterns implies a process of trial and error. This explains why the typeface took almost three years to produce, as the design staff at the typefoundry must have been exercising their own judgement to provide new versions for Renner, Heinrich Jost and Georg Hartmann to assess. Given that Renner returned to work in Munich in May 1926, his communications with the foundry in Frankfurt must have been carried out largely by post after that date.

Renner believed there to have been a regeneration of German type design at the turn of the twentieth century, due to the participation of artists, beginning with Peter Behrens and Otto Eckmann at the Klingspor typefoundry. But, he commented: 'They made no models for patterns that the engraving machine could follow. Rather their designs demanded the collaboration of a skilful punchcutter.'[49] Here Renner implied that, for his own part, he did supply finished drawings that served as artwork for mechanical production. Accepting the evidence of trial-and-error methods described above, it is reasonable to assume that Renner did not supply master drawings for each size to be cut by the typefoundry. Futura was very sensitively redesigned for each type-size in its original foundry version, for which credit must be largely due to the craft knowledge and industrial skills possessed by the production staff at the Bauer typefoundry (figure 53).[50]

Representative
Bought Magnifi
MECHANIC

52 Beton Medium, at 18 point size. Bauer, 1931. Designed by Heinrich Jost.

53 12 point size of Futura Regular (above) enlarged to the same x-height as the 48 point size (below). From type specimen, *Futura: die Schrift unserer Zeit*, c.1928.

47 A publicity booklet issued by the Bauer'sche Gießerei, *Wie ein Druck-Buchstabe entsteht*, gives an idea of the production process at Bauer. An English translation of this booklet was issued by Bauer's British distributor Soldans, entitled *From sketch to type*. A second edition of the German text, credited to Konrad F. Bauer, *Wie eine Buchdruck-schrift entsteht*, gives more details on technological processes. Lane, 'Twentieth-century punchcutters' (p.10), asserts that Futura was cut pantographically.
48 'Über die Schrift der Zukunft' (1928f) p.192.
49 'Die Schrift unserer Zeit' (1927g), p.109.
50 A member of the design staff at Bauer during the production of Futura was Adolf Bernd, who had trained with Rudolf Koch at the Offenbach school. Bernd was Heinrich Jost's assistant and worked closely with him on Futura. In a letter to Gustav Stresow of 20 December 1993, Bernd commented that, although Futura was 'the work of Renner', Jost was responsible for its successful development as a family of related weights and variants. Bernd himself worked on Futura Black, and was responsible for working out some of its letterforms.

54 Character outlines incised in copper plates that served as patterns for matrix engraving during the production of Futura (for the 20 point size of the regular weight). c.1925. Outlines have been extracted from intaglio prints made from the plates, and rendered positive & the right way round. Crossings out and other marks on the plates have been retained. (40 per cent.)

　　　　PAUL RENNER

55 Sütterlin-Schrift, a model for children's handwriting in use in Germany in the early 1920s.

Futura's contemporaries

Renner's rhetoric implied that Futura arose almost organically from the prevalent 'sense of form', from the *Zeitgeist*. Whether there can be a 'spirit of a time' that exists independently of individual activity is questionable, yet ideas of primary geometry and elemental form were current in German artistic circles in the 1920s.

It has been suggested that another influence on German sanserifs of the 1920s was Edward Johnston's London Underground sanserif of 1916, used initially for station nameplates. Some British writers in the 1930s referred to a delegation of German graphic artists who visited London and were very impressed by the design.[51] This visit by the Bund Deutscher Gebrauchsgraphiker took place in 1925. Renner did not make the trip to London, but Heinrich Jost, artistic adviser at the Bauer typefoundry, did. A report of the excursion was published in the journal *Gebrauchsgraphik*. It was mentioned that the visitors were impressed with the advertising posters in London, but no specific mention was made of the London Underground station nameplates.[52] Johnston was already an influential figure in Germany, due mainly to the translation by his pupil Anna Simons of his book *Writing & illuminating, & lettering*, published in 1910. Renner claimed not to have known of Johnston's sanserif before he designed Futura: he was so immersed in thinking about his own typeface that he did not notice the work of others.[53]

51 Megaw, in '20th century sans serif types', p. 28; and Carter, 'Sanserif types', p. 42. Jan Tschichold stated that he had been impressed by the Johnston sanserif on a visit to London in 1926, in 'Alfred Fairbank' (1946) in *Schriften*, vol.1, p.301. See also Max Caflisch, 'New Johnston' in *Typografische Monatsblätter* (Jhg 62, Nr 2, 1994) pp.1–8.

52 Gustav Stresow, 'Prototyp der Seriflosen? Eine Fußnote zur Druckschriftgestaltung'. In his authoritative 1938 article, Megaw commented that 'German designers were already at work on their solutions before the German delegation of 1924 [sic] enthused over Johnston's sans'. Denis Megaw was a Belfast typographer who had trained in Germany and made links with German typefounders. It is possible that he brought a copy of the drawing in figure 47 (which is now lost) from Germany himself, enabling him to reproduce it in his article. It is also possible that Jakob Hegner, for whom the drawing was originally made, brought it with him when he settled in England *c.*1938.

53 Letter to the Bauer typefoundry, 14 March 1940. In a letter to Renner of 16 April 1940, Anna Simons, who had returned to live in Germany in 1914, stated her opinion that the Johnston sanserif was not well-known in Germany until she illustrated it in an article in the yearbook *Imprimatur* of 1930/1.

PAUL RENNER

Another way in which Johnston may have indirectly influenced the development of geometric sanserifs in the early twentieth century is by his involvement in establishing models of this kind for teaching writing to schoolchildren. Although Johnston himself denied any direct responsibility for 'print script' (the geometric writing model introduced in Britain in 1922), he had illustrated similar letterforms in *Writing & illuminating, & lettering* as examples of the 'skeletons' of letters – their 'essential or structural forms'.[54] Furthermore, a German model for schoolchildren's writing exhibited similar geometric characteristics: this was the Sütterlin Schrift (figure 55), which was in use in the early 1920s.[55] Exercises in *Schriftschreiben* taught by Renner at the Munich Meisterschule also incorporated the task of drawing the basic, skeletal roman forms with a tool that produced a line of even thickness.[56]

It is futile to attempt an ascription of ultimate originality for the design of sanserifs in the twentieth century; it seems likely that many designers had similar ideas independently. In any case, as Renner himself admitted, the basic forms were already available in the nineteenth-century grotesk types.[57] One of Renner's stated intentions in designing Futura was the harmonious marriage of capitals and small letters, and it is this kind of practical intention that marks the significance of his contribution. Whereas, for instance, the *Bauhäusler* Herbert Bayer designed geometric forms ideologically, with all the lack of subtlety that ensues from compass and ruler, Renner designed pragmatically, for the sake of a usable typeface. Bayer's most famous design, his 'universal' alphabet from 1926, was never produced as type in the form that he proposed, because it was not workable – at least as a typeface for text, which is what Renner set out to design.

The formal characteristics of Futura

Renner stated later that 'grotesk' was not in his vocabulary when he designed Futura. This is untrue: in 1925 he declared his intention to renovate grotesk with certain artistic intentions not characteristic of that kind of type. Grotesk was to him 'a proletarian family, with an inglorious ancestry'[58] (the very aspect of the style that endeared it to Tschichold in the 1920s). Renner's starting point for his design was to use the forms of classical, Roman inscriptional majuscules as a basis

54 *Writing & illuminating, & lettering*, p. 240 & pp. 275–6.

55 Renner certainly knew of Sütterlin Schrift, as he was involved in a campaign to replace it in Munich schools by the more geometric script developed by Jacob Hulliger in Switzerland. (Letter from Fritz Wichert to Renner, 26 April 1932; Nachlaß Renner.) Renner also gave a report on the advantages of Hulliger script for use in Swiss schools. (Letter from the Educational Department of the Kanton Basel Stadt to Renner, 15 December 1932; Nachlaß Renner.)

56 'Vom Georg-Müller-Buch …' (1939d) p. 5. Letterforms produced in this way are shown in some examples of students' lettering supervised by Jan Tschichold at the Munich Meisterschule (NAL). See also Tschichold, *Schriftschreiben für Setzer* (Frankfurt am Main: Klimsch, 1931).

57 There was also a grotesk cut in 1920 by Wagner & Schmidt Stempelschneiderei, Leipzig, which featured certain geometric letterforms that prefigure Futura (especially in the capitals). Illustrated in Bertheau *et al*, *Buchdruckschriften im 20. Jahrhundert* (Technische Hochschule Darmstadt, 1995) p. 191.

58 'Vom Georg-Müller-Buch …' (1939d) p. 5.

for the capitals, and, by doing this, he certainly brought something fresh to the grotesk form, which did not customarily rely on classical rhythm in its capitals (figure 56).[59] He claimed to have begun with the same exercise that he taught his students – reproducing the Roman capitals with a tool that produced a line of even thickness. In his earliest published writings, Renner had praised the elemental form of classical capitals, derived from the simplest shapes: circle, square and triangle.[60] He recalled later: 'In contrast to the then fashionable Constructivists, I did not want to glorify the compass as a tool, instead I wanted to lead form out of the wilderness and back to its origins.' By giving the capitals their *Urform* – that is, without stroke contrast – he claimed to have arrived only by chance at something that could be categorized as grotesk (figures 56–8). Before the appearance of Futura, he could not recall ever having used a grotesk in his many years of work in designing books.[61]

In his published statements during the design and production of Futura, Renner clearly expressed his desire to suppress any visible reference to the calligraphic heritage of small letters, and to bring them under the influence of the static form that governed capitals. In order to produce a typeface attuned to the modern, technological age, Renner believed that the energy of small letters had to be curtailed in deference to the capitals, 'as the form of the Roman capitals is almost inalienable'.[62] Renner recalled his decisions concerning small letters in correspondence with the Bauer typefoundry in 1940, when he remembered designing Futura 'as if it was yesterday':

59 He also remembered being impressed from an early age by the simple clarity of Roman capitals, and had fond childhood memories of copying their forms from type used in commercial printing. (*Mechanisierte Grafik* [1931d] pp. 67–8.)
60 *Typografie als Kunst* (1922a) p. 39.
61 Letter to the Bauer typefoundry, 14 March 1940 .
62 'Das Formproblem der Druckschrift' (1930c) p. 31.

56 AKZIDENZ GROTESK   57 JOHNSTON SANSERIF   58 PAUL RENNER FUTURA

Renner based the proportions of Futura capitals on 'circle, triangle, and square'. He did not consider the circularity of the round letters to be as intrinsic to Futura's character as the forms of E, F, L, T and P. Renner made E, F and L half-square in width and, more importantly for him, the horizontal strokes of E were all the same length. He compared his designs with the forms of these letters in Johnston's sanserif, which he described as closer to a grotesk. Johnston's capital E had differing lengths of horizontal strokes, and was wider in relation to the other capitals than Futura's E. Renner stressed that the uncommonly narrow capitals E, F, L, T and P in Futura defined the character of the typeface to some extent and helped to differentiate between wordshapes. The strictness of principle behind these decisions was what Renner perceived as Futura's originality. (Letter to the Bauer typefoundry, 14 March 1940.)

In designing Futura, everything followed from the desire to carry the strict geometric structure of the capitals into the small letters also.... I consciously suppressed and eradicated all those small qualities that creep in to the design [*Formgebung*] of their own accord when the form is developed from writing – that is, handwriting; this resulted in ɑ instead of a or a: ɡ instead of g: l instead of l : t instead of t : ʊ instead of u or u.[63]

Renner's decision to start from zero, as it were, in designing Futura's small letters marked a decided change from the opinion about typeface design that he expressed before he became so concerned with the necessities of modernist form. In 1913 he had said that the role of the twentieth century's precise technology for type production was essentially imitative:

The task of the reproductive arts consists of rendering the 'tool-language' of the original as faithfully as possible: it must allow the contrast effected by the movement of the brush or pen to be perceived as logical. ...

But the production of entirely strange alphabets, in which the European writing tool, the broad pen, must inevitably be exchanged for another, is as useless an effort as inventing a new language, if this other tool is not subordinated to the broad pen as a means of reproduction.[64]

Renner's statements in the late 1920s demand exactly the opposite, that any trace of 'the writing hand' be obliterated:

Our printing type is not the expression of a movement like hand-writing; everything deriving from a left-to-right dynamic, all thicks and thins, which only entered into script with the quill, make no sense in printing type.[65]

Renner also had an aesthetic reason for ridding small letters of their 'dynamic': he sought to bind capitals and small letters by a common basis in static construction. Consequently, he always considered the small letters to be the true innovation in Futura. Stripped of any handwritten characteristics, they acquired a 'lapidary' character like the capitals.[66] Some would say that he was correct in 1913 when he stated that the trace of human hand movement is a comfort to the eye when reading. In a way, he was aware of the consequences of his experiment in form; he described classical capital letters as 'isolated within their own boundaries':

There is no flow from one to the other. The movement, the vigour these letters receive is through their simple appearance,

63 Letter to the Bauer typefoundry, 14 March 1940. Renner's account of the development of Futura's small letters here may have been slightly distorted in his memory, as the Bauer foundry's trial proofs and published type specimens show that two forms of ɑ and ɡ were developed simultaneously (see figures 62–4).

64 'Buchgewerbe und Bildende Kunst' (1913) pp. 72–4.

65 'Die Schrift unserer Zeit' (1927g) p.110. Herbert Bayer expressed a similar rejection of handwritten character in 'Versuch einer neuen Schrift'.

66 Letter to the Bauer typefoundry, 14 March 1940.

DAS BUCHGEWERBE
Ausstellung in Dresden
KULTUR UND PRESSE
Deutsche Möbelkunst
MEISTERKURSUS
Handwerkskunſt

59 Lines from Futura type specimen. *c.*1928. Showing (from top to bottom), Light, Regular and Bold weights in 36 point size. Note that the Bold weight eschews the pointed apexes in capital A, N, M, V, W, and small v and w. To maintain these points in bold weights would have required too great a reduction of the internal space of the characters. The points are flattened, so that the inner side of the stroke-junction can be opened out; in the case of Futura Bold the strokes become slightly thinner towards the junctions, to avoid the 'flecks' Renner spoke of. In addition, there is an exaggerated opening of the internal junction in these characters in most sizes. This is clearly shown on the copper matrix patterns (figure 54).

the crystalline clarity of the forms. Their life is, so to speak, of spiritual origin. The small letters are entirely different! Here is real life, expressive movement, ductus.[67]

Many people expressed concern to Renner that his renunciation of cursive features (like the curl at the bottom of small letter t) would result in incoherent wordshapes. But Renner insisted that the thematic similarity between letters constructed on geometric principles would provide coherence: 'It is not little marks, rather it is the "spiritual bond" that binds the many individual marks into a unity of form.'[68] Already in his book *Typografie als Kunst* (1922), he had described the function of strokes in capital letters as being to 'circumscribe surface areas' not to 'indicate direction' in themselves.[69] So Renner felt that he was dealing with the balance of shapes within and between letters as much as with the bodily parts of letters themselves. He seemed conscious of the fact that he

67 'Die Zukunft unserer Druckschrift' (1925g) p. 86.

68 'Futura: die Schrift unsrer Zeit' (1928a) pp. 4–5. Renner commented later that many of the typefaces that he considered to be Futura-imitations were 'miserable' because they lacked the consistency of a guiding concept behind the details. It was in order to maintain such a concept, he claimed, that Futura took so long to produce. (Letter to the Bauer typefoundry, 14 March 1940.)

69 *Typografie als Kunst* (1922a) p. 39.

PAUL RENNER

was constructing an 'idea' of a typeface, rather than a set of living letterforms:

> The impression of our printing types is not thrown onto the paper from left to right like handwriting, rather it descends with an impression from above. The script of the future will have to be an honest expression of all these technical processes.[70]

This romantic allusion to the technology of letterpress printing is characteristic of the declamatory tone of Renner's rhetorical articles on 'the new script', a tone that often mars the legitimate observations he made about the problems of designing letterforms. In an article of 1930 entitled 'The problem of form in printing type', Renner detailed the issues taken into consideration when designing Futura. His comments reveal a keen observation of optical phenomena in typefaces; he seemed to have made some study of optics, an interest that undoubtedly ensued from his training as a fine artist. Indeed, he was still guided by a classical requirement of harmonious form, of unity:

> Furthermore, we demand from a printing type a regular, pearl grey; no letter should be blacker than any other and no part of a letter should appear as a fleck. This grey on the opened pages of a book arises from the optical mixture of black letterforms with white paper. ... Generally, where two heavy bars intersect at a right angle or meet in a pointed angle, a zone forms that is not lightened by irradiation, or less strongly so. Dark flecks arise; one can notice them in almost all printing types. Only a few designers and punchcutters succeed in avoiding them.[71]

In typefaces with contrast between thick and thin strokes, this problem is perhaps more avoidable, but with a typeface like Futura, where the impression of monolinearity was intended, the problem of thick stroke junctions is pervasive. Renner must have learned this principle during the progressive moderation of strict geometric construction in the trial versions of Futura; it resulted in the thinning of curves as they meet stems in the final version. (See the various forms of small letter g in figure 54.)[72] As Renner observed, the problem is accentuated in bolder letterforms, and the bold weights of Futura show a subtle mastery of this kind of optical compensation, without ever appearing awkward (figure 59).

It became apparent in Renner's collaboration with the Bauer typefoundry that pure geometry would not result in apparently 'constructed forms':

70 'Vom Stammbaum der Schrift' (1927i) p. 87.
71 'Das Formproblem der Druckschrift' (1930c) pp. 30–1.
72 See also Walter Tracy's sensitive comments on the design of Futura in *Letters of credit*, pp. 93–6.

p p

60 The p on the left (from figure 47) was one of Renner's initial drawings for Futura. The second p is from 48-point Futura Regular, as finally released: it shows the subtlety of drawing which Renner explains in the passage quoted on this page. The stem of the first p seems to extend above the circle, whereas it in fact aligns with the vertex. This is corrected in the second p, which also avoids the thick junctions between the curved and straight strokes.

ss**s**

61 Detail of figure 59, showing the moderation of geometrical construction in the different weights of Futura. The bold letter sacrifices the semblance of geometry to achieve maximum boldness.

The most ample curve is not, as one might believe, the circle constructed with a compass, or the black ring encircled by two concentric circles. The artistic value of a typeface has only to prove itself before the human eye; that is, in the sphere of appearances and not the sphere of mathematical concepts. ...

If one wanted to attach a black ring made from two concentric circles to a vertical stem, this would not result in a p-form that one could use in the typefoundry. The circle actually appears wider than a circle, the horizontal parts seem less strongly curved and considerably thicker than the vertical parts. In the junctions of curve and stem flecks arise and, finally, the stem, even if it is in reality aligned at the top with the horizontal tangent to the curve, will actually seem to extend beyond the vertex of the circle. Therefore, anyone who wants to create a constructive script for the human eye, cannot achieve it with elemental geometric construction.[73] (Figures 60–1.)

Yet, some of Renner's original designs for the small letters in Futura were very quirky, due to an excess of geometrical construction. As he observed, the Roman capital forms are 'almost inalienable', and certainly lend themselves to a monolinear form, so the capital letters of Futura seem to have hardly changed after the first trial casting of the type (figures 48–9). Renner's stated objective was to align the form of the small letters with the capitals, so he had no specific model to follow.[74] His initial designs for a, e, g, n, m, and r all display the attempt to contort conventional forms into a geometric straight-jacket (figures 47–9 & 54). Some of the stranger forms of g and a disappeared early in the production period, along with the uncial form of e, but a, g, n, m, and r were all developed up to the release date along with a, g, n, m, and r.[75] An alternative ampersand and a long ſ were also developed (figure 54). In many of the printed proofs of test type cast in 1927, these forms were randomly interchanged, implying that the matter

73 'Das Formproblem der Druckschrift' (1930c) p.32.
74 Erich Schulz-Anker, in 'Syntax Antiqua, a sans serif on a new basis' (*Gebrauchsgraphik* Heft 8, August 1970) p. 64, perceptively remarked that Renner named the 'Mediäval' type forms as capable of development for the 'type of our time'; Renner did not simply say 'Antiqua' (roman) but 'Mediäval', the specific forms of old-face roman type, as he regarded modern-face roman to be too lifeless (*Mechanisierte Grafik* [1931] p. 54). Later, in 'Fraktur und Antiqua'

(1948c) p. 347, Renner called Futura a 'serifless roman form derived from a cross between classical roman and grotesk'.
75 Edith Tschichold suggested later that Renner had asked Jan Tschichold's opinion of the early designs for Futura during their first correspondence in 1925. She said that her husband had critical comments to make concerning the innovative forms of some small letters. ('Interview mit Edith Tschichold ...', p.184.)

was still undecided (figures 62–4). The п, ɯ, and r were the unconventional character-forms that disrupted the flow of a text least by departing only slightly from the conventional letterforms, and it seems that the typefoundry decided initially to release the typeface with them. They were present in the version of the typeface used to typeset an article by Renner in the literary periodical *Die Literarische Welt*, which was probably the first showing of Futura in its near-finished

AN DER SPITZE DER EUROPÄISCHEN Schriften stehen die römischen Versalien, aufgebaut aus Kreis, Dreieck und Geviert, den denkbar einfachsten und den denkbar gegensätzlichsten Formen. Seltsam strahlt die vornehme und edle Schlichtheit dieser Schrift in unsere Zeit, RENNER 2189427 MÜNCHEN 8416510 Baron & Ullrich 1808652

62 Proof of Futura Light, 24 point size (reduced). Bauer typefoundry. Dated December 1927, just after Futura had first come on to the market. It shows that some small letters were still being tested simultaneously in two different forms. Proofs after 1927 showed the increasing disappearance of the quirkier forms of the small letters.

63 & 64 Sheets of pasted-up proofs taken from trial-cut letters of Futura. Bauer typefoundry, *c.*1927. These sheets were used to assess and amend characters: for instance, the Bold small **s** has been corrected with white ink. (Greatly reduced.)

A B C D E F G H I J K L M N O P
Q R S T U V W X Y Z Ä Ö Ü Æ Œ Ç
a b c d e f g h i j k l m n o p q r ſ s t u v w
x y z ä ö ü ch ck ff fi fl ffl ſſi ſt ß æ œ ç
1 2 3 4 5 6 7 8 9 0 & . , - : ; · ! ? (' « » § † *

Auf besonderen Wunsch liefern wir auch nachstehende Figuren

a g m n ä & 1 2 3 4 5 6 7 8 9 0

A B C D E F G H I J K L M N O
P Q R S T U V W X Y Z Ä Ö Ü
a b c d e f g h i j k l m n o p q r ſ s t
u v w x y z ä ö ü ch ck ff fi fl ffl ſſi ſt ß
1 2 3 4 5 6 7 8 9 0 & . , - : ; · ! ? ' (* † « » §
1 2 3 4 5 6 7 8 9 0

65 (top) Character set as displayed on the back of the first Futura type specimen. Late 1927. The more conventional versions of a, g, n, m (which have now become standard) are shown in addition to the long f. However, the ball-and-stick r was presented as standard, without the offer of the more conventional version. The innovative versions of a, g, n, m and the non-ranging figures are illustrated and offered for supply on special request in this first published specimen.

66 (below) Character set as displayed on the back of the second edition of the Futura type specimen. c.1928. The now familiar version of small r was adopted and the innovative small letters were not featured. (Only the non-ranging figures were now offered on special request.) Note also the improvement in some of the ranging numerals between the first and second editions of the specimen.

Many roman typefaces produced in Germany were provided with ligatures for ch and ck letter combinations, including Futura. But, given that Germany had a greater tradition of gothic type, some German typefoundries did not produce fi and fl ligatures for roman type. Renner had remarked in his earliest writing about typography that these ligatures were essential for setting French and German, and Futura was provided with a full set of ligatures for f and ſ.

This second specimen shows subtle changes to the proportions of some small letters; b, d, g, p, & q in particular are less rounded than in figure 65.

Futura, Magere Paul Renner 1927 Bauersche Gießerei, Frankfurt a. M. 6, 8, 10, 12, 14, 16, 20, 24, 28, 36, 48, 60, 72	Hamburgers	
Kabel, Leichte Rudolf Koch Gebr. Klingspor, Offenbach a. M. 6, 8, 9, 10, 12, 14, 16, 20, 24, 28, 36, 48, 60, 72, 84	Hamburgers	
Futura, Halbfette Paul Renner 1927 Bauersche Gießerei, Frankfurt a. M. 6, 8, 10, 12, 14, 16, 20, 24, 28, 36, 48, 60, 72, 84	Hamburgers	

67 Showing of Futura Light and Regular (with Kabel in-between) in the first supplement (1927) to Wetzig (ed.), *Handbuch der Schriftarten*. Light shows a, m, g; Regular shows a, m, g.

state.[76] In the first type specimen marking Futura's release in late 1927, entitled 'Futura: die Schrift unserer Zeit', some of the text employs these characters, but they were not present in a second edition of the Futura specimen (*c.*1928; see figures 65–6).[77] In this second type specimen non-ranging figures were still offered, but they too soon disappeared from use. Sanserif typefaces had never included non-ranging figures before Futura, and it is another signal of Renner's fresh approach to this style of type that he designed a set.

a g m n ä &
1 2 3 4 5 6 7 8 9 0

a g m n ä &
1 2 3 4 5 6 7 8 9 0

68 Alternative small letters and non-ranging figures initially provided for Light and Bold weights of Futura.

Renner remarked later that, when Futura was originally released, it did not exclusively contain the unconventional small letterforms. He implied that two versions of each were consciously developed:

> It is not so that Futura was initially released with the Constructivist (to use this horrid word) small letters, rather it was in two forms from the outset: you will see yourself from the files, which unfortunately I no longer have, that the a and g forms were cut at the latest in early 1926, if not earlier.[78]

It seems, then, that the typefoundry decided to finally opt for the more conventionally designed characters, perhaps fearing that any quirks might affect the sales of the typeface. Some early press comments contained doubts about the unconventional small letterforms.[79] In publicity material, it was soon stated that a second form of r had been produced in addition

76 'Die alte und neue Buchkunst' (1927a) p. 3. The first trade advertisement for Futura was in *Archiv für Buchgewerbe und Gebrauchsgraphik* (Band 64, Heft 5/6, 1927). Press advertisements in 1927 did not feature the bold weight of Futura extensively, neither did the first edition of the type specimen. Only in a further advertisement in *Klimschs Druckerei-Anzeiger* of February 1928 were all three weights shown in detail (Light, Regular and Bold), as in the second edition of the type specimen.

This implies that the first issue of Futura was only fully completed in February 1928. (See also Lane, 'Futura'.) These dates are also discussed in a document about a copyright dispute concerning Futura & Elegant Grotesk (Stempel). See Burke, 'The authorship of Futura', p. 37.

77 This specimen formed part of a folder called *Futura – die sich die Welt eroberte*, which also included loose examples of Futura in use. The large amount of material in the folder implies that it may well have appeared one or

two years after the initial release. Unfortunately the type specimens are undated. Further evidence of initial confusion about which letterforms to use in the typeface is provided by showings in the first supplement (1927) to Wetzig (ed.), *Handbuch der Schriftarten* (figure 67).

78 Letter to the Bauer Typefoundry, 5 April 1940.

79 For example, see Julius Rodenberg, 'Neues aus den Werkstätten der Schriftgießereien' in *Gutenberg Jahrbuch* (1927) p. 230.

> **Wer hier nur die künstlerische Leistung sieht, wird wenig dagegen einzuwenden haben. Doch empfindet wohl jeder, daß die Formgebung, ja ich möchte sagen die Gesinnung dieser Titel an eine bestimmte Zeit gebunden ist; daß sie eben jener Zeit des Klassizismus angehört. Versuchen wir einmal diese Titel unbefangen anzusehen, ohne die Ehrfurcht vor den historischen Vorbildern! Ist es da nicht etwas sonderbar, am Eingang eines modernen Buches einen solchen Grabstein aufzustellen? Ein solches Doktor-**

69 Text set in Futura Regular (actual size) from *Mechanisierte Grafik* (1931).

to the first ball-and-stick form (r) in order to increase the possible applications of the typeface. Konrad F. Bauer commented on the disappearance of the unconventional small letters:

> These well-considered and well-drawn innovative forms inevitably had an effect that certainly was not intended by its creator. They appeared wilful and bizarre, not necessary and constructive. Therefore, in the process of further work these innovative forms had to be sacrificed one after another to the traditional forms.[80]

Renner, too, admitted that any deviation from easily recognizable letterforms was problematic, pointing out that typography was different from architecture in this sense:

> A definite re-orientation, of the kind seen today in architecture and furniture design, is not possible in script because the necessity of adapting it to purpose already provides a pressing reason for retaining the traditional form.[81]

Renner certainly held an affection at least for the alternative n, m, and r long afterwards: the ball-and-stick form of r was used in his book, *Mechanisierte Grafik* (1931); and in 1944 he maintained that his innovative designs for small letters had been serious attempts at reducing letterforms to their essential parts:

> Unfortunately the n and m forms were not introduced and the Bauer foundry brought the typeface on to the market with the more common variants, which found such passionate and unanimous approval that the original Futura was entirely forgotten in the process.[82]

Yet, in 1939, Renner admitted that his attempt to deny the written dynamic in n, m, and r had resulted in unacceptable letterforms: 'It seems that the forms of n, m, and r which press to the right are indispensable in all European script.'[83]

80 Bauer, reviewing recently released sanserifs in *Imprimatur* (Jhg 2, 1931) p. 68.

81 'Das Formproblem der Druckschrift' (1930c) p. 29.

82 Letter to Karl H. Salzmann, 1944 (Nachlaß Renner). Renner remarked that his preferred form of Futura was used in the books designed by Henry van de Velde for the Institut des Arts Décoratifs in Brussels.

83 *Die Kunst der Typographie* (1939c) p. 62. The m, n, and r resurfaced as alternate sorts for one of the copycat versions of Futura, Vogue (Intertype, 1930). See Mac McGrew, *American metal typefaces of the twentieth century* (New Castle: Oak Knoll, 1993) p. 328.

PAUL RENNER

70 Example of Futura in use. Included with the first edition of the Futura type specimen. Late 1927. 386 × 260 mm. Typography by Hans Leistikow.

71 Mock book advertisement. Included with the first edition of the Futura type specimen. Late 1927. 260 × 193 mm. This choice of subject matter was perhaps influenced by Renner's claim that ancient Roman capitals inspired those of Futura.

Although Renner was attempting to design a typeface with associations of universality, he nevertheless still considered the particular needs of the German language. For this reason, he described Futura as 'an eminently German typeface'.[84] When making his initial designs he deliberately gave the capital C and small c vertically-cut stroke endings, so that they could be closely spaced in relation to subsequent characters (compare the obliquely-cut upper stroke-ending of capital G).[85] In German the letter after C is often H or K, and, if the C is wide, its internal space makes a gap in the word-shape. Another significant feature of Futura, uncommon in previous sanserif typefaces, was the difference in height between capitals and ascenders. Renner deliberately emulated humanistic script by making the ascenders slightly taller than the capitals, thereby reducing the overall visual weight of the capitals in text (figure 69).[86] He commented that this was already an advantage of some roman typefaces for setting languages

84 Letter to the Bauer typefoundry, 9 March 1940.

85 Renner summarized his intention in a letter to the Bauer typefoundry, 14 March 1940.

86 See the illustrations of humanistic script in 'Drei Jahre Futura' (1930b). See also 'Type und Typographie' (1928e) p. 461.

Versalien

A Á À Â Ä Ä Ã Å Å Ă Ā Ą B C Ć Ĉ
Č Ç Ç D Đ Ď Ð E É È Ê Ë Ĕ Ē Ė Ę
F G Ĝ Ğ Ģ H Ĥ I Í Ì Î Ï İ Ī Ĭ Į
J Ĵ J Ɔ K Ķ L Ĺ Ł Ľ Ļ Ḹ L M M M
M N Ń Ň Ñ Ņ Ň O Ó Ò Ô Õ Ơ Ö Ő Ø
P Q R Ŕ Ř Ŗ S Ś Ŝ Š Ş Ş Ş T Ť Ţ
Ŧ U Ú Ù Û Ü Ű Ů Ŭ Ū Ų V W X Y Ý
Ŷ Z Ź Ž Ż Æ Œ Þ

Gemeine

a á à â ä ã å ă ā ą a á à â ä å
a á à â ä ã å α b β c ć ĉ č ç ç
d đ ď d̄ ḍ ð e é è ê ë ě ē ė ę ĕ
ɛ f g ĝ ğ ġ ɡ g ǥ h ĥ i í ì î ï
ı ī ĭ į i î j k ķ l ĺ ł ľ ļ ī ĭ
l m ɱ n ń ň ñ ņ ñ ɲ ñ o ó ò ô õ
ö ő ø p q r ŕ ř ŗ ɾ s ś ŝ š ş ş
š ſ s t ŧ ť ţ ŧ u ú ù û ü ű ů ŭ
ū ų v w x y ý ŷ ÿ z ź ž ż æ œ þ
ch ck ff fi fl ft ij fi ff ft ß & &

Hochstehende Gemeine

a   d   e   g   i   l   m   n   o   r   s   t   v

Normalziffern (auf Halbgeviert)

1 2 3 4 5 6 7 8 9 0

Versalziffern

1 2 3 4 5 6 7 8 9 0

Gemeine Ziffern (mit Ober- und Unterlängen)

1 2 3 4 5 6 7 8 9 0

Bruchziffern, zusammengegossen

% ½ ⅓ ⅔ ¼ ¾ ⅛ ⅜ ⅝ ⅞ ³⁄₁₆

Bruchziffern, zusammensetzbar

1 2 3 4 5 6 7 8 9 0 / 1 2 3 4 5 6 7 8 9 0

Zeichen

£ $ ¢ . , - : ; ! ? ([§ † * '
„ " » « — — – / ·

72 All of the characters available in metal type for Futura's
regular weight at 10 point.

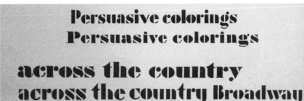

73 Sketch by Renner for Futura Black, showing how it developed to some extent from classic Fat Face display types.

74 Futura Black, as released in 1929.

EISEN- UND STAHLWERK
Handbuch für Geometer

TIROLER VOLKSTRACHTEN
Vereinigung der Kunstfreunde

NEUHEITEN DER SAISON
Die Mustermesse in Dresden

Silberbergwerk ZIGEUNERKIND

75 Samples (in 28 point size) of the variants available in the second wave of Futura releases. 1930. From the top: Semi-bold, Light oblique, Regular oblique, Bold condensed.

other than German, but that it became even more important in typesetting the German language, with its great number of capitals.[87]

Three weights of Futura were available on its first release in 1927/8 (Mager, Halbfett and Fett; Light, Regular and Bold), giving a versatile palette of weight differentiation. Futura Black, a stencil-form display face appeared in 1929 (figures 73–4). In 1930, the next group of variants was released, including a semi-bold, a slanted [*schräg*] version for Light and Regular, and a Bold Condensed variant (figure 75). In the type specimen for the second wave of Futura variants, Renner commented that they had been supplied due to demand from the

87 Renner's statements concerning the moderation of Futura's capital-height prefigured comments made about the same feature in Adrian Frutiger's programmatically-designed sanserif Univers, released in 1957. See John Dreyfus, 'Univers in action', *Penrose annual* (vol. 55, 1961) p. 19.

76 (above left) Second Futura type specimen folder (Mappe 2). *c.*1928. 262 × 195 mm. The cover reads: 'Futura, which conquers the world'.

77 (above right) Example from the second specimen folder. *c.*1928. 386 × 260 mm. Both the above items produced at the Bauer typefoundry under the direction of Heinrich Jost.

trade: compositors felt that a slanted variant was needed to make a distinction different from that made by weight.[88] The Bold Condensed variant, which Renner claimed was requested by customers for advertising, has an effortless quality to its adaptation from the standard width version. A weight between Mager and Halbfett, Futura Buchschrift, was added in 1932, intended specifically for book setting, as its name implies. Renner's principle of maintaining an even texture of colour throughout a text set in Futura permeates all of its variants, and it is this sober attitude that makes them seem like members of a 'modern' type family. Undoubtedly, much of the credit for the consistency within the Futura family must be due to Heinrich Jost and his staff at the Bauer typefoundry.

Renner himself believed that modern, sanserif typefaces were best suited to the requirements of modern typography due to their 'internally unified and well differentiated contrasts'.[89] He felt that the even colour-distribution achieved by Futura in text made it most appropriate for combination with photography, and therefore an essential 'building-brick' of the New Typography.[90] Indeed Futura was promoted as the typeface 'for photomontage'[91] (figure 78). When used for continu-

88 The type specimen was called *Futura: die Ergänzungs-Garnituren* (1930/1), in which Renner penned an essay, 'Drei Jahre Futura' (1930b). Philipp Luidl in *TGM Werkstattbrief 5: kursiv oder schräg* (Munich: Typographische Gesellschaft München, n.d.) commented that Renner must have deliberately chosen the term *schräg*

(oblique) as opposed to *kursiv* (italic) because he knew enough about the history of letterforms to realize that the slanted version of Futura was not a true italic: that is, it does not have cursive forms.
89 'Moderne Typografie' (1946f) p. 140.

90 'Drei Jahre Futura' (1930b) p. 2; *Mechanisierte Grafik* (1931d) p. 82; 'Die alte und neue Buchkunst' (1927a).
91 See note 47 in Robin Kinross's introduction to Tschichold, *The new typography*. See also the advertisement in *Gebrauchsgraphik* (Jhg 10, Heft 1, 1933) unnumbered page after p. 82.

ous text, Futura does give a restful, almost bland impression, which accords with Renner's objectives. Unlike grotesks, which have more compressed letterforms and heavier capitals, Futura seems classical, not only due to the form of its capitals, but also to the open, wide forms of the apparently geometrical small letters.[92] Used in traditional, symmetrical book design, as in Renner's own *Mechanisierte Grafik* (figure 69), Futura does not seem out of place, since it relies on notions of classical form – harmony and evenness of texture. Undoubtedly some modernist typographers spurned it for exactly this reason, preferring the rather rugged form of grotesks. Herbert Matter designed some posters and brochures for the Swiss Tourist Board in 1934–5, in which he inventively mixed photography with grotesk types; yet Renner had set up a typographic style for the Board's publicity material in 1933–4, which included the use of Futura (see figures 86–9). Jan Tschichold's book, *Die neue Typographie* (1928), could feasibly have been set in Futura, which was already on the market when the book was in preparation. Even if the typeface had not been quite ready, Renner could have secured its use for the book; instead Tschichold had it set in a grotesk. There may have been an element of personality clash in this decision; yet, when asked in 1960 why he had not used Futura for the book, Tschichold replied that he never really deemed it suitable for setting text.[93] However, the Czech-born modernist graphic designer Ladislav Sutnar seemed to use Futura almost exclusively, both before and after his emigration to the United States in 1939.[94] The artist and graphic designer Kurt Schwitters was a true Futura-enthusiast: his statements on Futura's 'noble' form rival the publicity material issued by the Bauer typefoundry itself.[95]

78 Example from the first type specimen folder (Mappe 1). 1927. 260 × 193 mm. The legend reads: 'Futura – the typeface of our time matches the picture of our time.' Note that the figure in this piece is dressed like a laboratory technician, as if photomontage was some kind of science. Produced at the Bauer typefoundry under the direction of Heinrich Jost.

92 Otl Aicher, in *Typographie* (2nd edn. Berlin: Ernst & Sohn, 1989) p. 182, likened the rhythm of Futura's wide small letters to 'a string of pearls'.

93 The British designer Ken Garland asked him the question. (Conversation with Ken Garland and Gerard Unger of 18 November 1993.) However, Tschichold did say that Futura was a 'step in the right direction' in *The new typography*, p. 74. He had his book *Schriftschreiben für Setzer* (1931) typeset in Futura, and featured it in his book *Typografische Entwurfstechnik* (1932). He also used it for the text in some

books published by the Bücherkreis, and for that organization's publicity material.

94 See the illustrations in Steven Heller, 'Sutnar', *Eye* (vol. 4, no. 13, summer 1994) pp. 44–57.

95 See the booklet by Schwitters, *Werbe-Gestaltung* (Hannover, n.d. [1930]). For a unified set of official documentation that he designed for the city of Hannover, Schwitters employed Futura, which had been chosen from amongst samples of several typefaces that he had prepared: 'From the different cuts of fraktur, roman and grotesk

typefaces that I showed to the Planning Office, they wanted grotesk as the simplest and clearest type, and from the different grotesk types they chose the Renner-'Futura' from the Bauer typefoundry in Frankfurt a.M., and about a dozen printers, who did not have this typeface, acquired it.' ('Über einheitliche Gestaltung von Drucksachen' [1930?], reprinted in Schwitters, „Typographie kann unter Umständen Kunst sein". Kurt Schwitters: Typographie und Werbegestaltung, p. 87. Schwitters used the term grotesk for Futura).

79 & 80 Cover and pages of type specimen for Plak. Stempel, 1928. A4.

Renner commented that Futura's claim to be 'the typeface of our time' had been justified by its world-wide success. Indeed it was a rapid and enduring commercial success, and is still one of the best-selling typefaces today.[96] Immediately after the Second World War, when production at the Bauer typefoundry was inevitably curtailed, Heinrich Jost wrote to Renner, saying that it was still their most requested typeface: 'I could sell 5 000 marks worth of Futura per day alone', he commented.[97] The Bauer foundry also had well-established branches in New York and Barcelona, which undoubtedly aided the rapidity of Futura's international success. The rights to market Futura in France were purchased by the Deberny & Peignot typefoundry, and Charles Peignot renamed the typeface 'Europe'.[98] Most typefaces intended to compete with Futura commercially (in both Europe and the USA) were either immediately or eventually modified (or provided with alternate characters) to bring them closer to Futura.

Renner himself designed a grotesk bearing some similarity to Futura as a display typeface for Stempel. It was called Plak (1928), and it was promoted as an accompaniment to Stempel's Neuzeit Grotesk family.[99] This seems a strange state of

96 See the table in Karow, *Font technology*, p. 217 for information about Futura's recent popularity. Futura seems to have become unfashionable among some graphic designers in the 1950s and 1960s, particularly in Switzerland, where the modernist typographers favoured typefaces like Monotype Grotesque, and the new grotesks, Helvetica and Univers. P. M. Handover commented that 'Sans serif was not invented by Erbar and Renner and Koch, and their designs now appear as only a phase: they are "dated".' ('Grotesque letters', p. 9). Yet, in America, Futura was used for the notable Volkswagen advertising campaign in the late 1950s, which,

by means of minimalist graphic design, attempted to rid the car of any parochial German associations. It is still used in advertising for Volkswagen.

97 Arnold, *Entstehung und Werdegang der Futura* (1985) p. 23. The Bauer typefoundry in Frankfurt was bombed in the Second World War, destroying its records of sales.

98 As 'Europe', Futura was used very tastefully for headings in *Arts et métiers graphiques*, the periodical in which Charles Peignot was listed as 'directeur'.

99 See *Chronik der Schriftgießerei D. Stempel AG. Frankfurt A.M: Sechzig Jahre im Dienste der Lettern. 1895–1955.* Presumably, Plak's name was derived from *Plakat*, meaning poster.

PAUL RENNER

affairs, since Neuzeit-Grotesk was a rival to Futura; moreover, Renner was still very occupied at that time with the second wave of Futura, released by Bauer in 1930. Plak was produced as wooden letters from 72 point to 624 point in size. Being a poster type, it was available exclusively in bold weights, but in three width variations. The widest variant bears similarities to some of Futura's geometric letterforms, but in the condensed variants, the letters necessarily become more grotesk-like (figures 79–80). Grotesk typefaces were developed in the nineteenth century for use at large sizes on posters, and Renner realized that grotesk forms were more adaptable than Futura in maintaining maximum weight with narrow width.

Futura was adapted for machine composition on the Intertype line-casting machine in 1934: the Light weight was duplexed with the Regular weight, and the Semi-Bold with the Bold. In the USA both Linotype and Monotype companies made close copies of Futura for machine typesetting: Monotype's was called Twentieth Century (1937) and Linotype's (made in association with ATF) was called Spartan (1939). Spartan became very popular for use in American newspapers. Futura was adapted officially for use on Linotype composition machines in the 1950s. Today, the Adobe typeface library has over twenty variants of Futura. Some of these variants were prepared after Renner's death, like the Extra Bold weight.

Renner's desire to rid type of any handwritten dynamic did result in a very original typeface, unlike anything that had come before. The subtlety of design in Futura surely enhanced its appeal: it seems at ease with itself, not suffering under a rationalized principle of construction like many subsequent geometric typefaces (for instance, Avant Garde Gothic, 1970).[100] Although Renner himself discussed Futura as partly a stylistic exercise – to capture the style of his time – he shared some of the ideals of the Bauhaus graphic designers in wanting to abstract letterforms to their simplest elements. He wished to universalize, to rid of any intrusive personal or local character. In this he did not consider himself to be imposing a sterile impersonality:

> If we demand today that a script be impersonal, non-individualistic, we are certainly not stating a preference for weak individuality over strong; rather we are saying that we demand *Sachlichkeit*, service, total submersion in the task. In general only strong individuality is capable of this.[101]

81 Futura-Heft. Bauer, *c.*1931. 193 × 130 mm.

100 Despite his scepticism about 'modernist' typefaces, even Neville Brody, in *The graphic language of Neville Brody* (London: Thames & Hudson, 1988) p. 24, commented that Futura was 'unequalled in its purity'.
101 'Das Formproblem der Druckschrift' (1930c) p. 30.

82 Chart using the Vienna method of pictorial statistics later known as Isotype. From Otto Neurath, *Gesellschaft und Wirtschaft* (Leipzig: Bibliographisches Institut, 1930). 310 × 460 mm.

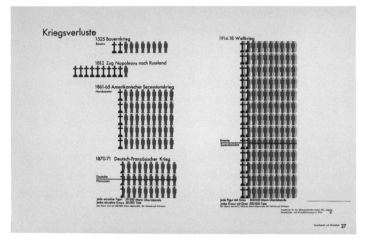

Renner commented that Futura was not like many quirky *Künstlerschriften* (artist-typefaces) that required the compositor to work in a style befitting the typeface, rather 'it provides the neutral elements of construction, in which every modern typographer can realize his own artistic concepts'.[102]

Both Renner and the Bauer typefoundry were understandably keen to stress the impersonality and *Sachlichkeit* of Futura when it was first released. The publicity for the typeface rested on its associations with the 'style of the era': stripped-down forms suited to the needs of Germany's reconstructed, industrialized landscape of the late 1920s. Consequently, any opportunity to stress the 'scientific' connotations of Futura were quickly exploited. In a small publicity booklet from *c.*1931 (known as the 'Futura-Heft'; figure 81) a series of quotations from 'doctors' were reproduced, attesting to the exemplary legibility of Futura. Most of these statements were vague assertions that the 'clarity and regularity' of Futura made it the most legible typeface yet produced.

The most persuasive testimony in the Futura-Heft is from Dr. Walther Moede of the Institute for Industrial Psychotechnics at Berlin's Technische Hochschule. He compared the speed with which subjects read a text set in Futura and a text set in the seriffed roman typeface called Romanisch. (The experiment was commissioned to find out if a certain chemistry journal would benefit from changing its typeface.) On average the Futura text took slightly less time to be read. Then the same task was performed with the text on a 'rattling' apparatus to aggravate the reading conditions. Futura again needed

102 'Drei Jahre Futura' (1930b) p. 2.

PAUL RENNER

slightly less time to be read.[103] Moede also carried out an experiment, which he deemed most conclusive, using a tachistoscope to test the recognizability of words of the same length in roman and Futura. The Futura words needed far fewer showings on the tachistoscope to be recognized. Moede concluded that this demonstrated the advantages of Futura 'for reading from great distances and for reading in weak and unfavourable lighting'.[104] Moede's comment implied that Futura would be most appropriate for signing, instead of books, although Renner most certainly intended the typeface for use in text. Bror Zachrisson has commented that, although the exact methods of investigation were not described, the Futura-Heft is notable for the 'manifestly scientific nimbus given to the statements'.[105]

Very soon after it came onto the market, Futura was adopted by the Gesellschafts- und Wirtschaftsmuseum in Vienna for its statistical charts, which were designed with the system later known as Isotype. Jan Tschichold worked with the team for a short time, probably in 1929, and it has been suggested that he may have advised Isotype's inventor, Otto Neurath, on this matter.[106] Otto Neurath's initiative to educate the public with easily-comprehensible statistics was a significant example of modernist activity; the charts themselves were also eminently simple, based on the principle of repeating simple pictorial icons to depict quantity (figure 82). Futura, used for headings and labels in these charts, was very well suited to the Isotype system, because Renner had similarly attempted to reduce letterforms to static, geometric shapes, repeated in sequence.

Both Isotype and Futura are traces of what Robin Kinross has called 'the faith of modernism: the belief in simple forms, in reduction of elements'[107] – not merely a stylistic choice, but a serious attempt to improve communication. By exposing the geometric basis of letterforms, Renner felt that he was revealing the fundamental features that enabled a typeface to be read – just as pre-fabricated components for housing projects in the New Frankfurt were derived from tried-and-tested solutions to building.

Renner believed that a truly contemporary typeface would have its form partly determined by the technology used to produce it: punchcutting – moreover mechanical punchcutting aided by the pantograph.[108] He proclaimed: 'The typeface

103 G.W. Ovink refers to this 'rattling' experiment by Moede in his *Legibility, atmosphere-value and forms of printing types*, p. 111. He commented that experiments had proven sanserif suitable for reading under these conditions, but that 'results obtained in this way should not be generalized.' Zachrisson makes the same point in *Studies in the legibility of printed text*, p. 68.

104 'Futura-Heft' (1930/1). Ovink chose certain letters from Futura, including some of the innovative small letter designs, for his own tachistoscopic experiments. He chose the alternative Futura characters so that his experiment might show how far one could stray from the 'basic form' of letters. Some confusion was caused by the small a and g, although the square-topped m and n caused little confusion. Ovink showed a small letter c from Futura, and stated that it was the finally released version, although it is simply a semi-circle, lacking the subtlety of the final design. This may explain Ovink's bad results for the recognizability of this letter and his conclusion that it is too narrow. Ovink, *Legibility, atmosphere-value ...*, p. 29.

105 Zachrisson, *Studies in the legibility of printed text*, p. 37.

106 Robin Kinross, *Otto Neurath's contribution to visual communication (1925–1945): The history, graphic language and theory of Isotype* (Unpublished MPhil Thesis. University of Reading, Department of Typography & Graphic Communication, 1979), pp. 28–9. See also Michael Twyman, 'The significance of Isotype' in *Graphic communication through Isotype* (University of Reading, Department of Typography & Graphic Communication, 1975), p. 13.

107 Kinross, 'The rhetoric of neutrality' (1985) p. 138.

108 'Die Zukunft unserer Druckschrift' (1925g) p. 87.

of our time must once and for all accept the obvious consequence of the invention of typefounding.'[109] Taking this sentence at face value, one might say that Futura could possibly have been designed in the 1450s by Johann Gutenberg, the inventor of typefounding. Futura's reductionist forms were really linked to the new *Zeitstil* of the 1920s that Renner perceived around him. Yet he denied this influence: 'The typeface of our time cannot be attained by superficially aligning historical letterforms with the forms [*Bauformen*] of the New Architecture.'[110] In Renner's words concerning Futura there is a technological determinism: he implied that Futura's skeletal letterforms were an inevitable consequence of modern processes of type manufacture. Yet he himself observed that this production process could be made to serve any form. Here, the fundamental difference between architecture and typography is apparent: Renner's theories about modern design were largely based on the New Architecture, which had always been foremost in design criticism. In architecture, the materials constitute the final structure itself, and therefore it makes sense to talk of 'technological form'; but in typography, materials, like lead type, are only the means to an end – the final product is merely an index, a graphic trace of the technology used to produce it. Indeed, there is a tradition of defying the constraints of the hidden metal frame of typography, as displayed in Robert Granjon's kerning italics and joining ornaments of the sixteenth century. Perhaps it is this kind of *trompe l'oeil* that Renner was trying to refute by ridding his typeface of any trace of handwriting. He suggested that it was more honest to employ mechanized processes of type manufacture to reproduce clean, geometric forms than to imitate handwritten letters.[111]

Yet Futura's letterforms, like any others, were arbitrarily imposed on the production process. In his essay on 'The problem of form in printing type' (1930) Renner described the artfulness and subtle visual adjustments required to create letters that seemed purely geometric. The internal logic of Futura stemmed from Renner's characteristic pursuit of a middle way: a fusion of classical proportions with the prevailing taste for geometric simplicity; its forms are not derived from modern technology, rather expressive of a notional modernity. Futura was a triumph of craft in alliance with industry – a design full of subtle and necessary inconsistencies.

109 'Futura: die Schrift unsrer Zeit' (1928a) p. 4.
110 'Futura: die Schrift unsrer Zeit' (1928a) p. 1.
111 Renner's fellow Munich type designer, F.H. Ehmcke, a traditionalist, commented: 'One believes oneself to be at the height of the time in striving to find the typeface for the age of the machine, the typeface that represents this machine character, and one hardly notices how romantically, how fundamentally *unsachlich* one is proceeding even in this.' (Ehmcke, 'Wandlung des Schriftgefühls'.)

PAUL RENNER

Renner stated: 'As paradoxical as it sounds: one cannot make the Mechanical mechanical enough if one wants to elevate it to the status of art and imbue it with spirit.'[112]

Orthographic reform

Futura became a central typeface of New Typography, but, in its final form, it was given the traditional character set with no attempt at orthographic innovation.[113] Renner evidently saw the virtue of rationalization in certain tasks of structuring information, but he resisted the total systematization that some of his contemporaries applied to the issue of orthography.

New Typography provided a platform for renewed discussion about simplifying German spelling. Renner, Tschichold and the *Bauhäusler* all called for the abolition of fraktur and all other type-styles derived from handwriting in favour of sanserif as a style expressive of the modern age. But Renner's views about capitalization and spellir g differed from those of younger German modernist typogι aphers in the 1920s.

German orthography had a peculiar history. In the early sixteenth century, when the florid forms of fraktur were developed in the chancery of Emperor Maximilian, capital letters were adopted for every noun (not only proper nouns). Attempts at redressing this imbalance of capitals date back to Jakob Grimm. His *Deutsche Grammatik* of 1822, as well as being set in roman type, restricted capitals to sentence beginnings and proper nouns. In the introduction to his *Deutsches Wörterbuch* of 1854 Grimm advocated this form of orthography in order to align German spelling with that in the rest of Europe. Grimm's rejection of both fraktur and conventional German orthography, based on sound historical knowledge, was a significant influence on Renner's views.[114]

Early in the twentieth century, there were two separate and idiosyncratic attempts at orthographic reform in Germany. The first was initiated by the poet Stefan George, who required a typeface for his published works that emulated his own handwriting. Under George's direction, the artist Melchior Lechter redrew some letters of the Berthold typefoundry's Akzidenz Grotesk, and a new typeface was cast in 1903. The modified characters mostly took on the form of uncial letters. George also echoed Jakob Grimm's principles by restricting

112 *Mechanisierte Grafik* (1931d) p. 97.
113 Some of Renner's articles about his typeface do however imply that Futura's skeletal form constituted the new *script* of his time, not merely a typeface. But Renner did not consistently develop this suggestion and it could be argued that it was an accidental implication, given the ambivalence of the German word *Schrift*, which can denote both handwriting and type. Most of Renner's articles use *Schrift* in their title, although a few use *Druckschrift* (printing type). See the list of Renner's published writings, pp. 208–10.
114 See the lengthy quotation from Grimm in Renner's *Das moderne Buch* (1947) pp. 11–14, and the original text in Grimm, *Deutsches Wörterbuch*, columns LI–LVIII.

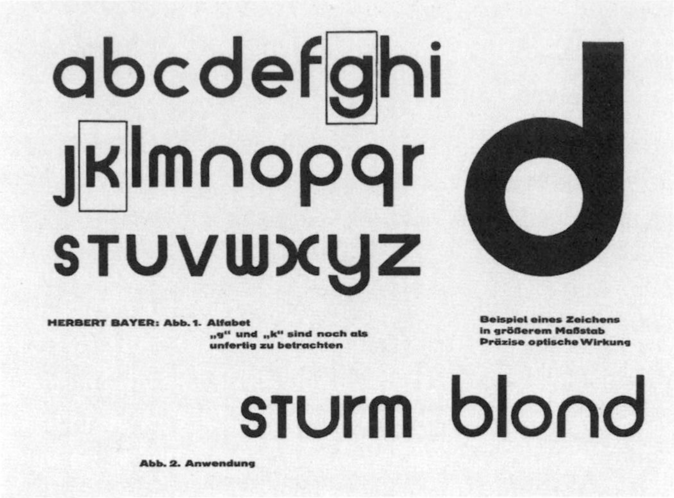

83 Herbert Bayer's 'universal' alphabet. 1926.

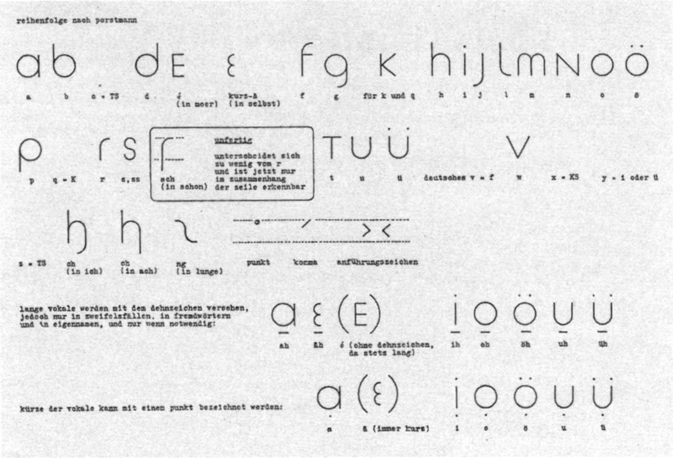

HERBERT BAYER: Abb. 1. Alfabet
„g" und „k" sind noch als
unfertig zu betrachten

Beispiel eines Zeichens
in größerem Maßstab
Präzise optische Wirkung

sturm blond

Abb. 2. Anwendung

84 Jan Tschichold's single alphabet. 1930.

115 Kaufmann's typewriter alphabet is illustrated in Ehmcke, *Schrift*, and in Herbert Spencer, *The visible word* (2nd edn. London: Lund Humphries, 1969).

capital letters to the beginnings of sentences and lines of verse. But George's orthographic style was not taken up outside of his elitist literary circle. The second attempted reform was made in 1911 by Hermann Kaufmann, who dispensed with small letters and produced a single alphabet of modified capitals for the typewriter. But Kaufmann's reform had no followers.[115]

More radical attempts at reform gained impetus from the book *Sprache und Schrift* by Walter Porstmann, published in Berlin in 1920. Porstmann was associated with the Deutscher Normenausschuß and contributed to the literature it produced on standards. Porstmann's suggested reform was to abolish capital letters altogether, while modifying the design of some alphabetic characters to enable phonetic transcrip-

PAUL RENNER

tion. Furthermore, Porstmann came from a scientific background and therefore his ideas were ideal fuel for those modernists who craved the aura of impersonality and rationalized efficiency surrounding the work of scientists and engineers.

Porstmann's words are to be found liberally quoted in Bauhaus literature. The teacher László Moholy-Nagy brought Porstmann's ideas to the Bauhaus, where some of his students began to explore them. Herbert Bayer, first a student and then from 1925 a teacher in the printing workshop at the Bauhaus, offered a graphic proposal for a single alphabet (that is, with no capitals). It was first published in 1926, and soon became known as the 'universal' alphabet (figure 83).[116] Jan Tschichold took Porstmann's ideas more seriously during his period at the Munich Meisterschule: instead of simply applying geometric construction to existing small letterforms, he adapted either majuscule or minuscule forms according to which version of each letter was most distinguishable, and designed the necessary phonetic characters. Tschichold's alphabet, published in 1930, was accompanied by a thoughtful article explaining the spelling system, suggesting primarily a new script, not a new typeface (figure 84).[117]

Renner first expressed his view on the orthographic issue as early as 1920, in a survey of leading typographers' opinions made by the periodical *Archiv für Buchgewerbe und Gebrauchsgraphik* (see also pp. 28–9 above). The survey was in response to a threefold reform proposed by the Bund der Deutschen Schrift (Association of German script): to restrict capitals in accordance with Jakob Grimm's suggestion; to import some phonetic spelling from stenography; and to get rid of fraktur. Renner was the only respondent who dealt specifically with the separate questions: he was fully in favour of Grimm's principles, but felt that phonetic spelling might result in confusion. He maintained these views until the end of his life, unswayed by the radical suggestions of the *Bauhäusler*. In *Mechanisierte Grafik* (1931) Renner commended 'Porstmann and his adherents' for having revived the issue of orthographic reform. He felt that they should not be 'reproached for radicalism'; he perceived their efforts as part of the general modern examination of 'traditional customs' in order to ascertain 'whether they still make sense, whether they still fulfil their purpose'.[118] Herbert Bayer claimed that his alphabet design was inherently most suited to all possible modern modes

116 The alphabet is featured in Bayer, 'Versuch einer neuen Schrift'.
117 Jan Tschichold, 'noch eine neue schrift' in *Typographische Mitteilungen*, supplement to Heft 3, March 1930.
118 *Mechanisierte Grafik* (1931d) p. 63.

of production: printing, handwriting, typing and stencilling. He implied that the single alphabet would make using a typewriter easier, given that the shift key would be redundant. The abolition of capitals would therefore save time and money. Indeed the use of capitals was abolished at the Bauhaus in October 1925, and a footnote printed on the Bauhaus letterhead, designed by Bayer, stated: 'text loses nothing when composed only of small letters, but becomes easier to read, easier to learn, essentially more scientific.'[119]

Renner regarded the use of a capital for every noun as 'squandering', robbing sentence beginnings of their rightful emphasis.[120] He was reluctant to admit that over-capitalization in German was an 'autocratic' feature, but admitted that it was certainly not 'democratic', and he understood why 'the youth enthusiastic for the "collective" want to get rid of capitals altogether'.[121] He agreed to a restricted use of capitals, but he objected to the 'illogical grounds' given by the *Bauhäusler* for their decision to rid of them completely. Renner suspected that the time which Bayer claimed would be saved by typing with only small letters, was only the writer's time. In Renner's view, 'orthography is only to be judged in terms of the service it renders to the *reader*'.[122]

Porstmann's advocacy of phonetic transcription struck Renner as misguided: it neglected reading conventions, and consequently neglected readers themselves. Instead of dictating a radical reform, Renner considered the issue according to users' needs: his concern was for *Leserlichkeit* (legibility/readability). To illustrate his doubts concerning the value of phonetic spelling, Renner gave the example of the two German words 'daß' and 'das', which had different meanings but the same sound in most dialects. Under a system of phonetic spelling these words would look the same, and Renner feared the loss of a distinction. He felt that written language, which did not have the rich 'expressive means' of spoken language, should not sacrifice anything that aided clarification.[123] And, he explained:

> We should not let ourselves be distracted from our faith in a functional orthography by supporters of a strictly phonetic orthography, who interpret the highly complex process of reading too mechanistically.[124]

119 Translated by Kinross in 'The rhetoric of neutrality', p. 138. Also translated (differently) by Hollis in *Graphic design*, p. 54. The original letterhead is pictured in Tschichold, *The new typography* (1928). The words in the note on the Bauhaus letterhead are a direct quotation from Tschichold's 'Elementare Typographie'.

120 'Type und Typographie' (1928f) p. 462.

121 *Mechanisierte Grafik* (1931d) p. 69. Later, in 'Nach der Entscheidung' (1942b) p. 202, Renner described the German custom of capitalizing every noun as 'a baroque pomposity that embarrassingly recalls Germany's most wretched period of petty monarchy [*Kleinstaaterei*] with its numerous princes and their most obsequious servants'.

122 'Gegen den Dogmatismus in der Kunst' (1928b) p. 313. Italics in original.

123 *Mechanisierte Grafik* (1931d) p. 66.

124 'Modern, traditionell, modisch' (1932b) p. 76.

PAUL RENNER

The unqualified advocacy of *Kleinschreibung* and phonetic spelling espoused by Tschichold and some Bauhaus graphic designers was a distinctly modernist initiative: they sought to modernize the visual form of language by reducing it to a universally valid system. This would have constituted a totalizing reform, which these designers did not have the power to impose.[125] Such power was potentially in the hands of the Soviet Minister for Culture, Anatole Lunacharsky, who expressed a wish in 1929 to abolish 'ethnic' scripts (including Cyrillic) in favour of adopting roman letterforms and *Kleinschreibung* as instruments in the service of international communism. Although a diluted element of this internationalizing ambition was present in the theories of the Bauhaus teachers, Herbert Bayer and Joost Schmidt, their alphabet designs seemed to contain as much aesthetic vanity as social conscience. The Bauhaus alphabets were artistic essays expressing Germany's new age of industrial efficiency and technological innovation; Josef Albers, a teacher on the preliminary course at the Bauhaus, based the explanation of his own 'economic' alphabet on the premise that 'time is money'.[126] Yet the similarly romantic claims made at the Bauhaus for the 'economic' nature of *Kleinschreibung* were unproven. Renner voiced the opposite view:

> It is understandable if one dispenses with capitals in typewritten letters. But the economic savings that are promised by their complete removal from the typesetting case could be as dangerous in certain circumstances as the desire to save lubricating oil in a machine.[127]

Renner seemed to be arguing that the tradition bound area of language was not susceptible to Fordist-style rationalization like some physical processes of manufacture. Language is integral to the expression of complex ideas and emotions, and as such, Renner sensed that it could not be straight-jacketed into rationalized clothing. He recognized that habit was an impediment to sensible reform in spelling, but he also realized that habit was a foundation stone of language usage that could not simply be disregarded. His arguments in the debate on orthographic reform portray the human face of 1920s modernism.

125 In a poll carried out by the Bildungsverband der Deutschen Buchdrucker in the May 1931 issue of its periodical *Typographische Mitteilungen* a majority of readers voted in favour of Jakob Grimm's principle for capitalizing sentence beginnings and proper nouns. See Kinross, 'Large and small letters: authority and democracy', p. 4. In his article 'Modern, traditionell, modisch' (1932b) Renner listed the basic principles for spelling reform formulated at a meeting of the Bildungsverband in August 1931. He proposed that these principles, which included the replacement of 'ph' with 'f', should be widely adopted.

126 Albers, 'Zur Ökonomie der Schriftform', p. 395.

127 *Mechanisierte Grafik* (1931d) p. 67.

5 **Crisis** 1932–3

Since Germany's protracted counter-revolution, which lasted well into the 1920s, disagreements in almost all areas of public life were exacerbated by an increasing sensitivity to the polarities of 'left' and 'right'. International communist organizations developed their own effective propaganda campaigns, but it was inevitably the Nazi Party that swayed the views of the majority by its effective manipulation of powerful myths concerning German national identity. In the Reichstag election of September 1930, the Nazis won 105 seats, second only to the Social Democrats. This represented a gain for the Nazis of 92 seats, or five-and-a-half million votes, over a period of just two years.

The Nazis were masters of irrational rhetoric, knowing exactly how to distort language for the purpose of creating scapegoats. The accusation of 'communist' was all too frequently tossed at artists and intellectuals whose work was in some way modern or progressive, regardless of whether the individual in question had any affiliation with the Communist Party. At this time in Germany, it was difficult to extricate matters of art and design from the prevalent political extremism. In this climate, even organizations that were largely unpolitical were destined to be split. A case in point was the Werkbund.

The course of the Werkbund

Perhaps the central problem of the Werkbund was its uncertainty about whether to promote a style or a philosophy of work. Hermann Muthesius, one of the Werkbund's founding fathers and a defining influence, stated in 1911, only four years after the founding of the organization, that most of the Werkbund's economic objectives had found acceptance, so henceforth it needed to concentrate on 'form', which he described as 'a higher intellectual need in the same way that cleanliness is a higher physical need'.[1]

Yet, only in the mid 1920s did an explicit, stylistic identity become attached to the Werkbund. By 1924, a notion of avant-garde style linked with Cubism, Constructivism, and De Stijl had established itself in design. Unornamented forms acquired associations of internationalism and functionality. The German economy had stabilized in 1923, and the Werkbund was then able to renew its exhibition programme: in 1924 it staged the

1 Hermann Muthesius, 'Where do we stand?' (1911) in Benton et al (ed.), Form and function, pp. 48–51.

Form ohne Ornament (form without ornament) exhibition in Stuttgart. Reductionist style became generally known as *Die neue Sachlichkeit* (the new objectivity/sobriety), a term first applied in 1925 by the curator of the Mannheim Kunsthalle, Gustav Hartlaub, to a touring exhibition of art by Georg Grosz, Otto Dix, and others.[2] Although the proclamation of a new *Sachlichkeit* implied that the old *Sachlichkeit* from the first two decades of the twentieth century was already felt to be out-of-date, the original sense of the term (see p. 34 above) was assimilated under *Die neue Sachlichkeit*, which came to denote all kinds of 'functional' design.[3]

The landmark exhibition that really established the Werkbund as 'modern' was the Stuttgart Weißenhof Siedlung in 1927, a model residential area with houses designed almost uniformly in what would become known as the 'international style' by architects including Walter Gropius, Mies van der Rohe, Peter Behrens and Le Corbusier. This exhibition proved to be a focal point for conflict between the conservative and avant-garde factions in German culture.[4]

A principal figure in the campaign against modernist architecture was Paul Schultze-Naumburg, an architect and founder member of the Werkbund. He was also an active member of the Bund Heimatschutz (Association for Protection of Homeland), founded in 1907, an organization dedicated to preserving *völkische* (national) styles in art. Independently of the Nazis, Schultze-Naumburg began to develop theories of art and design that linked style with race. The flat roof, a staple feature of the New Architecture, was to him 'immediately recognizable as the child of other skies and other blood'.[5] Only in 1929 did these racist theories concerning art and design become Nazi policy; in this year Schultze-Naumburg was appointed to lead the architectural school in the old Bauhaus building at Weimar. One of his first actions was to efface the building's murals by Oskar Schlemmer, without consulting the artist.[6] Schultze-Naumburg's racist views were also officially adopted by the Kampfbund für Deutsche Kultur (Fighting League for German Culture), an organization formed in 1930 by Alfred Rosenberg (editor of the Nazi newspaper, *Völkischer Beobachter*) after an inaugural meeting in Munich.

2 Renner seems to have known Hartlaub well: the Mannheim Kunsthalle is mentioned extensively in *Kulturbolschewismus?* (1932b). Hartlaub, who was victimized by the Nazis for his progressive views, wrote to Renner on 25 October 1932, pleading with him to deny that Hartlaub had sent him any material when he was preparing *Kulturbolschewismus?* (Nachlaß Renner).

3 See Willett, *The new sobriety*, pp. 111–23.

4 Certainly there was no consensus within the Werkbund itself. On the subject of New Architecture, which was synonymous with workers' housing, the architect Adolf Behne argued that it was wrong to make workers fit the ideas of middle-class socialists – namely, the architects. The Werkbund became a kind of clearing house for building in the new style after Richard Riemerschmid resigned as president in 1926, and Mies van der Rohe took over as the first vice-president. See Campbell, *The German Werkbund*, pp. 179–95.

5 Schultze-Naumburg quoted in Lane, *Architecture and politics...*, p. 134.

6 Willett, *The new sobriety*, p. 187.

Renner's view of the Werkbund's role

Paul Renner believed that the Werkbund was a necessary element in German culture, and that it could be adapted to new demands and circumstances in order to promote the values he had always understood it to represent: quality in both work and form.

In the early 1930s the Werkbund was torn by inner conflict whilst also providing an object of scorn for the Germanic reactionaries. Nazi-affiliated members slowly withdrew, displeased by the refusal of the organization's policy-makers to equate *völkische* styles with the national interest. Meanwhile, the leading modernists, such as Walter Gropius and Mies van der Rohe (the latter was vice-president until September 1932), were regarded by young members as too dogmatic in their views on aesthetic matters.[7] The Werkbund was losing influence among the press and public due to these internal conflicts, and it was this situation that Renner seemed intent on remedying in his flurry of appeals to the Werkbund Committee in 1931 and 1932, after his appointment as a Committee member in early 1931.[8]

Renner was initially involved in an internal Werkbund review of policy. Local groups, irritated by the tendency of the Berlin office to monopolize funds, initiated a revision of the organization's constitution, in order to devolve power to its branches. On 15 July 1931 Renner sat on the constitutional committee, which also included Mies van der Rohe, Hans Poelzig, Lilly Reich, and Walter Riezler.[9] Renner also contributed a suggestion for the revision of the Werkbund's second statute: its aims. He proposed the Werkbund as 'a focal point for all those who feel responsible for all designed work in our country'. The quality of such work was a 'gauge for the culture of a people', and should therefore be promoted by example and by publicity. Renner's only stipulation about the form of design was that it be honest; primarily he stressed the spiritual value of 'quality' work, feeling that it should 'help those people whose life is employed in this designing effort, whether in craft or industry, amidst divided labour or not'.[10]

Renner's idealism remained intact, and he must have felt strongly about the fate of the Werkbund to step up his polemical activity within the Committee. He circulated his thoughts to the Committee members and attended several meetings of the Inner Council and Executive Committee.[11] He felt that the

7 See Campbell, *The German Werkbund* (pp. 207–42), for a comprehensive summary of the Werkbund between 1930 and 1932.

8 Renner's appointment is reported in the Werkbund's yearly report for 1931.

9 Campbell, *The German Werkbund*, p. 211n.

10 Renner's suggestion is included along with others in a document called 'Entwurf für eine Neufassung der Satzung des Deutschen Werkbundes, Berlin' (BASK: file DWB III). Renner's page is not dated but another contribution is dated 25.10.31.

11 Renner's memos are dated 12 April 1932, and 10 May 1932. He was present at Executive Committee meetings in Berlin on 28 June 1932, and 14 October 1932 (BASK: file DWB III).

Werkbund should regain strength as a public influence amidst the increasing politicization of German culture and the injection of racial arguments into questions of art and architecture by the Nazis. Renner analysed the public perception of the Werkbund. He had been careful in the 1920s not to fall prey to wide-eyed wonder at the technological possibilities of the new age, which had seduced some of his younger contemporaries; his scepticism was still evident here in 1932, although he characteristically attempted to pursue a middle course. Firstly, he upbraided Schultze-Naumburg for his 'demagogic hate-rhetoric' against modern architecture. However, Renner also criticized the Werkbund's prevailing enthusiasm for everything new, which was evident from the advance publicity for its exhibition, *Die neue Zeit* (The new era; this exhibition never actually took place). He remarked that the Werkbund had a reputation for 'steering progress-drunk into the new era; it is sacrificing the legacy of the old culture with a light heart to enjoy the age of the machine with the minimum of burdens and inhibitions'.[12] Renner pleaded for a strong and focussed Werkbund to act as a positive cultural force beholden to no political party. He hoped that such an organization would be so influential that political parties would have to bow to its influence, and not vice versa. In hindsight, this seems a desperate hope, and Renner must have been moved to make such pleas by the worsening situation in political and cultural life.[13]

Renner's engagement in controversy

The culmination of Nazi propaganda linking art and race was the 1937 exhibition 'Entartete Kunst' (Degenerate art) held in Munich. But before the Nazis came to power, Paul Schultze-Naumburg embarked on a lecture tour of German cities to expound his racist theories about German culture. His talk in Munich was so well received that he gave a second, which Renner attended. Schultze-Naumburg showed slides of Asian art and of modern, avant-garde Western art, describing the distorted representations of human figures in them as products of perverse minds. Renner gave an account of the lecture:

When the young Munich painter Wolf Panizza ventures to interrupt: 'But where is the good modern art?', he is beaten to the ground with knuckle-dusters by the Nazi guards in the hall and kicked in the stomach with boots. Covered in blood, with a broken

12 Renner, 'An die Vorstandsmitglieder des DWB!' (10 May 1932; BASK: file DWB III) pp. 9–10.

13 Renner seemed to have had few allies in his demand for a strong stand against Nazism. One Werkbund member who often expressed similar views in print, was Walter Riezler, a Munich musicologist, who was editor of *Die Form* until the end of 1932. Like Renner, he advocated a middle way, neither dogmatically modern nor traditional, yet staunchly independent of party politics. The two men seem not to have known each other well, but Riezler congratulated Renner on his *Kulturbolschewismus?*, and reviewed it favourably in *Die Form*. (Letter from Riezler to Renner, 21 April 1932; BASK: file DWB III.)

cheekbone and a ripped ear, he had to be taken to hospital, where, as the leader of the Kampfbund für Deutsche Kultur and editor of the *Völkischer Beobachter* [Alfred Rosenberg] remarked at the end of the lecture, he had time to reflect on his question and the answer he had received.[14]

Renner was outraged by this conduct. He proclaimed:

> If we are concerned about German art, let us protect it from nationalist associations who want to fight for it with slogans and knuckle-dusters. They profess to fight for German culture and yet they are prepared at any moment to betray to fascism the prerequisite and living condition of any culture: intellectual freedom.[15]

Renner supported his friend Hans Eckstein, a fellow member of the Münchner Bund, in organizing a protest in all of Munich's cultural organizations about the incident at Schultze-Naumburg's lecture. But support for the Kampfbund was strong in Munich; the Münchner Bund refused to join the protest and Renner began to distance himself from this conservative regional group of the Werkbund.

Kulturbolschewismus?

The definitive statement of Renner's views on Nazi cultural policy is contained in his booklet *Kulturbolschewismus?* This essay began life as a speech for a second public meeting to be held in Munich, with Thomas Mann among the speakers.[16] Recalling this plan in 1939, Renner stated that 'Munich had to be warned once more of the danger threatened by National Socialism'.[17] The gathering was still being discussed in January 1932, but it never took place. However, Renner was so shocked by the information he gathered from his Werkbund friends in preparation for his speech that he felt he should publish his thoughts. He hoped that his essay would find a publisher 'despite the terrible times'.[18] He sent the manuscript to two German publishers, who both rejected it, so he submitted it to his friend Eugen Rentsch in Zurich. The anti-Nazi polemic of Renner's essay was obviously too dangerous for German publishers to handle in early 1932.[19]

Around 1930 the expression 'cultural Bolshevism', which Renner questioned (literally with a question mark) in the title of his essay, had become a reproachful refrain directed against the New Architecture by the Nazi press-organ, *Völkischer Beobachter*, around 1930. In his essay, Renner attempted to

14 *Kulturbolschewismus?* (1932b) p. 9.
15 *Kulturbolschewismus?* (1932b) pp. 61–2.
16 By the 1930s, Thomas Mann was a frequent public speaker and he was regularly harangued by Nazi thugs. See Nigel Hamilton, *The brothers Mann*, p. 243.
17 'Aus meinem Leben' (1939a) p. 12.
18 Letter to Peter Meyer (editor of the Swiss Werkbund magazine, *Das Werk*), 4 January 1932 (Nachlaß Renner).
19 'Aus meinem Leben' (1939a) p. 12. One of the German publishers was S. Fischer Verlag. (Letter to Dr Kronberger-Frentzen, 19 February 1932; Nachlaß Renner.)

85 Cover of *Kulturbolschewismus?* 1932. 220 × 145 mm. Type: black; image: light red.

counter the anti-semitic and anti-communist rhetoric of the Nazis with an appeal to reason: his approach was one of common sense and humanitarianism. In his opinion, the Kampfbund's 'struggle' directed itself 'against the old cosmopolitan openness of the Germans to the whole world, against the whole humane tradition'. He remarked that the 'German' culture defended by the Kampfbund was not the culture of all Germans: '... instead it is a culture in which only those national comrades who are national [*völkisch*] in a narrow sense can participate; it is the culture of a particular German "Nordic" race.'[20] Renner perceived that the struggle for this culture was being fought on two fronts: against the humanist concept of culture from the West and South; but most bitterly against the materialism and Bolshevism of the East.

With their unique brand of logic, the Nazis equated being 'Eastern' with being Jewish. Renner rejected entirely the notion that great German art was conditioned by the blood of the artist. He felt that German culture had been enriched by a mixture of races and influences. He observed that those Germans who blamed the success of Jews for a lack of their own success were in danger of 'causing this noble word "German" to acquire a fatal aftertaste'.[21] Furthermore he soberly observed that certain 'Jews' who had been singled out by the Nazis (such as Mies van der Rohe and Oskar Kokoschka) had no Jewish ancestry. Equally he disputed the myth that the New Architecture was 'Bolshevist', claiming that the pioneers of the new style were German and Dutch, as well as Russian. Indeed Renner implied that Germany's geographical situation between two divergent sources of culture (France & Italy on one side, and Russia on the other) caused a fruitful tension that led directly to the development of the New Architecture in Germany.

Renner considered the New Architecture a valid attempt to derive a style appropriate to the needs of his day, and he admitted that the political system of Soviet Russia may similarly have been an attempt to find a contemporary form of government. However, he commented that his era tended to over-value revolutions, and particularly the Russian one. Instead of the recent 'historical dramas', Renner perceived the true character of the 'new era' in a 'totally undramatic course of events, the slow solidification of a new collectivist disposition'.[22] He believed that the hothouse atmosphere of political

20 *Kulturbolschewismus?* (1932b) p. 6.
21 *Kulturbolschewismus?* (1932b) p. 17.
22 *Kulturbolschewismus?* (1932b) p. 42.

extremism in 1932 was due to the distortion of perspective caused by the First World War. This was a remarkably prescient analysis of the Weimar era for one still living in it:

> We live in a new era that gives lie to the proposition that everything has been done before. But even here in Germany it is so difficult to ascertain from the manifold layers of events, from the currents and counter-currents of the unprecedented New, in what way our time is different from any other. This stems from the fact that we still live in the shadow of World War. It is still so near to us that we have lost the ability to assess anything that lies further back. We speak of a pre-war era and a post-war era, as if the war was the cleft that divides the old era from the new. What happened before the war seems to have sunk into an abyss. Voices from the nineteenth century sound muffled, as if emanating from a tomb, and we know absolutely nothing of the eighteenth century any longer. And therefore everything that has happened in the narrow space of the last fourteen years has gained a false perspective, like an object photographed from far too close-up.[23]

Astutely, Renner remarked: 'Not America or Russia, but the densely-populated lands of Middle Europe are the site in which the decisive events in the spotlight of world-historical relevance are being played out.'[24]

Renner's views, then, were well-considered and not stridently polemical: he was sceptical of materialism and its Soviet offshoot, but admitted its role in a dialectic. Such equivocation did not obscure the fact that, from the simple-minded view of Nazi watchdogs, Renner was suspiciously progressive. *Kulturbolschewismus?* provoked a response in the *Völkischer Beobachter*. Renner later commented that this Nazi retort was 'less yobbish than expected', although the article in question simply descended into anti-semitism.[25] In contrast, on sending Thomas Mann a copy of the booklet, Renner received a congratulatory reply:

> I can hardly say how good it is today, when stupidity, falsity and objectionable hostility press so alarmingly from all sides, to hear goodness, truth and amiability expressed, especially when they appear in such a pure and noble form as yours.[26]

Arrest

Jan Tschichold commented late in his life that it was not certain that things would go Hitler's way in Bavaria in 1933.[27] Munich was a conservative city, yet it had a well-known cosmopolitan tolerance of diverse points of view: this apparent

23 *Kulturbolschewismus?* (1932b) pp. 29–30.

24 *Kulturbolschewismus?* (1932b) p. 31.

25 Rudolf Paulsen, 'Kulturbolschewistische Attacken', *Völkischer Beobachter*, Wednesday 30 March 1932. Zweites Beiblatt/90. Ausgabe. Renner later commented that his earliest book *Typografie als Kunst* (1922a) was added to the Nazi list of 'undesirable and shameful literature', but in 1933 the original German edition was already out of print. ('Aus der Geschichte der neuen deutschen Typographie', 1947, p. 6. Nachlaß Renner.) The Nazis may have been induced to censure this book because it had been issued in a Russian translation by the Soviet State publishing house in 1925 (see p. 207 below).

26 Letter from Mann to Renner, 17 April 1932 (Nachlaß Renner); also reproduced in Luidl, 'München – Mekka der schwarzen Kunst', p. 202.

27 Tschichold, 'Jan Tschichold: praeceptor typographiae', p. 20.

contradiction was an aspect of the city treasured by those who loved it, including Paul Renner. It may also have created an ideal milieu for Nazism to thrive: more than any other city, Munich served as a base for the gradual acquisition of power by the Nazis. Indeed, during the Third Reich, Munich was christened *Hauptstadt der Bewegung* (Capital City of the Movement).

In the Bavarian parliament, the Nazis had increased their presence, holding the second largest number of seats next to the Catholic Party (BVP). In the March 1933 election, called by Hitler after his appointment as Chancellor in January, the Nazis won a large majority in Bavaria.

Renner had already come into conflict with the Nazis by testifying as a witness for the artist Erich Wilke in a case brought by Wilhelm Frick, head of the Munich political police, who went on to become Nazi Minister of the Interior.[28] Renner also gave a lecture at the Berlin Kunstgewerbemuseum early in 1933 in which he denounced all methods of propaganda.[29] Still, *Kulturbolschewismus?*, as a document of Renner's resistance, constituted the prime piece of evidence against him. Presumably as a result of this publication, he was more closely observed, although, after his arrest, some of his activities during the preceding ten years were brought up by Nazi officials as evidence of his 'Bolshevist' tendencies. (Already in 1926, Renner had been accused in a trade periodical of being a 'Bolshevist'; see p. 59 above.)

During March 1933 Renner supervised the design of the German exhibit at the fifth Triennale exhibition in Milan. At this international exhibition, the German display was entrusted to the Werkbund, which decided to restrict its contribution to the products of the German graphic design trades. Renner took charge of selecting material and designing the display; the architect Walther Schmidt also contributed to the final layout of the German stand. Renner's particular contribution was a slide show illustrating the historical progression of style in letterforms. He used four projectors, and each series of slides in the sixty stages of the sequence featured an image of script alongside illustrations of other arts from the same period.[30]

On 31 March 1933, just four days before his arrest, Renner was visited in the Munich Meisterschule by Dr Sievers, a longtime Werkbund supporter from the Foreign Office, and the

28 Renner, 'Interview mit Paul Renner' (1947) p. 6.
29 Letter to Franz Roh, 17 September 1946 (Getty: file 850120).
30 Description contained in the Werkbund report 'Vorstands-Mitteilungen Nr 3' dated 12 April 1933, Berlin (GNM, ABK Riemerschmid I, B-146). See also the notes by Luidl about slides possibly used by Renner in Milan in the catalogue pages (p. 599) accompanying 'München – Mekka der schwarzen Kunst'.

director of the National Gallery in Berlin, Eberhard Hanfstaengl. They were sent to verify that the material chosen by Renner for the exhibition was suitable in terms of foreign policy. Several items were found unfit for display, and Hanfstaengl complained specifically that there was an imbalance in favour of roman type over gothic. Renner was not happy with this interference and his obstinacy was noted. The Foreign Office requested the Werkbund to send written reassurance that its wishes would be complied with.[31] Otto Baur, who had assumed a provisional leadership of the Werkbund and was keen to appease the Nazis, complained to Richard Riemerschmid, the president of the Munich Werkbund division, that Renner was not obeying the wishes of the Foreign Office representatives. In Baur's opinion, Renner's conduct was endangering a plan to install further pro-Werkbund staff in the Foreign Office.[32]

After the Nazi success in the national election on 5 March 1933, their programme of arresting dissidents began in earnest, and Renner must have been fully aware of its effects. Indeed his colleague Jan Tschichold was arrested in the middle of March, a few weeks before Renner's own arrest. Tschichold received notice of his dismissal from the Meisterschule after only the first few days of his internment.[33] As director of the Meisterschule, Renner complained on Tschichold's behalf, but Tschichold remained in prison for four weeks.[34]

31 Letter from Auswärtiges Amt to Deutscher Werkbund, 4 April 1933 (GNM, ABK Riemerschmid I, B-146).

32 Letters from Baur to Riemerschmid of 5 April & 6 April 1933 (GNM, ABK Riemerschmid I, B-146). See also Campbell, *The German Werkbund*, p. 247.

33 'Interview mit Edith Tschichold ...', in Deutscher Werkbund, *Die Zwanziger Jahre...*, p. 188. It seems that the Nazis took advantage of Tschichold's temporary indecision about his career. In January 1933 his resignation from the Munich Meisterschule had been accepted in order for him to take up a post at the Höhere Graphische Fachschule in Berlin, which was led by Georg Trump at that time. (A premature announcement of Tschichold's move to Berlin was printed in *Typographische Mitteilungen*, Jhg 30, Heft 3, March 1933, p. 92.) But, on visiting Berlin after the Nazi take-over, Tschichold decided that he wanted to stay in Munich. Renner was annoyed by what he regarded as Tschichold's capriciousness in this matter and told him that he should personally ask the municipal authorities if he could remain in Munich despite his resignation. Before he could do this, Tschichold was arrested due to the initiative of a Sturmabteilung officer who was his neighbour. Edith Tschichold later commented that the Tschicholds' cleaning lady, who had heard them express anti-Nazi sentiments, also informed on them ('Interview mit Edith Tschichold...', p. 191). In 1944, Renner still harboured some indignation at Tschichold's conduct over his employment, suggesting that Tschichold's losing his job was partly his own fault for having placed himself 'between two stools'. (Letter to Karl H. Salzmann, 1944; Nachlaß Renner.) Mies van der Rohe wrote to Renner in May 1933, asking his opinion of Tschichold, who had applied for a position teaching the *Reklameklasse* at the Bauhaus. It is not clear whether Tschichold applied for this position before or after his dismissal from his Munich post. (Letter from Mies van der Rohe summarized by Luidl in the catalogue pages [p. 605] accompanying 'München – Mekka der schwarzen Kunst'.)

34 Tschichold wrote to Renner on 17 April 1933 thanking him for his efforts, which had contributed to the shortening of Tschichold's imprisonment. He also expressed regret that the visit paid by his wife to Renner (presumably to ask for help) resulted in unpleasantness for Renner also. (Letter summarized by Luidl in the catalogue pages [p. 604] accompanying 'München – Mekka der schwarzen Kunst'.) Indeed Renner felt that his intercession on behalf of Tschichold and their mutual friend Franz Roh, who was arrested at the same time, had provoked the same Sturmabteilung officer who had arrested Tschichold and Roh to press for Renner's arrest. (Letter to Karl H. Salzmann, 1944; Nachlaß Renner.) Many years later, Edith Tschichold alleged that, when she called on Renner for help after her husband's arrest, Renner told her that, for his own part, he had 'connections' ('Interview mit Edith Tschichold ...', p. 189). Edith Tschichold claimed that Renner considered her husband to have had too many dubious Russian connections. In this interview of 1979, Edith Tschichold still seemed bitter towards Renner, who, she claimed, had hardly suffered under the Nazis compared to her family. She lamented that there were no Nazis in the Tschicholds' circle of friends for them to call on, which resulted in their decision to leave the country as soon as they could. Some idea of the uncertainty that Jan Tschichold and his wife must have suffered during his four weeks in 'protective custody' can be gained from Stefan Lorant's engrossing book, *I was Hitler's prisoner* (Harmondsworth: Penguin Books, 1935). Lorant was the editor of a Munich periodical when he was similarly put into 'protective custody', a euphemism to hide the fact that no charges were made.

One can only guess what Renner's thoughts were about this situation. He must surely have been afraid that he would also shortly be arrested, although he was a more established and respected figure in Munich than Tschichold. Tschichold had been arrested for no good reason – he had never been a member of the Communist Party, as the Nazis were to allege, and he was a subscribing Social Democrat for only a short time. By contrast, Renner had explicitly criticized the Nazis in print, which gave them a better reason to arrest him; also, his intercession on Tschichold's behalf must have counted against him. Perhaps there were people of influence whom Renner knew he could call on in an emergency, but he had taken a significant stand against the Nazis and he maintained this position. Certainly he did not attempt to ingratiate himself with the new regime.

During Renner's activity in designing the Milan exhibit, the authorities increasingly harassed him. Both Renner's office at the Munich school and his apartment were searched on 25 March 1933.[35] Annie Renner told the intruders in her home that her husband was in Berlin. A caretaker let the 'political police' into Renner's office at the Meisterschule and they seized photographic slides featuring examples of photomontage that the authorities described afterwards as 'Russian propaganda against Germany'.

Around this time Renner received a visit 'in the dead of night' from Alexander Oldenbourg, the President of the Deutscher Buchdrucker-Verein, and a close confidant of Renner. Oldenbourg warned Renner that the Nazis were closing in on him and offered to hide him in an attic room.[36] Yet Renner chose to remain in public view. Many designers and members of the Werkbund maintained hope that the state would not interfere in their work. Renner may have clung to some optimism, but his comments in *Kulturbolschewismus?* (1932) had shown that he perceived the potential disaster in the Nazis' politicization of culture. In a contribution to a survey on the 'state of graphic design' for *Gebrauchsgraphik* in January 1933, Renner had commented: 'Political idiocy, growing more violent and malicious everyday, may eventually sweep the whole of western culture to the ground with its muddy sleeve.'[37] Renner's comment was duly noted, and later used as evidence against him.

35 Principal sources for the account of Renner's arrest and dismissal in this chapter are: a lengthy report by the Direktorium des Stadtrats Unter-suchungs-Ausschuß of 25 August 1933, which documents the evidence against Renner (Bay HStA; file MInn 80151); and Renner's own recollections from 'Aus meinem Leben' (1939a).

36 'Aus meinem Leben' (1939a) p. 10.

37 Modified from E.T. Scheffauer's translation as it appeared in *Gebrauchsgraphik* (Jhg 10, Heft 1, January 1933) p. 35. In contrast to the other contributions by *Gebrauchsgraphiker* to this survey, Renner's work is not illustrated, as he did little advertising design prior to 1933.

PAUL RENNER

Renner was taken into custody at 23:30 on 4 April 1933, and released the next day, on the condition that he report to the police every other day. Renner's almost immediate release was due to an indirect contact with Rudolf Hess, Hitler's deputy. Luise Renner, Paul's daughter, was engaged to Heinz Haushofer, son of Karl Haushofer, who was a noted Munich academic, mentor to Rudolf Hess, and occasional adviser to Hitler.[38] Heinz Haushofer wrote a letter to Hess on 25 March 1933, the day on which Renner's apartment and office were searched (over a week before his arrest): in his letter Heinz Haushofer described Renner as a 'true German' and 'a wholly outstanding figure as a man and a teacher'. Consequently, on Renner's arrest, Hess made a telephone call, pleading for leniency in Renner's case and asking for him to be retained in his professional position if possible.[39]

In the official Nazi reports on Renner's case, *Kulturbolschewismus?* proved to be the most incriminating evidence against him. Renner seems already to have sensed the trouble that his essay was attracting and had withdrawn it from the German book trade. Most copies remained unreachable in Switzerland, and, in order for the Nazi officials to see the booklet, copies had to be borrowed from the State Ministry of Education and Culture. The file of evidence against Renner compiled by the investigating body of the Munich City Council listed the most offensive pages of *Kulturbolschewismus?*, and it was remarked that Renner even insulted the Führer. One suspects that this was taken more seriously than any ideological issue.[40]

Renner's public defiance of National Socialist trends must have been noted by some observers in the Munich printing community for some time, because Renner's accusers were soon able to compile a comprehensive list of his supposed offences. His participation in the 1926 Tonhalle gathering with the Mann brothers weighed against him because both Thomas and Heinrich Mann had become enemies of Nazism and were forced to flee the country early in 1933. Renner's appointment of Jan Tschichold to a teaching post at the Munich Berufsschule in 1926 incriminated Renner further. Tschichold had evidently proclaimed himself 'an outspoken Bolshevist' at a public meeting in Leipzig in 1930, which, according to the Nazi investigation committee, should have precluded him from retaining his teaching post.[41] Renner was

38 Karl Haushofer had originated the notion of *Lebensraum*, although it was perverted by the Nazis to their own ends. He had been close to the NSDAP since 1920, but was never a member.

39 Heinz Haushofer recalled in his personal memoir of his father-in-law Renner that a bibliophile named Schulte-Strathaus, who had influence with Rudolf Hess, was responsible for securing Renner's release. (Luidl & Lange [ed.], *Paul Renner*, p. 19.) Schulte-Strathaus, who, like Renner, had edited some issues of the periodical *Die Bücherstube* in the 1920s, was indeed a member of the Nazi Party; but the documentary evidence implies strongly that Heinz Haushofer intervened personally via Hess. After the first officially sanctioned public displays of anti-semitism, Karl Haushofer warned the Nazi leadership of alienating world opinion and he consequently began to distance himself from the regime. The Haushofer family eventually fell foul of the Nazis, particularly after Rudolf Hess, who was close to the Haushofers, flew to Britain on a misguided solo peace mission in 1941. Karl Haushofer's other son, Albrecht, was suspected of involvement in the assassination attempt on Hitler in 1944, and consequently both he and his family were hounded. Albrecht Haushofer was executed by the Nazis as a traitor in 1945. Heinz Haushofer and his wife Luise (née Renner) were imprisoned briefly in 1944. Karl Haushofer and his wife were also imprisoned in Dachau in 1944, and after the war, in 1946, they committed suicide together.

40 Renner had pointed out that the artist Oskar Kokoschka, who was accused of being Jewish, was an Austrian, and that 'he is distinguished from his equally comfortable countryman Hitler in being blond, not brunet'. (*Kulturbolschewismus?* [1932] p. 14.) It seems a remarkably simple observation – that Hitler hardly matched the Aryan ideal – but it was very seldom made. Ironically, photographs of Renner himself show that his chiselled and handsome features matched the Aryan ideal of warrior-like German manhood purveyed in Nazi painting and iconography. He was what used to be known as a 'Siegfried'.

41 Tschichold's alleged self-description is reported in the Munich page of the *Völkischer Beobachter* (Ausgabe 68 of 22 March 1930). In the Nazi reports, Tschichold is referred to as 'Johannes Tzschichold' or 'Iwan Tschichold', ignoring his use of the name Jan since 1926.

accused of concerning himself over-enthusiastically with Tschichold's initial employment, and speaking out in his favour at every opportunity, even in the face of attacks from the press. Renner later commented that 'Tschichold was never a Bolshevik, and I am proud to have once acquired him for Munich'.[42]

Certain stories told by colleagues at the Munich school surfaced after Renner's arrest, revealing that his actions had been observed by a 'National Socialist cell' in the Meisterschule. Renner later suspected that his friend Hans Baier, the Municipal Educational Director, had let many complaints fall into the wastebasket:

> Once he paid me a totally unexpected visit in the school; it seemed as if something had annoyed him. He asked me to go with him into the office of one of my school directors; there, after a short greeting, he sat at the typewriter and typed a few lines. Then he came back with me to my office and compared what he had just typed with a letter from his pocket and said: 'I thought so, it's the same machine.' I never knew what was in the letter and I never asked.[43]

An incident at the school explicitly cited in the Nazi reports was an occasion when Renner allegedly expressed his scorn for the swastika. Three students were sent to him to be punished for having painted the Soviet star on the wall of the lavatory. Renner was reported to have said: 'How dare you degrade the Soviet star to the level of the swastika, that symbol of the sewer.'[44] Renner protested that he had actually adhered to the official regulations on political neutrality, and simply scolded the students for having daubed such an emotive sign in a place such as the toilet. In 1939, Renner recalled:

> It was that period when the struggle between National Socialism and communism had chosen public toilets as a battle-field. Even at the stops on the D-train 'Heil Hitler!' fought 'Heil Moskau!' and the swastika fought the Soviet star.[45]

A Municipal Education Inspector named Bauer (whom Renner described as one of the 'decent Nazis') told Renner that copies of *Kulturbolschewismus?* had been sent to the authorities by some of Renner's colleagues, who denounced Renner and suggested themselves as successors to his post at the Meisterschule.[46] The Nazi authorities received pleas for Renner's reinstatement from the curatorium of the Meisterschule and from Alexander Oldenbourg. Renner's dismissal

42 'Aus meinem Leben' (1939a) p. 10.
43 'Aus meinem Leben' (1939a) pp. 11–12.
44 Renner's alleged words were 'das Zeichen des Aborts' (Bay HStA; file MInn 80151).
45 'Aus meinem Leben' (1939a) p. 11.
46 Letter to Franz Roh, 7 September 1946 (Getty: file 850120). In July 1933 Bauer drew up a more balanced report on Renner's case than that of Munich City Council.

PAUL RENNER

was demanded by the leadership of the Sturmabteilung, the Munich division of the Kampfbund für Deutsche Kultur, and the regional group of the Reichsverband Bildender Künstler Deutschland (Reich Group of German Fine Artists). This last organization was one of many art and design organizations to which Renner had belonged before 1933. He was also expelled at the end of April from the Bund Deutscher Gebrauchs-graphiker (Association of German Graphic Designers), which published the magazine *Gebrauchsgraphik*.

During the enquiry into his character, Renner received a letter from his friend Alexander Oldenbourg, who had collab-orated with Renner in setting up the Meisterschule. Olden-bourg (evidently assuming that Renner would be re-instated) suggested that he should henceforth favour gothic script in teaching exercises at the Meisterschule, in order to avoid incurring further wrath from the Municipal Educational Authority. (Gothic script was becoming a firm aspect of the Nazi propaganda machine at this time.) Oldenbourg urged Renner to acquire some new gothic typefaces from the type-foundries, thereby correcting the imbalance in favour of roman typefaces among those already held at the school.[47] However, even if he had wanted to, Renner had no time to act on Oldenbourg's suggestions. He was temporarily relieved of his post at the Meisterschule on 11 April 1933, although he still received his salary pending further review. Renner's case was examined under the statutes of the Gesetz zur Wiederher-stellung des Berufsbeamtentums (Professional Civil Service Restoration Act), which was instituted by the Nazis on 7 April 1933 (three days after Renner's arrest and release).

In attempting to dismiss Renner, the Nazi authorities sought to establish firm links between creative work and political ideology. Although Renner had often expressed the view that art and life should be united in creative work, he cannot have envisaged the facile injection of politics into culture carried out by the Nazis. At first, the authorities attempted to convict Renner according to statute 2a of the new law, under which 'officials are to be released from their post, if they belong to the Communist Party or communistic sister- or ancillary-organizations, or have been active in a com-munistic way'.[48] On arrest, Renner had to fill out a question-naire in which he stated that he belonged to no political organization. Renner's advocacy, albeit qualified, of the new

47 Oldenbourg wrote to Renner in his capacity as President of the Deutscher Buchdrucker-Verein, but he sent his letter (dated 8 April 1933) to Renner's home address. Letter quoted by Luidl in the catalogue pages (p. 605) accompanying 'München – Mekka der schwarzen Kunst'.
48 Bay HStA; file MInn 80151.

styles in art and design in *Kulturbolschewismus?* was distorted into evidence of communist sympathy, and, considering his profession as a teacher, it was implied that he sought to indoctrinate his students with graphic examples. The slides of photomontage seized by the police and held as evidence against Renner were considered subversive because of their anti-German content. Photomontage had become a significant feature of Russian graphic design, often used in publications sponsored by the Soviet regime. In Germany it had also been developed as a tool of left-wing satire, employed for some notable attacks on Hitler's reputation by the artist John Heartfield.[49] Renner demanded the right to defend himself concerning the photomontage material seized from his office, and he did so in a deposition. Characteristically he adopted an intellectual tone: he described the material, which he intended to use in lectures, as 'incunabula of photomontage', and therefore historically important. The Nazis retorted that this was no reason to show 'communistic' pictures. They asserted that the use of such material reflected 'the communistic disposition of Renner', in order to convict him under statute 2a of the Gesetz zur Wiederherstellung des Berufsbeamtentums. However, the Nazis admitted: 'Insofar as it does not concern artistic questions, one cannot speak of "communistic activity" in Renner's behaviour'. Renner could only be convicted under statute 2a if his 'artistic activity' could be established as 'communistic'. The Nazis then had to face the consequences of their own loose employment of political terminology: the officials realized that they could not adequately judge Renner's design activity 'because it is not clearly established what is to be understood as communistic art in the field of graphic design'.[50] They solved this problem by suggesting a stylistic link between his typeface Futura and the forms of the New Architecture, which was commonly held to have Russian associations. Renner's renunciation of the traditional forms of gothic type in Futura was deemed anti-German. Additionally, Renner's accusers judged his ideas on orthographic reform to be linked with the principles of abstract art: his aim here too was reductionist and anti-traditional.

Finally, Renner was permanently dismissed from his position at the Meisterschule on 16 February 1934 by the Bavarian Reichsstatthalter Franz von Epp, not on the grounds of communist activity, but on grounds simply of 'national untrust-

49 One of the satirical examples of photomontage seized in Renner's office read 'Des Kaisers Kulis' (concerning the Kaiser's shorts). This was most probably a book-jacket design by John Heartfield for the novel *Des Kaisers Kulis,* written by Theodor Plivier, and published by Malik Verlag in 1930.

50 Bay HStA; file MInn 80151.

PAUL RENNER

worthiness'. Renner later recalled that the phrase used to describe him was 'politically untrustworthy', commenting that 'the combative methods of the Nazis always employed the least coy distortion of the German language'.[51] Renner was only one of hundreds of officials who were dismissed in Munich alone. Those who belonged to communist organizations were easily dismissed and the official files on their cases often contain only a single item of correspondence. The file on Renner was extensive: his case was complicated, given that design was not an overtly political activity. The Nazis expended a great deal of effort in twisting Renner's work to fit the regulations; even in a totalitarian state the Germans had a flair for petty bureaucracy.

Renner offered a reasoned explanation for his possession of slides featuring photomontage. But the Nazi administration was impervious to reason. Renner was not a communist; as Joan Campbell has pointed out, like many members of the Werkbund his views tended towards a 'German socialism' that had more in common with National Socialism than communism.[52] It would be simplistic and inaccurate to draw direct links between the beliefs of certain Werkbund members and those of the Nazis; yet, for example, the *Führerprinzip*, the principle of appointing a dictatorial leader, had been echoed even by Renner in describing his opinion on the role of a successful school principal, like himself: the ideal candidate was a figurehead, leading by strong example.[53]

Renner's status as a Modern branded him as subversive. By his support of New Architecture and New Typography he associated himself with the avant-garde. The new styles of design were products of an elite, and were consequently antipathetic to the populist notions of traditional village life promoted by the Nazis. They propagated strong myths about German identity that were intended to stir the hearts of the majority. The Nazi accusations of communist influence in artistic activity were a convenient propaganda exercise designed to remove potential dissidents. Futura, attuned to the new taste for unornamented form, was labelled anti-German by the authorities. In 1928 the graphic design magazine *Gebrauchsgraphik* (printed in German and English) had adopted Futura as its typeface for text, followed by the Werkbund journal, *Die Form,* in August 1931.[54] The scope of these periodicals was truly international, in dealing with design from all over

51 'Aus meinem Leben' (1939a) pp. 12–13.

52 See Campbell, *The German Werkbund*, p. 234.

53 'Werkbund und Erziehung' (1932f) pp. 332–5. See also the discussion between Hans Eckstein and F. H. Ehmcke of the educational policy in Munich's trade schools (as reformed by Georg Kerchensteiner) in *Das Werk* (Jhg 19, Nr 4 & 9, 1932). Eckstein praised the modernity of the schools in only attempting to train 'professional capability' instead of 'original creative potential'. Ehmcke retorted that the Munich graphic school was lucky to have such a gifted artist as Renner in charge, otherwise the quality of its work might suffer.

54 *Gebrauchsgraphik* retained Futura for its text until it ceased publication in 1944, long after it had become the official organ for the Fachgruppe Gebrauchsgraphiker (Graphic Design Division) of the Reichskammer für Bildende Künste (Reich Chamber of Fine Arts). See Aynsley 'Gebrauchsgraphik as an early graphic design journal, 1924–1938', p. 59. *Die Form* was typeset in Futura from 1931 until its demise in 1934. In May 1933 Wilhelm Wagenfeld, the Bauhaus-trained product designer, complained to the Werkbund Committee that Futura was being spurned in some Werkbund publications, which he perceived as a sign of capitulation to the reactionary pressures of Nazi cultural policy. (Campbell, *The German Werkbund*, p. 262.)

Europe and America. Futura emerged as a principal component of typographic modernism; by differentiating itself from roman and gothic with its simplified forms, the typeface carried an aura of international neutrality. Although Jan Tschichold and the Bauhaus typographers were strongest in arguing that sanserif constituted a rejection of 'national' styles in letterforms, Renner also proposed his Futura as a universal letterform. It was easy for the Nazis to make a facile link between such a preference for stylistic uniformity and the international communist effort.

Ironically, after his arrest and release, Renner received the Grand Diploma of Honour for his work on the German exhibit at the Milan Triennale, which had finally opened on 10 May 1933. The judges were especially impressed with the slide show presentation.[55] Richard Riemerschmid had written a letter on 21 April 1933 confirming to the Nazi authorities that Renner's guiding presence was needed in Milan during the few weeks before the opening.[56] Renner travelled to Milan, but a Nazi guard (in brown-shirt and jack-boots) was assigned to follow him. The guard, who did not aid in setting up the exhibit, was a conspicuous shadow, especially when he tried to follow the entourage surrounding the King of Italy, who took a great interest in the German exhibit.[57] Afterwards, Renner's involvement in the Triennale was not mentioned in some press reports.

The material shown in the German exhibit at Milan included book typography (from the luxurious Bremer Presse limited editions to cheap books), packaging, illustrated periodicals, stamps, and a special section for typeface design, featuring work by Rudolf Koch and Renner himself. Futura was shown in a specially typeset quotation from Mussolini: 'We dare not plunder the inheritance of our fathers, we must create new art.' The German display of graphics received a great deal of attention and plaudits; members of the Italian military were reported to have been impressed.[58] Indeed the Italian monarchy later awarded Renner the Officer's Cross for his work. This exhibition seems to have been decisive in spreading the popularity of Futura around Europe.[59] Specifically in Italy, a sanserif inscriptional letter, very close to Futura in form, was developed in public lettering on buildings for the Fascist regime. The allusion to classical, Roman majuscules in Futura capitals accorded neatly with the undoubted intention

55 Letter from H. K. Frenzel to Renner, 3 October 1933 (Nachlaß Renner).

56 GNM, ABK Riemerschmid I, B-146.

57 Haushofer, 'Paul Renner – ein Eindruck' in Luidl & Lange (ed.), *Paul Renner*, pp. 19–20.

58 A report on the opening of the Triennale is included in *Gebrauchsgraphik* (Jhg 10, Heft 6, 1933) pp. 70–1.

59 Attilio Rossi, the editor of the Milan-based graphic design periodical, *Campo grafico*, which dealt with modernist Italian design, recalled later that Renner's Milan exhibit had a great influence on him and his colleagues. Futura was used extensively in *Campo grafico*. (Rossi's recollection in the introduction to Carlo Pirovano [ed.] *Campo grafico 1933–1939*. Milan: Electa, 1983, p. 11.)

of the Italian Fascists to evoke imagery from the Imperial Roman past.[60]

Around the time of his arrest Renner was still involved in Werkbund business. The organization was being press-ganged into *Gleichschaltung* – the process of enforced political alignment by which organizations succumbed to Nazi control. Despite the attempt in 1932 to distribute power more evenly among the regional groups, the organization was still dominated by the central Berlin office under Ernst Jäckh, a natural bureaucrat, who actively sought to secure a degree of autonomy for the Werkbund by negotiating with Hitler, Joseph Goebbels and Alfred Rosenberg personally. Jäckh had a meeting with Hitler on 1 April, and met with Alfred Rosenberg on 5 April.[61] The meeting with Hitler was preceded by a lengthy consultation with the Executive Committee of the Werkbund, at which members gave their views on the future relationship of the organization with the government. Renner attended this consultative meeting along with Walter Gropius, Mies van der Rohe, Otto Baur, Peter Bruckmann, Hans Poelzig, Richard Riemerschmid, Martin Wagner and several others.[62]

In June 1933 Renner participated in a vote deciding the future course of the Werkbund. Ernst Jäckh proposed the election of two Nazi architects as president and vice-president. Both candidates were members of the Kampfbund für Deutsche Kultur, to which the Werkbund would then become affiliated if Jäckh's recommendations were approved. The proposal was discussed at a committee meeting in Berlin on 9 June 1933 by Walter Gropius, Hans Poelzig, and Martin Wagner, among others. A telephone link was set up so that the members of the Münchner Bund could vote. Richard Riemerschmid, the President of the Münchner Bund, Renner and Walther Schmidt (the architect who collaborated on the Milan display) were documented as having agreed to the election of the new president.[63] Renner may have considered this compromise the best hope for maintaining the Werkbund's relative independence. Alternatively he may have simply given up hope by this point and acquiesced, with the intention of withdrawing completely from Werkbund affairs. The election of a Nazi Werkbund president was finally approved on 10 June 1933, although Gropius and his friend Martin Wagner voted against the motion. Wagner, former chief city architect of Berlin, warned of grave consequences from collaboration with the Nazis.

60 Some of these inscriptions are illustrated in Armando Petrucci, *Public lettering: script, power and culture* (Chicago: University of Chicago Press, 1993) figures 118–20.

61 Campbell, *The German Werkbund*, p. 246.

62 'Vorstands-Mitteilungen Nr 3', 12 April 1933, Berlin (GNM, ABK Riemerschmid I, B-146).

63 Notes on meeting of 9 June 1933, perhaps written by Richard Riemerschmid (GNM, ABK Riemerschmid I, B-146).

The Munich division was expelled from the Werkbund after Richard Riemerschmid refused to be dismissed from its presidency. It finally disbanded in February 1934, but, by this time, Renner's name had disappeared from the list of members. In early 1934 the Werkbund lost any last vestige of independence when it became affiliated to the Reichskulturkammer (Reich Chamber of Culture), the organization set up by Goebbels to wrest power from Rosenberg's Kampfbund.

A brief stay in Switzerland

During the review of his case, Renner embarked on a working trip to Switzerland, where he stayed until after his final dismissal from his Meisterschule position. Shortly after his temporary suspension from duty, Renner received an invitation from Siegfried Bittel, the General Secretary of the Swiss Railway, who also had the task of re-organizing the Swiss Tourist Board. Bittel asked Renner if he would like to serve as a typographic consultant on this project, and enclosed a first-class ticket to Bern with his offer. Bittel had seen Renner's work at the Milan Triennale and had read of his dismissal in the newspapers; he may also have seen a lengthy article Renner wrote in *Die Form* about publicity for the tourist industry.[64] Renner persuaded the 'ever-obstructive' authorities that his trip to Switzerland would be a useful way of spending his time until a decision was made on his position at the Munich Meisterschule, from which, in the meantime, he still received his salary. At this point, he maintained hope of returning to his post because the successor of Hans Baier (who had been dismissed from the Munich Education Office) was keen to retain Renner. So Renner travelled to Bern, where he stayed until April 1934, and then he moved to Zurich. (So Renner's final dismissal from his Meisterschule post occurred while he was away in Switzerland. It is not clear how long he remained in Zurich). Renner described his work for the Swiss Railway and Tourist Office as the formulation of guidelines for a typographic style (see figures 86–9).

Renner believed in later years that his stay in Switzerland saved him from further victimization. Indeed, he ran into some trouble when he visited Germany from Switzerland in December 1933 to attend his daughter Luise's wedding. He heard that a certain Munich artist, who was a member of the

64 'Verkehrswerbung, deutsche Lebensform und Kulturpropaganda' (1932e). There had also been an exhibition of international tourist publicity organized by the Münchner Bund in 1931, which Renner and Jan Tschichold may have helped to organize.

PAUL RENNER

Faust den Gurt, die andere den Hosenstoss gefasst, so kann der Hosenlupf beginnen. Entschieden ist der Sieg, wenn der eine Kämpfer auf dem Rücken liegt. Rohe und gefährliche Griffe sind verpönt. Ein freundschaftlicher Handschlag vor und nach dem Kampf ist üblich, seit nach Kunst und Regel geschwungen wird. Aus Älplerbräuchen und Älplerfesten sind die grossen nationalen Schwingfeste erwachsen. Ein erstes schweizerisches Schwing- und Älplerfest war das berühmte Hirtenfest zu Unspunnen im Jahre 1805. Doch erst seit der Gründung des eidgenössischen Schwingerverbandes in Zürich im Jahre 1894 sind die allgemeinschweizerischen Wettkämpfe der Schwinger zu regelmässig wiederkehrenden grossen Anlässen geworden.

54

86 & 87 Two double-page openings from booklets for the Swiss Tourist Board. *c.*1934.

88 & 89 Two double-page openings from a large-format booklet, *Die Schweiz*, published by the Swiss Tourist Board. Autumn 1935. 345 × 245 mm. Designed to Renner's specification. The listings pages are printed letterpress on coated paper. The main text pages are printed gravure on uncoated paper. Text in Futura with Beton used for sub-headings.

Munich Nazi Party, had started rumours that Renner was spreading anti-German propaganda in Switzerland. Renner asked Bauer (the 'decent Nazi' in the Munich administration) to set up a meeting with this artist, so that he could make his accusation to Renner's face. The artist refused to meet Renner, but while Renner was waiting in Munich for the meeting, he missed his daughter's wedding. His family waited anxiously for his return. Renner later believed that he would have ended up in some concentration camp if Rudolf Hess had not intervened once more at the request of Karl Haushofer, who attended the wedding.[65]

Switzerland was a natural destination for those escaping Nazism, although the Swiss authorities did not welcome refugees. Renner's colleague Jan Tschichold managed to find work there, through helpful contacts, and eventually became a Swiss citizen in 1942. Some designers, including the leading lights of the Dessau Bauhaus, Walter Gropius and Moholy-Nagy, fled Germany in another direction, passing through Britain on a seemingly inevitable path to the USA, which was to become the foster home of European modernism. But Renner returned from Switzerland and settled quietly in his house on the German side of Lake Constance, in semi-retirement at the age of fifty-five. Now that the initial trouble concerning his dismissal had blown over, the authorities did not harass him further (for the time being at least). Perhaps he was protected to a certain extent by his links with members of the Haushofer family, who were close to the Nazi regime's leaders.

One of the Meisterschule's co-founders, Alexander Oldenbourg, asked Renner for his advice about who should succeed him as principal of the school. Renner recommended Georg Trump, who had taught at the school between 1929 and 1931. Renner asked Trump personally to be his successor, and in September 1934 he returned from teaching in Berlin to take up the Munich post.

65 Letter to Franz Roh, 17 September 1946 (Getty: file 850120). In a letter to Luise of 19 April 1946, Renner expressed his gratitude for Karl Haushofer's intervention: 'I won't forget your father-in-law. I will never forget that I owe my life to his recommendation and his intercession on my behalf with R.H.' (Nachlaß Renner.)

6 Typography in a dictatorship
1933–45

During the Third Reich, National-Socialist views of culture were marked by a certain schizophrenia, or perhaps it was simply opportunism. Progressive and backward-looking cultural policy were both represented by factions within the Party. Hitler's propaganda minister, Joseph Goebbels, had a liking for certain modern trends in art and design, whereas Alfred Rosenberg, founder of the Kampfbund für Deutsche Kultur, rejected modernism as a danger to the 'olde-worlde' values of the German *Volk*.

Threads of modernism from the 1920s were not simply severed with the accession of the Nazis to power. Some aspects of modernist design survived into the Third Reich, so long as they did not conflict with broader ideas in Nazi policy. The main priority of the Nazis was rearmament and, consequently, the increase of efficient industrial production. Rationalization, for instance, was adopted by the Nazi government as a means towards achieving a more powerful nation. Even some aspects of modernist style were tolerated in state-sanctioned design: for instance, tubular steel furniture, an icon of modernist design from the Bauhaus, remained in production, because tubular steel was a favoured material in another area, aircraft production.[1] The Nazis soon realized that modernity, which they continued to denounce in abstract terms for propaganda purposes, was integral to their military and economic aims.[2]

In practice, the Nazis were not at all dogmatic about their stylistic choices: in state-commissioned architecture, the modern style survived after 1933 for some industrial buildings, in addition to the bombastic neo-classicism of Albert Speer.[3] The 1936 Olympiad in Berlin was a perfect opportunity for the Nazis to stress their attachment to the classical heritage, which Hitler was as keen to appropriate as Mussolini was. Roman and sanserif letterforms were used instead of gothic for publicity of the event (see also figure 90).[4] State-sector commissioning bodies even employed some modernist graphic designers to convey an image of Germany as a modern, progressive nation. Herbert Bayer, whose work is regarded as central to New Typography, carried on working in Germany until 1938, when he left for a successful career in America. Bayer designed some documents for National Socialist purposes, including the display and catalogue for the 'Deutschland' exhibition that coincided with the Olympics. Here Bayer

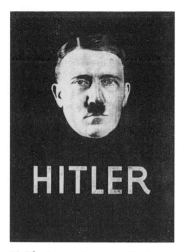

90 Election poster. 1933. Designer unknown. The lettering suggests that the Nazis had no firm policy initially about eschewing sanserif in favour of fraktur.

1 See Heskett, 'Modernism and archaism in design in the Third Reich', and Campbell, *The German Werkbund*, pp. 13–24.

2 Jan Tschichold later accused the Nazis of hypocrisy in persecuting modernist intellectuals like himself: 'The Third Reich was second to none in accelerating technical "progress" in its war preparations while hypocritically concealing it behind propaganda for medieval forms of society and expression.' ('Belief and reality' [1946] in McLean, *Jan Tschichold: typographer*, p. 133.)

3 See Lane, *Architecture and politics...*, pp. 205–16.

4 See the illustrations of graphic design for the Berlin Olympics in *Gebrauchsgraphik* (Jhg 13, Nr 7, 1936).

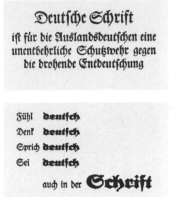

91 Slogans on stickers from the early years of the Third Reich. The top example reads: 'German script is an indispensable protective weapon for Germans abroad against menacing de-Germanization.' Bottom: 'Feel German/think German /speak German/be German/even in your script.'

5 When asked about his contribution to the *Deutschland Ausstellung* booklet Bayer's only comment was: 'This is an interesting booklet insofar as it was done exclusively with photography and photomontage, and was printed in a duotone technique.' Quoted by Benjamin H.D. Buchloch in 'From faktura to factography' in *October* (no. 30, Fall 1984) p. 118. In the copies of these documents in his personal collection, Bayer later painted out all those elements that made explicit Nazi references.

6 See Ute Brüning's essay 'Bauhäusler zwischen Propaganda und Wirtschaftswerbung' in Nerdinger (ed.), *Bauhaus-Moderne im Nationalsozialismus*, pp. 24–47.

7 Lehmann-Haupt, *Art under a dictatorship*, p.171.

utilized the most advanced technological methods for combining images and type – a principal tenet of modernism in graphic design.[5] However, Goebbels turned down at least one of Bayer's designs for being 'too modern'.[6]

Sanserif letterforms did not immediately disappear from view in 1933: then, as now, ideology was often not a major factor in choosing a typeface for a printing job. Choice of typeface would also have been determined by mundane factors, such as availability. But gothic type certainly experienced an officially sanctioned revival in the early years of the Third Reich.

Gothic script during the Third Reich

Gothic script formed part of the Nazi regime's cultural propaganda, and its usage was promoted by official bodies. Germany stood alone in its use of gothic, and the Nazis capitalized on this situation by accentuating the popular notion that gothic script was inherently German. Slogans were printed on stickers to promote the use of 'Deutsche Schrift' as the only suitable clothing for the German language (figure 91); competitions in gothic lettering were held among art students and school children, and the winning results were published in magazines and calendars.[7] Several exhibitions about gothic script were held in major museums during 1933 and 1934, including one in the Frankfurter Kunstgewerbemuseum called 'Die schöne Deutsche Schrift' (The beautiful German script), which was organized by the Kampfbund für Deutsche Kultur and the Deutscher Buchdrucker-Verein.

The sanctity of gothic type was enshrined in the programme of literary censorship that led to the book-burnings of 10 May 1933. The student organizations in universities, which led this campaign, under Nazi influence, and with the agreement of certain librarians and academics, drafted twelve proclamations concerning the unsuitability of certain texts. The Hauptamt für Presse und Propaganda der Deutschen Studentenschaft (Central Office of the German Studenthood for Press and Propaganda) published these proclamations under the title 'Wider den undeutschen Geist' (Against the un-German spirit) and posted them in public. They constituted an anti-Semitic tract, calling for loyalty to the German language: the seventh thesis stated that Hebrew texts translated into

German were a misuse of the German script: 'German script is only for the use of Germans.'[8]

Printing trade journals reflected a more catholic taste in typography than most publications but, from 1933, these periodicals also began to acquiesce to the prevalent mood of nationalism by adopting more gothic type.[9] After Paul Renner's dismissal from the Munich Meisterschule in April 1933, the periodical published by the school, *Graphische Berufsschule*, which Renner had edited, soon changed its text typeface from Futura to a contemporary gothic design (figure 92). Another specific case in which Futura was sacrificed to gothic was in the documents designed by Kurt Schwitters for the city of Hannover (see p.109 above). An official decree from the Hannover City Press Office of 14 June 1933 dictated that 'Deutsche Schrift' was henceforth to be used in all official documentation, due to the new era of 'national uplift'.[10] But there was no uniformly official adoption of gothic type; indeed the Nazis' initial advocacy of gothic seemed to wane after only a few years of the Third Reich. Within the NSDAP, the *völkische* faction tussled with the modernist element for a position of influence on German culture. Hitler initially steered a course between these tendencies, but in 1936 he came out in public support of the vaguely modernist preferences of his propaganda minister, Goebbels. In a speech to Party members he stated: 'Your cosy gothic souls fit badly with the age of steel and iron, glass and concrete, of female beauty and manly strength, of heads held high and defiant spirit.'[11] Roman and sanserif were not yet outlawed, and continued to be used, especially in advertising, a field in which Futura enjoyed enduring success.

The gothic types of the Nazi era

In the 1930s a new kind of gothic typeface arose, in which traditional forms were simplified to give a brute impression. Such typefaces were deliberately marketed by the typefoundries to capitalize on nationalistic feeling, bearing names like Großdeutsch, National, Deutschland, Tannenberg and Element (figure 93, overleaf). Most calligraphic elements were eliminated from the letterforms; in some cases they were reduced almost to a kind of gothic-sanserif form.[12] Gothic capital letters were simplified so that they became more roman in form; in this sense, the Third-Reich gothics went some way towards

92 Cover of *Graphische Berufsschule*, Jhg 1935, Nr 1. A4. After Renner's dismissal from the Munich Meisterschule, the school's house periodical took on an increasingly gothic typographic dress. This cover shows the use of gothic type mixed with photography, in the manner of the modernist 'Typofoto' style. Georg Trump, who took over from Renner as principal of the school, had been a leading practitioner of this style. Issues of *Graphische Berufsschule* after 1933 also increasingly contained Nazi texts: the issue pictured here features extracts from *Mein Kampf* and from writings by Goebbels.

8 Proclamations quoted by J. M. Ritchie, 'The Nazi book-burning' in *Modern Language Review* (vol. 83, 1988) p.636.

9 An editorial in the periodical *Deutscher Drucker* (Nr 481, October 1934) pp.17–18, called for fraktur to be used in the modernist 'Typofoto' style.

10 Decree reproduced in Schwitters, *„Typographie kann unter Umständen …"*, p.95.

11 Hitler quoted in Walter Wilkes's introduction to Bertheau *et al, Buchdruckschriften im 20. Jahrhundert*, pp.xxi–xxix.

12 There is some confusion between these terms in any case: in America, sanserif typefaces have been called 'gothic'. See p.82, note 17 above, and Handover, 'Grotesque Letters', p.5.

National
Element
Gotenburg
Tannenberg

93 Some of the gothic typefaces
released in the early years of the
Third Reich: National designed by
Walter Höhnisch, 1934; Element
by Max Bittrof, 1934; Gotenburg
by Fritz Heinrichten, 1936; Tannenberg by E. Meyer, 1934. Element,
the most rationalized of these typefaces, was promoted by the Bauer
typefoundry as 'The German script
of the New Typography'.

13 See also Renner's comments in *Die
Kunst der Typographie* (1939c) p. 288.

14 See the article by Friedrich Friedl,
'Max Bittrof: visual engineer', *Eye*
(vol. 3, no. 9, 1993) pp. 72–7. Also, for a
perceptive analysis of form in 1930s
gothic typefaces, see Willberg, 'Schrift
und Typographie im Dritten Reich'.

15 Koch died in 1934, and the Offenbach school where he taught became
thoroughly Nazified, as can be seen from
publications about the school: see *Graphische Jugend* (Jhg 2, Heft 10, October
1934) and *Graphische Nachrichten* (Jhg
15, Nr 3, March 1936). In the first of these
journals, an autobiographical article by
Koch was published: 'Rudolf Koch: Der
Deutsche' p. 325. Here he described his
longing for some kind of identity, a
yearning for a sense of belonging. For
Koch it was perhaps his craft and reli-
gion that helped to fill this void, for
others it may have been Nazism. Ehmcke,
who can be seen as Renner's polar
opposite in the debate on fraktur, was
investigated by the Nazis himself in
1933 and was under threat of losing his
job at the Munich Kunstgewerbeschule.
See Philipp Luidl, 'Ehmcke – Erneurer
und Traditionalist' in *75 Jahre Werkbund* (Munich: Deutscher Werkbund
Bayern, 1982).

modernizing gothic type.[13] Max Bittrof, in his typeface
Element, pared down gothic forms to their lineal basics, and
consequently produced a typeface that was a perfect accompaniment to the swastika.[14]

In this kind of typeface, gothic forms were rationalized
in the same way that classical forms were in the Nazi architecture of Albert Speer and Paul L. Troost. Troost's Haus der
Kunst in Munich (1937) took the essential forms of classicism
and simplified them into a kind of modernized austerity:
colonnades became unreasonably long, columns were not
fluted, pediments and architraves were undecorated, consisting of simple blocks of white concrete or marble. Consequently,
the impression of imperial power was enforced with a reference to the style of twentieth-century functionalism. Albert
Speer's monumental buildings and the spectacles that he
orchestrated in Leni Riefenstahl's propaganda films were
glamorous public displays of power, which, by fostering the
myth of the thousand-year Reich in the public imagination,
surely helped to perpetuate the regime's activities. Gothic type
was a less obtrusive – although more pervasive – aspect of the
Nazi propaganda machine. For most Germans, gothic type
must have been unthinkingly accepted as a homely custom;
yet it is such details of material life that accumulate to make
a culture and a national identity, and which can thus be distorted into totems of power by ideologues. Of course, one cannot assume that the designers of gothic typefaces during the
Third Reich were ardent Nazi-supporters (some of the types
must have been produced by many anonymous workers at the
typefoundries). Although the words of well-known gothic sup-
porters like Rudolf Koch and F. H. Ehmcke often conveyed an
epic sense of nationalism similar to that of most Nazi propaganda, these men were romantic nationalists, concerned with
abstract ideas of culture. Neither of them belonged to the Nazi
Party.[15]

Renner resettles in Germany

After his brief working interlude in Switzerland, Renner
returned to his country home at Hödingen on Lake Constance
in 1934. He already had a long career in book design and
teaching behind him, and the tumultuous events of 1933
must have proved an emotional strain. He had been censured

by the German authorities, and consequently began to live in a kind of 'inner emigration'.[16] After his dismissal from his official post in Munich, he was forbidden to earn any kind of regular salary from an employer, and his pension was cancelled. This must have resulted in some bitterness, and encouraged a feeling of being an exile in his own country.

Renner was able to find some occasional work by renewing contacts with former clients. In addition to working on type-face designs, he designed books and book covers occasionally for Otto Maier Verlag in Ravensburg and R. Piper Verlag in Munich. His royalties from Futura were still paid: his contract entitled him to 2.5 per cent of inland sales and 1 per cent of foreign sales. This does not sound like much, but, given the world-wide success of Futura, it supplied him with a steady income. Consequently Renner was able to spend much of his time painting. He was granted permission in 1938 by the Reichskammer für Bildende Künste (Reich Chamber of Fine Arts) to travel to Italy and Switzerland in order to paint the landscape. Also, Renner now devoted a great deal of time to writing.

Die Kunst der Typographie

Renner was invited to sit on the international jury to judge book design at the Paris World Exhibition in 1937. His intensive examination of outstanding book design during a week there inspired him once more to set down in writing his thoughts about typography. This resulted in his best-known book on typography, *Die Kunst der Typographie* (The art of typography, 1939). This lengthy and comprehensive book is much more of a practical manual than his earlier *Typografie als Kunst* (1922); it is also a more accessible practical guide than Tschichold's *Die neue Typographie* (1928), which had really been more concerned with typography as an ideological programme. Renner's own 'modernist' book on typography, *Mechanisierte Grafik* (1931), was even less concerned with details of practice than Tschichold's book, but Renner had promised in *Mechanisierte Grafik* that he would write a further book dedicated to practical matters.

Due to Renner's earlier dismissal from employment as 'nationally untrustworthy', the publishing firm of Frenzel & Engelbrecher (which also published the periodical *Gebrauchs-*

16 This description was suggested by Heinz Haushofer (himself a distinguished biographer) in 'Paul Renner – ein Eindruck' in Luidl & Lange (ed.), *Paul Renner.*

94 Jacket design by Albrecht Heubner, 1939. 244 × 160 mm.

graphik) requested permission from the NSDAP to publish Renner's new book. The book had no political content, and the Nazi party gave permission for publication.[17] *Die Kunst der Typographie* is informed by Renner's long experience in practising and teaching typography. It is reasonable to assume that the principles and exercises that formed the basis of the curriculum at the Munich Meisterschule are summarized in this book. Renner's text strikes a balance between aspects of aesthetic theory and procedural detail: indeed, the principal theme of the book is that preconceptions and prejudices concerning typographic solutions are not to be trusted. Establishing solid rules for practice struck Renner as mistaken, because such rules were bound to ignore the interdependence of many factors in any individual case. In the field of the 'creative arts' (*bildende Kunst*) he held that the eye is the only arbiter, commenting: 'While the compositor's work involves mathematics, aesthetic worth cannot be assessed by verifying the measurements of the type, it can only be checked by viewing a proof on the intended paper size.'[18] Another theme of the book is Renner's characteristic desire to balance technical and aesthetic aspects of creative work. Yet, while his text is underpinned by the practice of letterpress typography, Renner concentrated on the final visual effect, instead of giving step-by-step guidelines for typesetting. He stated in his introduction: 'Typographic design [*Formgeben*], which is the theme of this book, has less to do with technical demands than with practical and aesthetic matters.'[19]

Renner's pedagogical strategy

Renner began his book by considering the placing of a single word on a blank sheet, which, whilst he admitted it was an unrealistic task, he nevertheless suggested was a useful starting point. Such an exercise, along with the design of columns for the double-page spread of a book, were for Renner 'fundamental tasks, from which we can learn the general formal laws, so that we can apply them later to a particular circumstance'.[20] Once again, Renner affirmed his belief in book design as the fundamental task of typography. He dealt methodically with all the parts of a book (including title-pages, contents lists, footnotes and quotations), and his lengthy section on book design does raise many fundamental questions of typography, seeming to justify his decision to use the relatively

17 Letter from the Nationalsozialistische Arbeiterpartei: Reichsleitung, 28 December 1939. The letter stipulated: 'This communication should not be used for advertising purposes' (Nachlaß Renner).
18 *Die Kunst der Typographie* (1939c) pp. 14–15.
19 *Die Kunst der Typographie* (1939c) p. 10.
20 *Die Kunst der Typographie* (1939c) p. 11.

PAUL RENNER

neutral milieu of continuous text setting as an instructional framework. His model for the basic unit of a book was the symmetrical double-page spread containing justified columns of type. In this respect, his view had changed little from his earliest detailed discussion of typography before the First World War (see pp. 31–4 above). Indeed, most of his principles for good justified typesetting are repeated here from his initial formulation of typographic rules in 1917.

Yet Renner did take account of developments in typographic style since his earlier writings on typography. Asymmetric arrangements, in departing from the expected, comfortable position of type on a page, could be striking, he admitted, but he believed that symmetrical layout was unarguably the best solution for books. The reason for this, he maintained, was that the show-through of ink on the opposite side of paper is distracting if the text areas are not backed-up in register against each other, as in a symmetrical, justified arrangement. This observation is partly tied to the technology of letterpress printing, in which the type may sometimes penetrate the paper slightly, and show more strongly on the reverse side than if the book was printed by offset lithography.

Renner still championed the traditional proportions of margins, with the largest at the bottom of a page, 'because we hold the book by the lower margin when we take it in the hand and read it'.[21] This indicates that he envisioned a small book, perhaps a novel, as his imagined model. Yet he struck a pragmatic note by adding that the traditional rule for margin proportions cannot be followed as a doctrine: for example, wide margins for pocket books would be counter-productive. Similarly, he refuted the notion that the type area must have the same proportions as the page:[22] he preferred to trust visual judgement in assessing the placement of the type area on the page, instead of following a pre-determined doctrine.

Lists and tables

Renner's lengthy treatment of book design and his implicit confidence in the status of the book as the highest form of typographic achievement did not, however, prevent him from considering other areas of typography in some detail. He devoted a whole section to 'Lists, tables and forms', regarding them as complex configurations of information worthy of detailed consideration. His recommendations in this section

21 *Die Kunst der Typographie* (1939c) p. 47.

22 *Die Kunst der Typographie* (1939c) p. 51. Jan Tschichold later enshrined this principle in his essay on 'Non-arbitrary proportions of page and type area' in *Print in Britain* (vol. 11, no. 5, September 1963, Design supplement, pp. 2–8; original German text in Tschichold, *Schriften*, vol. 2).

of *Die Kunst der Typographie* stem from a desire to convey the sense and structure of information with the greatest clarity. This structural approach was a fundamental principle of New Typography as Tschichold had defined it, and had always been evident in Renner's writing about typography. Yet, a very significant aspect of New Typography, which Renner applied in *Die Kunst der Typographie*, would perhaps not have been an integral part of his approach to designing lists and tables before the mid-1920s: he advocated an almost unqualified use of asymmetric layout.

In listings of any sort, given that the text is no longer constituted in a linear string of words, but consists instead of discrete elements repeated in sequence, Renner recommended that the best arrangement was for items to 'begin vertically underneath each other' – what one would call in English today 'ranged left'.[23]

Part of Renner's approach to designing lists and tables was the elimination of the brackets, rules and boxes that had traditionally cluttered such typesetting. Perhaps he was satisfying his own desire for a simple and elegant design, in the hope that it would also make the information clearer for the reader. This was 'elemental typography', then, in the sense that Tschichold had first described it in 1925. Indeed, the examples of listed and tabular matter shown as illustrations in *Die Kunst der Typographie* bear a great similarity to examples of such tasks carried out by compositors under the tutelage of Renner, Tschichold and Trump at the Munich Meisterschule, which had also displayed a restrained use of typographic material in a calmly asymmetric layout (figures 95–6).

In his introduction to the book, Renner stated that typography must fulfil three criteria: it had to work in technical terms, in aesthetic terms, and it had to fulfil the purpose conceived by the client who commissioned the design.[24] This formulation ignores the needs of potential readers, but Renner's comments in the body of the book do indicate a very thoughtful approach that has readers' interests at heart. Renner undoubtedly based his interpretation of readers' strategies and eye movements in reading lists, for example, on his own experience, but nevertheless he was trying to generalize from this experience: it was an exercise in imaginative sympathy. In this respect his approach to designing complex information prefigured the kind of user-centred approach that became

23 *Die Kunst der Typographie* (1939c) p. 116.
24 *Die Kunst der Typographie* (1939c) p. 9.

PAUL RENNER

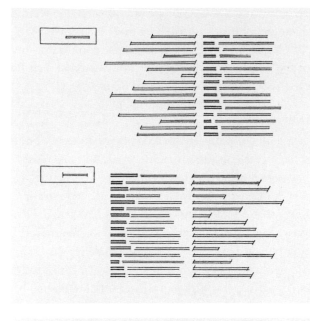

95 (left) Two schematic representations from *Die Kunst der Typographie* showing alternatives for designing a list of personnel. In each diagram, the surname of the person is in bold, with their forenames following on directly. The italic lines (denoted by diagonal ends) contain the duties of each person. Renner recommended the second example, with everything ranged left, so that the beginning of each line of duty-description can be easily accessed.

96 (below) Two possible configurations for a booklist from *Die Kunst der Typographie*. The top example is appropriate for a bookseller's catalogue (the date, author and title are in bold). Renner suggested the second alternative for an occasion when all the bibliographical details might need to be accessed easily. Here he adopted the principle of aligning categories of information in columns, making a kind of table.

1878. **Hogarth, Wilhelm. Zergliederung der Schönheit,** die schwankenden Begriffe von dem Geschmack festzusetzen. Übers. von C. Mylius. Mit 1 Titelvignette u. 2 Kupfertafeln. London 1754. 4⁰. Pappbd. d. Zt. mit schönem goldbedrucktem Überzugspapier.   15.—
Erste deutsche Ausgabe.
1879. **—. Sammlung Hogarthscher Kupferstiche.** 12 Hefte mit 71 (von 75) Tafeln. 4⁰. Umschläge.   6.—
Es fehlen die Tafeln 46—48, 50. — Einige Kupfer stockfleckig, Tafel 69 stark wasserfleckig.

Arldt, Th.	Die Entwicklung der Kontinente und ihrer Lebewelt.	Leipzig, W. Engelmann	1907
Blaringhem, L.	Mutation et Traumatismes. Etude sur l'évolution des formes végétales.	Paris, Felix Alcan	1908
Davenport, C. B.	Statistical Methods with special reference to Biological Variation, 2nd edition.	Neuyork, John Wiley & Sons	1904

accepted amongst some designers in the 1960s and acquired the label of 'information design'. As an attempt to relate typographic form to the task of reading, *Die Kunst der Typographie* is surely a prime example of modernist exposition – a refutation of the notion that typographic decisions were a trade secret.[25]

Renner approached his subject in terms of how type works visually, not how it worked as pieces of metal, which lends his text some qualities of enduring interest. (Indeed *Die Kunst der Typographie* was republished in 1948 and 1953.) Renner was

25 Renner believed that he and his former colleague Jan Tschichold had sought at the Munich Meisterschule to develop an 'architectonic' typography, a systematic approach, instead of 'muddling through' like traditionalist typographers, such as Walter Tiemann and F.H. Ehmcke. (Letter to Tschichold, 15 September 1947.)

interested in making the technology of type serve the form, and not vice versa.[26] He was generally more concerned with making life easier for the reader than for the compositor; he discussed the 'artistic' aim of the typographer a great deal, but never as if a beautiful array was an end in itself.

'Jobbing setting'

Despite a certain antipathy to the field of advertising – due, no doubt, to the increasing Americanization of German culture that he had seen around him since the 1920s – Renner treated the tasks of designing publicity documents in *Die Kunst der Typographie* with detached seriousness.[27] In his view, it was the designer's responsibility to be faithful to the manufacturer's intention and to find a style appropriate for the imagined consumers of the product being advertised. Yet he was able to build on the principles of basic text setting that he had previously set out in his discussion of book design.

Consequently, Renner's approach to 'jobbing setting' was conservative in stressing that order depends on some foundation in continuous text. If there is no perceptible 'base type', which he suggested should be a legible text typeface, then there is no basis for any particular emphasis that is placed on a certain part of the text: 'The levels of emphasis will have been robbed of their foundation'.[28] Also, the spatial arrangement of the text had to be grounded in sense: 'A merely formal typography begins with the decorative division of space; in contrast, an organic, meaningful and purpose-serving typography does not divide up surfaces, it divides up the text.'[29] Renner reasserted his belief in the classical task of the artist to produce a harmonic whole from these elements:

> The actual artistic task, however, consists in giving the whole a form [*Gestalt*] – despite the unavoidable sections demanded by practical considerations – in which no part seems isolated, in which every part is ordered with respect to every other, and everything is in tune.[30]

Standardization

Renner's attitude to national standards concerning typography was ambivalent and resists simplification. In *Die Kunst der Typographie* he re-affirmed his faith in the application of standards to paper-formats and typographic layout for official and business documentation. He devoted many pages to a listing

26 His attitude to ranged-left text setting was, in some respects, an exception to this approach (see pp. 186–8 below).

27 Renner's preference for matters of book design over publicity design was always implicit, but hardly ever rose to the surface in any explicit disdain. In an essay on the 'The modern artist's poster' (1946e) he did comment that, in Scandinavia, the need for posters was not great in 'these fortunate, least American of countries' (p. 228).

28 *Die Kunst der Typographie* (1939c) p. 152.

29 *Die Kunst der Typographie* (1939c) p. 149.

30 *Die Kunst der Typographie* (1939c) p. 162.

PAUL RENNER

and description of DIN standards: in those cases that were addressed by a standard that he deemed useful, like the DIN-standard for A4-format periodical design (including guidelines for typographic layout), he implied that no more thought need be given to the problem, because the standard was so well conceived.[31]

But Renner's enthusiasm for DIN standards did not stretch to the area of book design. He considered the proposed DIN book-format standards (1926) to be ill-conceived and counter-productive, for a number of convincing reasons. He believed that standardization of book formats would be beneficial, so that 'the book trade would finally experience the blessing of a standardization that has long since been carried out in other branches of industry'; but he perceived the desire for ration-alization to have gone too far, too soon, in ignoring certain 'artistic' principles. He argued that the traditional range of aesthetically pleasing book formats should have been stan-dardized: 'Instead of this an attempt was made to introduce new formats departing from the common and proven formats, an unprecedented step in the history of standardization.' DIN formats seemed to him of no benefit in book printing: the prin-ciple of the DIN system was that each paper size was created by folding sheets successively in half; but, as Renner observed: 'A book in A5-format can never be printed on the same paper as a book in A4-format, because the direction of the paper-grain (running along the length of the paper-roll, which is far more robust than the width) must always run perpendicular to the lines of type if the bound book is not to warp.' Along with other Moderns of the 1920s Renner had humbly praised the achievements of 'engineers'; yet he believed that paper-format standards for books had suffered from a surfeit of engineering initiative and a lack of artistic advice.[32]

To support his criticism of the DIN formats as applied to books, Renner had conducted a survey among a number of German publishers shortly before his dismissal from the Munich Meisterschule. In his circular letter, he summarized his opinions (as given above), and added that the greater part of German novel literature had appeared in the satisfying format of 180 × 120 mm (3:2).[33] Almost none of the publishers who replied to Renner's circular used DIN formats for books. Some admitted to having produced some technical booklets for edu-cational establishments in A4-format, but those publishers

31 *Die Kunst der Typographie* (1939c) pp. 174–81.
32 *Die Kunst der Typographie* (1939c) pp. 83–4.
33 Circular letter from Renner, 10 February 1933 (Nachlaß Renner).

who had carried out some standardization of formats had done it in-house with their own personal choices. Some of the respondents to Renner's survey commented that his preference for the traditional, small-book format was restrictive.[34] Here again Renner's comments had revealed his preferred definition of the ideal book: the slim and handy novel. Perhaps this kind of book gave him most pleasure in designing and reading. During his periods as a practising book designer, Renner had mostly been concerned with books of 'literature', although his experience in teaching at the Munich Meisterschule involved him in designing more complex kinds of text. In *Die Kunst der Typographie* Renner did not restrict his consideration of books to the novel-form. Indeed he stated that handiness was no criterion for reference books, which had to contain as much text as possible, and were therefore justified in being unwieldy, given that they would generally be laid flat on a table while waiting to be consulted. Renner suggested in a later article that these two forms of the book, the handy novel, and the weighty reference book, were the polarities between which all other kinds of books were ranged.[35]

Renner's attempt to fuse roman and gothic

Apart from his famous sanserif, Futura, Paul Renner designed both a gothic and a roman typeface. His gothic typeface design, Ballade, is nourished by the calligraphic tradition, spurning the rationalized forms of other 1930s gothics. His roman typeface, Renner-Antiqua, was also based on his own formal writing; indeed both typefaces seem to have arisen from a desire to discover a middle-ground between gothic and roman through an exploration of their shared basis in writing with a broad pen.

It may seem strange that Renner designed a gothic typeface, considering the public statements he made in favour of the abolition of gothic. But his typography and lettering had always shown an equal affinity for roman and gothic, except during his focussed advocacy of sanserif in the 1920s, and it seems likely that he returned to his interest in gothic letterforms after his dismissal from the Meisterschule. Of Renner's surviving sketches and calligraphy (which date mostly from after 1933), over half seem to be in the gothic idiom (see figures 97–8).

34 Letters from Julius Springer and Max Jänecke to Renner (Nachlaß Renner).
35 'Moderne Typografie' (1946f) p. 141.

PAUL RENNER

HBFCPMK
LTRSDW
ZOEAXUV
YGINQJ
agcedqobphlk
trfmnuijvwx
yszſtß,.;:!?

ABCDEFGI
JHKLMNO
PRSQTUW
YVXZabcde
fghijklmnop
qrsſtuvwxy!
zſtflſtftſißß?„

97 & 98 Two examples of scripts by Renner showing characteristics of both gothic and roman. (After 1933.)

The notion of mixing gothic and roman was not new. The printer, Johann Friedrich Unger, had made an attempt to produce a hybrid style of type in the early 1790s. Unger collaborated with Firmin Didot in designing a neo-classical fraktur, but the initial versions cut by Didot were unsatisfactory. The final form was cut by Unger's resident punchcutter Gubitz, and was announced by Unger with an essay in 1793 (see figure 11).[36] Unger-Fraktur was rediscovered around the turn of the twentieth century at the Enschedé foundry in the Netherlands; Renner used it extensively in designing literary editions, showing his early affinity for romanized styles of gothic.

The twentieth century brought a renewed enthusiasm for moderating gothic with roman. The typefaces designed by Otto Eckmann (1900) and Peter Behrens (1901) made steps in this direction, simply by doing without the customary gothic flourishes. The book-artist and type designer E.R. Weiss also designed some notable gothic typefaces that tend towards roman – one in each of the three main historical styles: Gotisch (textura), Rundgotisch (rotunda), and fraktur. All three display a simplification and widening of the traditional forms.[37]

36 J.F. Unger, 'Probe einer neuen Art deutscher Lettern' in Sichowsky and Tiemann (ed.), *Typographie und Bibliophilie*, pp. 24–9. See also Konrad F. Bauer, 'Zur Geschichte der Unger Fraktur' in *Gutenberg Jahrbuch* (1929) pp. 287–96; and Renner, *Typografie als Kunst* (1922a) p. 132.

37 See Burke, 'German hybrid typefaces 1900–1914' in Peter Bain and Paul Shaw (ed.), *Blackletter: type and national identity* (New York: Princeton Architectural Press/Cooper Union, 1998), pp. 32–9.

Renner approached the designing of a modern gotico-antiqua from the roman side. Figures 97 & 98 show some of his alphabet designs that are not easily categorized as either simply roman or gothic. They benefit greatly from Renner's expertise with a broad pen, which gives the characters a vital unity. Yet these alphabets suffer from a lack of traditional identity; by definition they are compromises between two familiar and strongly-established styles, and cannot escape giving the impression of experimentation. Renner himself seemed to have arrived at this conclusion. Although he retained the opinion that he formed in the late 1920s – that gothic was a *cul-de-sac* in terms of stylistic development – he commented later: '... gothic scripts must remain gothic; if one attempts to weaken their stylistic features, then one takes away their character and makes them, in the most favourable cases, what script was before its gothicization: a littera antiqua.'[38] He opted to accept the division between gothic and roman, but his two typefaces in these respective styles are both coloured by his experiments.

38 'Fraktur und Antiqua' (1948b) p. 347.

Es läßt sich im Leben nichts, gar nichts nachholen, keine Arbeit, keine Freude, ja sogar das Leid kann zu spät kommen. Jeder Moment hat seine eigentümlichen, unabweisbaren Forderungen. Die Kunst zu leben besteht in dem Vermögen, die Reste der Vergangenheit zu jeder Zeit durchstreichen zu können.   Hebbel

Tagung der deutschen Buchhändler
auf der Frühjahrs-Messe zu Leipzig
In Stadt und Land

99 Ballade. Berthold, 1937. 12 and 28 point sizes of the regular weight, and 48 point size of the semi-bold weight. The customary forms of fraktur are somewhat softened (by maintaining full curves on the small e, o and a, for example), yet Ballade retains a certain spiki-ness with the broken curves on small m and n. Renner also eschewed the traditional gothic form of small k, which is confusing to the modern reader, in favour of a more roman version.

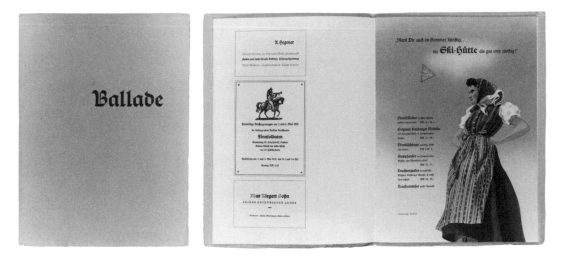

Ballade

Ballade was released in 1937 by the Berthold typefoundry. While remaining true to the gothic heritage, it also reflects an attempt to bring elements of roman to the letterforms (figure 99). Renner himself said that it could be seen as a 'modification of Schwabacher' (the style of gothic that prevailed for the setting of German texts until it was ousted by fraktur in the mid-sixteenth century). Like Schwabacher, Ballade's letterforms are wider and rounder than those of fraktur.[39] But Renner's gentle typeface did not match the spirit of late 1930s Germany, and it seems to have found little favour. Yet his attempt to provide a new variation within the gothic tradition shows that he perceived gothic to be worthy of fresh consideration, despite its adoption as part of Nazi propaganda.

Renner-Antiqua

Renner-Antiqua (released by the Stempel Typefoundry in 1939) exhibits the same preference for condensed letter-widths and heavily accented diagonal stress that can be found in Renner's calligraphy. The curved letters, like small o and e, almost break at their thinnest points, giving a near-gothic rhythm to the typeface (figures 102–8).

The first proofs of Renner-Antiqua are dated 1936, although there was some initial indecision as to whether it was to be called 'Antiqua' or 'Mediäval'. As Renner himself explained on one occasion, *Antiqua* was the generic word for roman in the nineteenth century when the only roman types generally available were in the modern-face idiom (also called

100 (left) Cover of type specimen for Ballade. Berthold, 1937. 280 × 205 mm. Brown on grey.

101 (right) Pages from Ballade type specimen, showing the kind of *völkische* imagery used to advertise gothic type during the Third Reich. Left-hand page: red and black; Right-hand page: four-colour process.

39 *Die Kunst der Typographie* (1939c) p. 286. Stresow also remarks that Ballade possesses some characteristics of Schwabacher in 'Paul Renner', p. 69. Caflisch, in *Die Schriften von Renner, Tschichold und Trump* (p. 19), stated that Ballade tends toward 'Gotisch' or 'Rundgotisch'.

ABCDEFFeGHIKLMNOPQRSTTeUVVe
WWeXYYeZÆŒÇØ$£ ` ´ ^ ¨ °

mabcdefghijklmnopqrstuvwxyzäöüæœøçn
mchckfffifltßstčt.,-:;!?'()'',,«»&m1234567890m

102 Renner-Antiqua. Stempel, 1939. From a proof of the 36 point size (reduced to 64 per cent).

Hamburg

Hamburg

Bamberg

Quamquam mihi semper

HAMBURGER Senatsmitglieder

Hamburg

Quamquam mihi semper

103 All the variants of Renner-Antiqua designed by Renner. Compiled at the Stempel type-foundry from proofs and drawings. Only the regular weight and italic were produced. The bold weights tend towards a gothic impression, especially the bold condensed weight (bottom).

104 Text set in Renner-Antiqua and Kursiv. From *Typografische Regeln* (1947). Actual size.

Titel gehört, auf eine eigene Seite zu bringen. Die Rückseite des Titels soll frei bleiben. Den Schmutztitel setze man in eine Zeile; bei Antiqua in nicht zu großen Versalien, bei Fraktur in Cicero oder Korpus gesperrt. Interpunktionszeichen werden auf den Titeln gewöhnlich nicht gesetzt; man will sie aber wieder einführen. Bei kurzen Titeln und bei römischen Versalien sind sie entbehrlich.

Der in den schönsten Schriften gesetzte Titel verunstaltet ein Buch, wenn keine Rücksicht auf die Grundschrift genommen wird. Auch berühmte Drucker sündigen dagegen. Die größeren Schriftgrade des Titels und der Rubrikzeilen müssen zu der Grundschrift des Buches passen. Sie müssen deshalb nicht unbedingt von der gleichen Garnitur sein. Oft ist man durch Rücksicht auf leider Vorhandenes

klassizistische Antiqua); in Germany at least, old-face roman typefaces became common again in the wake of William Morris's Kelmscott Press and were called *Mediäval*, a term stemming from Morris's predilection for the Middle Ages, and his gothicized version of the Jenson type model.[40] It is difficult to categorize Renner-Antiqua (as it was finally called) in terms of standard classifications of roman typefaces. It has a strong calligraphic, old-face influence in the small letters, but the capital letters have almost vertical stress, quite mannered serifs, and incline towards the proportions of modern-face. They bear some similarities to capitals by the eighteenth-century Dutch punchcutter Fleischmann, for whose work Renner held a particular affection (he even used a picture of Fleischmann as a frontispiece for his 1922 book *Typografie als Kunst*). Marrying the calligraphic element with an appropriate form of serif seems to have been a long process in the development of the type, and it is perhaps this unresolved mismatch of elements that makes Renner-Antiqua a less successful outcome of Renner's gothic/roman experiments than his Ballade typeface. However, the italic for Renner-Antiqua is a truly elegant design. It has certain affinities with gothic in some letterforms, like small g, but in general, Renner-Kursiv has a fluidity that is lacking in the roman (figures 104–6).

The typeface was adapted for use on the Linotype system in 1940 (Stempel manufactured typeface material for the Linotype company in Germany). It found some use in newspapers, particularly the *Süddeutsche Zeitung*, which was still set in Renner Antiqua at the end of the Second World War.

105 (above left) Renner's drawings for Renner-Kursiv. *c.*1938.

106 (above right) Detail of drawing, probably a preparatory sketch for Renner-Kursiv. 1930s.

40 'Fraktur und Antiqua' (1948b) p.347.

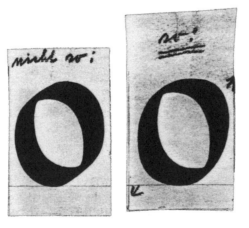

107 Letter from Renner to the Stempel typefoundry, giving detailed corrections to proofs of Renner-Antiqua. 1942.

108 Renner's correction to the shape of the small o in one of the bolder weights of Renner-Antiqua. His notes read: 'Not like this: *like this!*' (Actual size.)

PAUL RENNER

But Renner's working relationship with Stempel seems not to have been as satisfactory as that with the Bauer and Berthold foundries. He stipulated changes to be made to the typeface as late as 1942, implying that he was unsatisfied with its initially released form (figures 107–8).[41] In late 1942 the foundry had four of his designs in production and Renner remarked that, after four years' work, not one of them was ready. There are certainly proofs of many other, unreleased designs for roman and italic typefaces by him in the Stempel archives. One roman has the working title 'Hapag', implying that it was being designed for the Hamburg-America ocean liner company of that name. There were several modern-face italics, and the 'Renner-Grotesk' that was eventually turned into Steile Futura for the Bauer foundry (see pp. 193–5).[42]

The Nazi ban on gothic

Renner's gothic typeface, Ballade, did not have long to prove its worth, due to a sudden change of Nazi cultural policy with regard to letterforms in 1941, when gothic script was officially outlawed by the regime as a Jewish abomination. The Nazi decree, dated 3 January 1941, described gothic script as 'Schwabacher-Jewish letters' that infiltrated printing along with the Jewish ownership of printing businesses (figure 109).[43] Roman was now proclaimed the 'Normalschrift' (standard letter) to be used in all printing, beginning with those publications that already had a foreign circulation. This last stipulation revealed the true reason behind the about-turn. World conquest was within Hitler's sights: in September 1940, Germany, Italy and Japan had signed a pact to establish a new world order. Hitler's armies had already occupied France, the Netherlands, Belgium, Denmark and Norway – all of which were countries where roman type was used. In order to make Nazi communications understandable to people in these outlying regions of the new Reich, a more 'international' form of printing was needed.[44] The gothic ban must also have aided the regime's initiative to recruit labour for the war effort from the new regions of the Reich; Albert Speer commented that language was a problem in this operation.[45] It became apparent that fraktur was an obstacle to world domination, so, with their characteristic opportunism, the Nazis changed policy overnight. Ironically, the Nazi motive for outlawing gothic

41 Renner complained in a letter of 30 August 1942 to Stempel that progress at the foundry was very slow, also commenting that certain changes that he requested were not carried out when he asked (Stempel).

42 Here is a list of the fonts designed by Renner for Stempel. The dates refer to payments. He was paid 500 RM for each of the variants listed:

07.02.39	Mediäval & Kursiv [Renner-Antiqua]
19.03.41	Halbfette Renner-Antiqua
22.11.41	Schmalfette Renner-Antiqua
12.02.42	Fette Renner-Antiqua
11.05.42	Carus-Antiqua (Faustina)
04.06.42	Hapag (Antiqua & Kursiv)
19.06.42	Schmal halbfett Renner-Antiqua ($^3/_4$ fett)
01.07.42	Carus-Kursiv (Faustina)

43 The decree was signed by Martin Bormann, who controlled Nazi domestic policy by vetting all ideas submitted to Hitler, presenting them as he saw fit, and finally acquiring unquestioning agreement from Hitler for Bormann's own suggested solution. A translation of the decree is given by Steinberg, 'Secret decree reveals Hitler's real attitude to gothic type'.

44 A circular letter of 13 January 1941 to city councils from the 'Reichsminister und Chef der Reichskanzlei' (Reich Minister and Head of the Reich Chancery; signed by Dr Lammers, one of Bormann's lackeys) reiterated Hitler's decision to have all newspapers and periodicals set in roman rather than gothic, 'because foreigners who can read the German language, can hardly read this script.' (Reproduced in Schwitters, „Typographie kann unter Umständen…", p. 97.)

45 Speer, Inside the Third Reich, p. 220.

Nationalsozialistische Deutsche Arbeiterpartei

Der Stellvertreter des Führers

München 33, den
Braunes Haus

Stabsleiter

z.Zt. Obersalzberg, den 3.1.1941

Reichs-
Studentenführung
Eing. 9.JAN.41
B.B.Nr.
Z. d. A.

R u n d s c h r e i b e n

(Nicht zur Veröffentlichung).

Zu allgemeiner Beachtung teile ich im Auftrage des Führers
mit:

Die sogenannte gotische Schrift als eine deutsche Schrift
anzusehen oder zu bezeichnen ist falsch. In Wirklichkeit
besteht die sogenannte gotische Schrift aus Schwabacher
Judenlettern. Genau wie sie sich später in den Besitz der
Zeitungen setzten, setzten sich die in Deutschland an-
sässigen Juden bei Einführung des Buchdrucks in den Besitz
der Buchdruckereien und dadurch kam es in Deutschland zu der
starken Einführung der Schwabacher Judenlettern.

Am heutigen Tage hat der Führer in einer Besprechung mit
Herrn Reichsleiter Amann und Herrn Buchdruckereibesitzer
Adolf Müller entschieden, dass die Antiqua-Schrift künftig
als Normal-Schrift zu bezeichnen sei. Nach und nach sollen
sämtliche Druckerzeugnisse auf diese Normal-Schrift umge-
stellt werden. Sobald dies schulbuchmässig möglich ist,
wird in den Dorfschulen und Volksschulen nur mehr
die Normal-Schrift gelehrt werden.

Die Verwendung der Schwabacher Judenlettern durch
Behörden wird künftig unterbleiben; Ernennungsur-
kunden für Beamte, Strassenschilder u.dergl. werden
künftig nur mehr in Normal-Schrift gefertigt werden.

Im Auftrage des Führers wird Herr Reichsleiter Amann
zunächst jene Zeitungen und Zeitschriften, die bereits
eine Auslandsverbreitung haben, oder deren Auslandsverbreitung erwünscht ist, auf Normal-Schrift umstellen.

F.d.R.:   Verteiler: gez. M. Bormann.
           Reichsleiter,
           Gauleiter,
           Verbändeführer.

109 The Nazi decree that outlawed gothic type. 1941.

was a perversion of the argument used almost 100 years earlier by Jakob Grimm when he stated that gothic type was shutting Germany off from the rest of Europe.

The 'Jewish' aspect to the Nazi argument was a fantasy, as one might expect. S. H. Steinberg, in a very perceptive analysis of the decree, remarked that by linking the term 'Schwabacher' to Jewishness the Nazis created associations with the leading Jewish banker of the 1930s, Paul von Schwabach. Steinberg believed that the official Nazi printer, Adolf Müller, who is mentioned in the decree, must have contributed to this argument, as the term Schwabacher would have been in his vocabulary. Schwabacher was a specialist's term, and Steinberg suggested that this 'may have encouraged Hitler to pronounce this nonsense without fear of being laughed out of court'.[46] The imprecise grasp of the terminology and history of gothic

46 Steinberg, 'Secret decree ...', p. 11.

PAUL RENNER

scripts amongst the German public came to the aid of the Nazi propaganda machine in this case. Steinberg also remarked that the term for the new official roman script was carefully chosen: 'Normalschrift' was a neutral term, reflecting the international comprehensibility intended by the regime for its printed matter. Moreover, it had connotations of industrial standardization appropriate to the war effort; indeed it was the kind of term used in the rhetoric of modernist typographers in the 1920s.

The Nazis had therefore changed their policy on the very issue that they had exploited in their arrest of Renner in 1933. In his book, *Mechanisierte Grafik* (1931), Renner had echoed Jakob Grimm's views by stating:

> It is not clear why, in a time when all nations are seeking a communal humanity, only Germany should revert to a type that does not ease comprehension and endangers the preservation of the language of German minorities in neighbouring countries.[47]

Renner's argument is thus very close to the reason given by the Nazis for their ban on fraktur. Given that his booklet *Kulturbolschewismus?* was scrupulously studied by the Nazi watchdogs for evidence of 'cultural Bolshevism', his other writings may also have been scrutinized at this time: Renner's view concerning the invalidity of gothic in an international context may have been noted. Renner himself speculated that his writings may have had some influence on the regime. In 1944, he reflected on his stand against fraktur:

> And on the issue of script the Party had the gall to first of all give free rein to the proponents of fraktur and then to brush it aside as Jewish. The Führer himself was always against fraktur: perhaps my "Kunst der Typographie" (which was actually supported and recommended by the Party) was shown to him at some point, I don't know. But in any case, I was the first here to be able to write publicly as an opponent of fraktur, unimpeded by the Party, long before the script decree. And I am proud that even in a dictatorship I did not let them put a gag on my mouth.[48]

Soon after the gothic ban, Renner wrote an article welcoming the belated primacy of roman in Germany, once again taking the opportunity to point out that gothic had never been inherently German.[49] After the demise of the Nazi regime he was able to be more open in his views on the matter:

47 *Mechanisierte Grafik* (1931d) p. 60.
48 Letter to Karl H. Salzmann, 1944 (Nachlaß Renner).
49 'Nach der Entscheidung' (1942b) pp. 201–5.

DIE NEUE REICHSKANZLEI steht wie das benachbarte alte Haus auf geschichtlich jungem Boden.

Jahrhunderte hindurch kannte das mittelalterliche Berlin-Cölln hier den ausgedehnten, zwischen Spree und Landwehrgraben *Hallgarfen hingegen um* des Tiergartens. Während die ersten Kurfürsten diesen Wald lediglich durchforsteten und ihr Jagdwild in ihm *meinem arm* begann der Große Kurfürst die Umgestaltung des Waldes zu einem Park, den wir heute im wesentlichen unverändert vor uns

110 Proof from the Bauer type-foundry dated 26 November 1942 of a 'Mediäval' typeface designed by Renner. 16 point size. Likely to be the typeface Renner was working on for Albert Speer's architectural office in Berlin. This typeface was never released.

The motives that led to this step may have been loathsome, but this decree itself was an undeserved gift from the heavens, of the kind which occasionally deliver goodness from those whose intentions are bad.[50]

Renner seems to have been tangentially involved in an official reconsideration of the state-sanctioned letterform during the Third Reich. He had some discussions with a 'Graphiker' [graphic designer] at Albert Speer's architectural office in Berlin concerning an official typeface. The Office of the Generalbauinspektor für die Reichshauptstadt (Inspector-General of Building for the Reich Capital [Berlin]) had been set up in 1937 by Speer, Hitler's favourite architect, with the specific intention of keeping it independent of the NSDAP. Speer's office acquired a reputation as a sanctuary for non-Party members, because Hitler allowed Speer to choose his own staff, instead of forcing him to employ second-rate members of the Nazi Party. Speer commissioned non-Nazis like Peter Behrens and Paul Bonatz (both former Werkbund members) to design buildings for the new Berlin cityscape. Renner may have heard through ex-Werkbund colleagues that Speer's office was a potential source of work, free of direct Nazi control. Renner made designs for a typeface in co-operation with the Bauer typefoundry, proofs of which were sent to Speer's office in Berlin during 1943. Renner's correspondent there remarked that bureaucracy prevented a simple ministerial decision to choose Renner's typeface instead of the customary

50 *Das Moderne Buch* (1947d) p. 11.

'Speer-Schrift' for use on buildings. It is unclear whether Renner's design was a version of Futura or a new seriffed roman. There are proofs dating from late 1942 of a 'Mediäval' he designed for Bauer that is likely to be the typeface under discussion (figure 110). Renner also prepared a sketch of seriffed capital letters indicating how they would look when incised in stone (figure 111). The project seems to have come to nothing, although Renner was paid 10 000 marks for his efforts. This money would have been welcome, given that Renner had lost his pension on dismissal from the Munich Meisterschule.

Evidently, it was not simply the case that all those who had once come into conflict with the Nazi regime remained out of favour. Whether designers who are now regarded as 'modern' were able to continue working under the Nazi regime must have depended on a complex set of political, personal and financial factors, which are difficult to assess today. Designers were employed by the regime because of personal contacts and friendships, not the cleanliness of their records as Nazis. Hence the continued activity of some Werkbund members during the Nazi period, steering clear of the authorities, and achieving 'quality' work in the traditional Werkbund spirit.

7 **Survival** 1945–56

Most leading modernist designers had emigrated from Germany in the early years of the Third Reich, long before the Second World War. Many of them had successfully begun to rebuild their careers in the USA, Switzerland or Britain. These refugees of the diaspora must certainly have adapted their ideas to new circumstances. Some, like Moholy-Nagy in the USA, persisted on principle with a view of design free from political ties and cultural boundaries. Others, like Jan Tschichold, were scarred by their experience in Germany. Tschichold's work in Switzerland quickly veered away from his earlier 'elemental typography'. He criticized his own former belief that New Typography was the only approach suitable for the modern era: the dogmatism inherent in his evangelism for the New Typography was, he now believed, a symptom of the 'German bent for the absolute', which had also resulted in Nazism and the Third Reich.

Paul Renner also felt sad and betrayed by his treatment in his homeland. But, in 1945, at the age of 67, he was not in a position to carve out a new career for himself in a new culture. He continued painting and writing, living in 'inner emigration' at the southernmost edge of Germany. When the Allied and Russian troops entered Germany at the end of the Second World War, Renner's home in the region of Baden Württemburg fell into the newly established French zone. He welcomed this final release from the tyranny of the Third Reich: although he felt that Germany was now 'ripped apart', he knew that this was not the fault of the Allied forces, and he expressed a certain admiration for the French troops, whom he found to be quite friendly. Furthermore he found that some of the French officers 'even have sympathy and understanding for spiritual Germany'.[1]

He described the reaction of his wife, Annie, to the liberating Allied forces: 'When the first tank came into the village in 1945, my wife, who was standing at the window, took the beautiful yellow narcissi from a glass that stood next to her on the window sill and threw them down. No people in history has so welcomed the "enemy", I believe, than in Germany early last year'.[2]

Renner and his family had been hounded by the Gestapo in 1944, after the July assassination attempt on Hitler, in which some of Renner's relatives had been implicated. In November 1944, two Gestapo agents had arrived at his house

1 Letter to Tschichold, 31 May 1946.
2 Letter to Tschichold, 31 May 1946.

with a warrant for the arrest of his whole family. They were saved by intervention from the leader of the local farmers' association. Indeed Renner's frustration with the Nazi regime did not really end after Hitler's defeat, because he was informed of rumours that he had eventually become a member of the NSDAP. Renner was furious about these rumours, which seem to have emanated from ex-colleagues in Munich. He knew how dangerous such gossip could be from his experience in the Nazi years, when his 'life hung by a thread' so often, and he still did not feel that this danger had passed.[3] He feared that he might be arrested if the American troops heard the rumours, and noticed that the bogus information contradicted Renner's answer to their questionnaire, in which he had stated that he was never a Party member. He carried with him at all times a statement by the former, regional NSDAP leader, confirmed by the current mayor, that he had never been in the Nazi Party. He was sorrowful that some former colleagues were telling such lies about him. In a letter to Franz Roh, he reflected: 'I want nothing more to do with these people.'[4] And, in a subsequent letter: 'In 1933 I was younger and fuller of optimism; when I now see that the methods of the Nazis have begun to operate in those people who were anti-Nazis, then one loses hope and gives up the fight.'[5]

Renner's wife, Annie, suffered heavily from migraines as a lasting reaction to the worries of the Hitler era. In a letter to Jan Tschichold, Renner commented that she would like to go and live in Switzerland, rather than stay in Germany, which Renner now felt to be an empty shell of a country. Tschichold, then working in London, must have been thinking of moving to America, because Renner wished him success in a 'further transplantation across the great water'. He observed that Mies van der Rohe had been able to carry out his ideas more successfully in the USA than he could have in Europe: 'Perhaps more might have come of me in America. Now it's too late.'[6]

But Renner's hope had not been fully extinguished by the war. Immediately after its end, his pension from the Munich Meisterschule was reinstated.[7] He wasted no time in becoming active in restoring some dignity to Germany's cultural life – rather impressive for a man of his age. He was soon embroiled in efforts to revive the Deutscher Werkbund: he became a representative of the new regional group for his area, South Baden, and attended occasional committee meet-

3 Letter to Franz Roh, 7 September 1946 (Getty: file 850120).
4 Letter to Franz Roh, 7 September 1946 (Getty: file 850120).
5 Letter to Franz Roh, 17 September 1946 (Getty: file 850120).
6 Letter to Tschichold, 20 April 1948.
7 Letter from Landeshauptstadt München to Renner, 6 December 1945 (Nachlaß Renner).

ings in various cities. He also continued to engage in public debate about issues of culture and design.

Renner's response to the Tschichold/Bill dispute

A few years after he had settled in Switzerland in 1933, Jan Tschichold began to develop a refined traditionalism in his book design work. It is possible that he was encouraged to set aside New Typography for pragmatic reasons: he needed to work, and he probably had to conform to the traditional ideas of those book publishers from whom he received that work. But Tschichold also claimed that he had principled reasons for moving away from a strict adherence to New Typography. In any case, he found that a classical form of book typography best met the demands of the large range of literary and historical books he had to design.

The dispute between Tschichold and Max Bill that took place in the April and June issues of *Schweizer Graphische Mitteilungen* for 1946 is a central document of Tschichold's 'conversion' from modernist to traditionalist typographer; but it was also a defining moment for the reborn New Typography in Switzerland, which went on to thrive in the 1950s and 1960s (and still does to some extent).[8] Max Bill had studied at the Bauhaus and, although he was also a painter, sculptor and architect, he had made his living in the 1930s principally from graphic design. Bill accused Tschichold of deserting the progressive principles of New Typography that Tschichold himself had clarified and put into practice in the 1920s and 1930s. Bill was spurred to write his article, 'Über Typografie' (On typography), by a statement Tschichold made at a lecture given in Zurich in December 1945: Tschichold stated that New Typography had only proved itself suitable for advertising and jobbing printing. Bill regarded Tschichold's retreat into the 'age-old' classical forms of symmetrical book typography as a denial of contemporary technological possibilities and imperatives. He argued for a rejection of typographic schemas, both traditional and modernist, in favour of a constructive, elemental typography derived from the basic materials of the craft, as Tschichold had first defined it in 'Elementare Typographie' (1925).

Tschichold's thoughtful answer to Bill, entitled 'Glaube und Wirklichkeit' (Belief and reality), explored the personal, moral

8 See the account by Kinross, *Modern typography*, pp. 106–8.

and political aspects of typographic work. In Switzerland after the Second World War, Tschichold was recommending a stylistic pluralism, with a personal preference for classical symmetry; he commented that the sober forms of Bill's 'functional' typography might not suit the pragmatic demands of certain jobs and clients.[9]

Paul Renner's response to this dispute was a philosophical attempt to resolve a middle course between the two positions. The two disputants had raised fundamental issues about modern typography, and Renner brought his views on this matter to the debate. He contributed an article entitled 'Über moderne Typographie' (On modern typography) to *Schweizer Graphische Mitteilungen*, published almost two years after the initial exchange.[10] Before having his article published, Renner entered into correspondence with Tschichold, in order to clarify his ex-colleague's position. Renner told Tschichold that he had defended him to certain Swiss members of the Werkbund, who were enraged by Tschichold's conservatism. Renner could not accept that Tschichold was really anti-modern and requested that he relate his position in a letter to Renner, so that Renner could clarify it in print. He remarked to Tschichold that he did not want the young typographers of post-war Germany to get the impression that the teaching they had done at the Munich school was some kind of 'youthful error': 'Should we let the Nazis succeed in negating this work?'[11]

In his article Bill had affirmed a belief in matching typography with a *Zeitgeist*. He argued that certain forms, like ranged-left typesetting, were inherently better suited to the means of production (in 1946) than others. In his reply Tschichold accused Bill of suffering from 'naïve worship of so-called technological progress', as Tschichold himself had done as a young man.[12] He refuted some of Bill's assumptions: for example, ranged-left typesetting was no easier to achieve by machine than was justified setting. Modern methods and tools of production could produce typography in both symmetrical and asymmetric styles without any difficulty. The 'modern' aspect of Bill's typography was principally stylistic in its deployment of certain forms as expressive of the modern age. Tschichold offered a definition of 'modern' as synonymous with 'contemporary': both traditional and new typography could be modern, and one should refrain from 'investing the word "modern" with value judgments'.[13]

9 Interestingly, one of the sins of which Tschichold accused Max Bill was the rejection of indention to mark a new paragraph, which was also a blind spot for Renner at this time (see pp. 187–8).

10 In a letter to Tschichold of 31 May 1946, Renner referred to Tschichold's 'rejection of New Typography', which implies that he had already read Bill's article, or heard about Tschichold's previous lecture from Swiss friends. (Unfortunately Tschichold's side of this correspondence seems not to have survived.)

11 Letter to Tschichold, 15 September 1947. Renner wrote to Tschichold initially in early 1946 to inform him that his name had been put forward as a potential candidate to take over leadership of the Leipzig School of Printing. Renner had been asked first, but he considered himself too old, and therefore suggested Tschichold, who in turn replied that his Swiss citizenship made such an appointment difficult. Renner apologized for putting Tschichold in a difficult position, but believed that he would make a contribution in Leipzig that would provide healthy competition for the staff at the Munich school, who were reluctant, in his opinion, to enter public debate. He prized Tschichold, because he had always been a 'confessor' (letter of 31 May 1946).

12 Tschichold, 'Belief and reality' in McLean, *Jan Tschichold: typographer*, p. 134.

13 Tschichold, 'Belief and reality', p. 138.

Renner's view on what was modern in typography steered clear of stylistic questions. During his correspondence with Tschichold, he made reference to the work that Tschichold was then doing for the Penguin publishing house in London:

But anyway, I worked with you for seven years and cannot believe that you would now suddenly desert our front against irresponsible *Epigonentum* [imitation], especially as I regard your current work on cheap books as an eminently modern task.[14]

In his published text about the Tschichold/Bill dispute, Renner characterized it as a classical conflict, which was informative in itself. He did not seek to reduce its value by taking sides; once again this was characteristic of his reasoned resistance of extreme positions. It is worth quoting from his published article here at length, in order to get a sense of his argument:

... this hunt for knowledge we call Dialectic. With every thesis someone believes himself to be telling the truth; he only notices that it is merely half truth when he meets the other half of the truth as antithesis. Then he either insists stolidly on his half-truth, or he brews a synthesis from the half-true and the half-false. Usually nothing more comes from this than a new thesis, which will soon be met by a correcting antithesis. In this dialectical movement the spirit is pursuing a goal only attainable in infinity. Controversies like that of Bill and Tschichold (in numbers 5 [sic] and 6 of 1946 of this periodical) are therefore so informative; the conflict of their opinions corresponds to the inner conflict in which the typography of our era now finds itself, and therefore it would not be at all useful to take sides rashly. Bill seems at first glance to have the better position, because he is more definite, one-sided. He is a Bauhaus student; his typography today, however, is much more mature than Bauhaus typography, which once so shocked and stirred the soul of the young calligraphy teacher at the Leipzig academy Johannes Tztschichold [sic] that he henceforward named himself Iwan. He first became Jan when I summoned him in 1926 to the Munich Meisterschule, for I could not present the inhabitants of Munich with an Iwan. The road from Johannes to Iwan was also a dialectical movement, and it shows how serious Tschichold always was with his transformations. Seeming to go from one extreme to another, he was honestly seeking that 'mean', of which it is unjustly said that it suits undecided characters and the mediocre, whilst in antiquity it was prized as 'golden'. The 'middle' is, in any case, more energized than the one-sided extreme; it is the fruitful eye-of-the-storm in dialectical opposition; and this is best served by he who feels the conflict in his own

14 Letter to Tschichold, 15 September 1947.

being. The typography that was fostered between 1926 and the unfortunate year of 1933 at the Munich Meisterschule was already a synthesis of the middle, equally distanced from the older Bauhaus typography and Tschichold's initial elemental typography, as from the classicism of the bibliophile publisher. What things could have developed, if the Nazis had not put such a sudden end to this work!

Tschichold today is working as hard as he can with the best Englishmen on a timelessly-valid typography of the book; I am not anxious for his future development: perhaps the arch-conservative English surroundings will once more make him a revolutionary. We could only call his work 'unmodern', however, if we define the concept of the Modern in an inordinately narrow way. Nobody would agree with Tschichold when he says that modern typography today has to restrict itself to jobbing setting and that the typography of the book must follow the well-trodden road of tradition. Yet, admittedly, one must have a healthy optimism to expect a typographic renewal of the book from the Bauhaus, which published the golden words of Moholy 'Legibility – communication should never suffer under an *a priori* aesthetic' in a book with lines of 52 ems in length.

The Bauhaus style is, as Jugendstil and the arts and crafts of the Wiener Werkstätte once were, a station on the way to the style of our time. One should not linger too long at these stations if one does not want to miss the connection.[15]

Renner's description of Tschichold's changing his name as an instance of dialectic is an interesting observation. He had raised this issue in correspondence with Tschichold:

> Like all other arts, typography is always gripped in a development: and I would not have employed you at my school twenty years ago if I had not known that you were full of inner tension between the old and the new; the Iwan alone I did not like so much, and would also never have been able to push his employment through the Artistic Advisory Council of the City, if he had not been grafted on to Johannes. I could not have employed a pure Bauhaus man, because that avant-garde, seen from the point of view of exceptions like you, who was really familiar with tradition, had begun to develop downright stubborn and sterile grey hairs from 1920, without developing itself further.[16]

Renner did not equate the 'modernist' style that had emanated from the Bauhaus with a truly modern typography; it may have been modern at a certain point in time, but time moved on. Consequently he did not respond to the principal strain in Bill's polemic, which derided Tschichold for abandoning the

15 'Über moderne Typographie' (1948f) p. 119.
16 Letter to Tschichold, 31 May 1946.

search for a 'style of the time'. Bill's typography of the 1940s, consisting of cool columns of ranged-left sanserif, was an early taste of the 'Swiss typography' that would soon become a new international, modernist style. With its exclusive use of sanserif typefaces and its rejection of ornament, this style can be seen to have developed from some of Tschichold's earliest recorded principles. Bill's reassertion of a puritanical element-arism in typography was perhaps a protest against the separa-tion of modernist style from its ideological roots – it had become just another option in a palette of styles. In Switzer-land, which had remained neutral during the Second World War, and had not therefore been racked by the Nazi regime, it was perhaps easier to have maintained an attachment to the trappings of modernism. The notion that a form of typo-graphy could be innately linked to ideas of clarity and progress flourished in a country that vehemently protected the com-forts of its democracy. Tschichold remarked, however, that he felt as if Bill was seeking to deny him the freedom to work in the way that he believed to be right:

> *He who calls for the suppression of freedom of thought and artistic expression carries on the gloomy business of those who we thought were defeated. He commits the worst crime, for he buries our high-est good, the sign of man's worth – freedom.* Which perhaps a man must first lose, as I did, before he can discover its true value.[17]

Renner too had suffered at the hands of the Nazis, and the mental ravages of this experience still tormented his family after the war. From Germany, it seemed that the world had been turned upside down. Renner was trying to recover some foundations laid by Tschichold and himself before the Third Reich, but, as an old man wearied by the tactics of the National Socialists, and, moreover, a man of a liberal disposition, it is not surprising that Renner pursued a continuing middle course in the Tschichold/Bill dispute, and did not seek to polarize the issue.[18]

Ideas for the modern book

Soon after the war, Renner became involved in the Börsen-verein der Buchhändler in der französischen Zone (Associ-ation for the Book Trade in the French Zone).[19] He contributed to the periodical organ of this body, and also gave a closing speech at its inaugural conference on 11 August 1946. His text

17 Tschichold, 'Belief and reality', p. 139. Italics in original.

18 Evidently, the editor of *Schweizer Graphische Mitteilungen*, Rudolf Hostettler, was rather incredulous about the whole affair. See Hochuli, *Book design in Switzerland*, p. 76.

19 This provincial activity was somewhat enforced by the difficulties of travelling between national zones.

112 Cover of *Das moderne Buch*. 1947. 200 × 125 mm. Type black; rules and publisher's signet red.

for this speech formed the basis of a small booklet published in Renner's local town of Lindau, *Das moderne Buch* (The modern book, 1947; figure 112). This booklet contains an interesting meditation on the meaning of 'modern' in the post-war context.

The term 'modernism', as applied to artistic and cultural matters, seems only to have become widely used after the Second World War. Neither Renner himself (nor any of his German contemporaries in design, as far as I have observed) used the term or its German equivalent (*Modernismus*) between the wars.[20] However, Renner often spoke of 'the Modern'.[21] As someone who had lived in Germany through the Weimar period, which is generally regarded as the crucible of twentieth-century modernism, Renner was still concerned to pursue a modern course in design during the Third Reich and after the Second World War. His brand of modernity does not conform to a simplistic, retrospective notion of 'modernism', which might assume an alignment with the avant-garde and persistent radical innovation.

The meaning of 'modern'

Renner believed 'modern' to be a 'misunderstood and often misused word'.[22] He quoted the dictionary definition of modern as the 'opposite of antique'. So it was important, he believed, to distinguish the Modern from the simply modish: for those people who still adhered to the principles of the Werkbund, like himself, he suggested that the definition of modern was sometimes not very far from antique.

Renner therefore resolved the Modern to be that which is 'as rational and purposeful as possible, and which at the same time has the simplest and most pleasing form'.[23] So he made a distinction between what is simply contemporary and what is truly modern, asserting that something is not unmodern simply because it is old: he believed that rebels who delight in exposing tradition and rejecting it simply because it is old, have not really broken free from the grip of tradition.[24] In Renner's view, the achievement of modernity required a constant process of revaluation. In terms of book design, he demanded that 'we should never tire of letting the idea of a truly modern book be eternally renewed in our spiritual eye, of re-examining it over and over and making its realization better and better'.[25] Modern form was for him inherently

20 An anti-modernist polemic published in Britain, Sir Reginald Blomfield's *Modernismus* (London: Macmillan, 1934), adopted the German term to make it clear where the pernicious influence originated. Blomfield's refusal to accept that functional objects are '*ipso facto*' beautiful (pp. 71–3) bears a similarity to Renner's view, quoted on p. 68 above.

21 A noun is easily created from an adjective in German by giving it an initial capital, so this is how I shall distinguish it here – as the Modern. In his article of 1946, 'Glaube und Wirklichkeit', Jan Tschichold used the term 'Modernisten' to describe those like himself who had been censured by the Nazis for their progressive beliefs. (In *Schriften*, vol.1, p. 313. See above: p. 147, note 2.)

22 *Das moderne Buch* (1947d) p. 5.

23 *Das moderne Buch* (1947d) p. 6.

24 *Das moderne Buch* (1947d) p. 7. See also 'Die künstlerische Leistung des Typografen' (1950) p. 398.

25 *Das moderne Buch* (1947d) p. 5.

unstable, in need of constant redefinition. In another essay, from 1950, he summarized this idea: 'The truly Modern, that is, the undistorted expression of an objective *Zeitgeist*, is only what we hold today to be timelessly perfect. This is not the same in all periods, because the insight into the timelessly valid changes from generation to generation.'[26] The Modern was not a fixed style, but an abstract, guiding principle:

> For the Modern is an idea, an unending task, never to be entirely resolved. We seek it on a narrow ridge, which drops away on one side into thoughtlessly adopted convention and on the other side into the Modish, which is mostly a somewhat foppish exaggeration of the Modern at any one time. This ridge is no comfortable middle way.[27]

Perhaps it is best to call what Renner described here modernity, rather than modernism. His notion of modernity plainly had an inherent social mission: being more modern meant getting better. Such an eternally-renewing modernity is firmly grounded in ideas of social progress that have their source in the Enlightenment. Renner had a strong sense of service to one's time, and made clear his part in the Enlightenment tradition: 'Every generation is posed the task of leaving behind better relationships than those in which it grew up.'[28]

The form of the modern book

In 1863 the poet and critic Baudelaire offered a definition of 'modern' art: he suggested that it was the attempt to balance 'modernity' – the 'transient, the fleeting, the contingent' – with the 'eternal and the immutable'.[29] There is an echo of this desire to balance immediate needs with timeless principles in Renner's continued definition of modernity as a potential mixture of old and new. In the 1920s he indicated a belief in some eternal values in the arts; in 1947, his essay on 'the modern book' reaffirmed this view of modernity.[30]

Although Renner believed that the design of books was a process of constant revaluation, there were certain principles in designing the form of continuous text that he evidently felt to be 'timelessly valid'.[31] Once again, he stated clearly that, for the sake of his discussion, he was concerned with the *Lesebuch*, the book that is read from beginning to end – a novel, for example. The conventional form of text seemed to him still 'modern': justified columns in a symmetrical double-page opening; customary text type-sizes between 8 and 12 point;

26 'Die künstlerische Leistung des Typografen' (1950) p. 409. For evidence of how little Renner's view of modernity had changed in over forty years, see the views from 1910 expressed on p. 33 above.

27 *Das moderne Buch* (1947d) p. 7.

28 *Das moderne Buch* (1947d) p. 24. In another post-war essay, Renner commented that, while the Enlightenment was usually described as a positive turning point in the history of mankind, it also marked the beginning of 'the most inhuman and hardest of all ages, the age of technology and the machine'. Renner may not have believed that technological innovation signified progress, but his belief in the progress of humanity was clear: 'Regarded as a generation, the youth are not younger; at least they represent a later and in many respects more experienced generation than that to which the old people belong'. ('Diktatur oder Demokratie in der öffentlichen Kunstpflege' [1947b] p. 180.)

29 Quoted in Harvey, *The condition of postmodernity*, p. 11.

30 Renner's critique of materialist theories of design in the 1920s reflected the central premise of Baudelaire's definition in isolating 'time-bound' and 'timeless' characteristics of creative work. (See pp. 68–9 above.)

31 This epithet recurs regularly in Renner's writings after the Second World War, and formed part of the title of one lengthy article: 'The artistic achievement of the typographer: an essay on the timelessly valid' (1950).

an average line length of 20 cicero (9 cm); and interlinear space balanced in accordance with type-size and line length to achieve comfortable readability. Furthermore, a sober text typeface was essential: 'It must have a certain impersonality; it is therefore aptly called a bread-and-butter type [*Brotschrift*]; it should not be a confection, instead, like the daily bread, something that one can eat at any meal, and easily digestible.'[32] The specific measure Renner gave here (and had always given) for an ideal line-length assumed his preferred small octavo format as a pre-condition. If Renner's view of text design had been less defined by the traditional form of the book object and more sensitive to the meaning of words, he might have indicated an ideal line-length in terms of a number of words or characters. Yet, with the traditionally restricted range of text type-sizes that he cites, his customary 9 cm line-length had proved an effective solution. One might today contest the principle of mirror-image symmetry using justified text, but Renner's other principles still seem reasonable; certainly, they have survived as the basis of good text design, and have even found some confirmation in legibility research.[33]

Renner first described these principles during his typographic practice before the First World War, when his typography can be described as having been firmly traditional in style. Yet his criteria for good text design changed little throughout his 'modernist' period. He remarked that the principles of traditional book typography should only be questioned once they had been mastered.[34] He did not perceive any development in the way that people read, and so he considered these basic conventions, in that they still worked, to be modern. In this respect his views did not differ greatly from those of contemporary typographic traditionalists in Britain, like Stanley Morison and Beatrice Warde. There was some overlap of principle between the 'new traditionalism' and the New Typography: both movements placed an emphasis on clear communication with the reader, but their visual means were different: the new traditionalists felt that the best way to achieve clarity was by comforting the reader with the type-forms of tradition, whereas the New Typographers felt that these got in the way.[35] Indeed, Renner's views on book design only departed significantly from new traditionalism in his acceptance of a sanserif typeface for continuous text – ideally the one that he himself had designed.

32 'Moderne Typografie' (1946f) pp. 142–3.

33 See Spencer, *The visible word*, p. 35.

34 'Die künstlerische Leistung des Typografen' (1950) p. 401. Yet, Renner believed that, once a sound knowledge of principles had been acquired and one could justify one's decision to a critic, individuals had only to act according to their own conscience. But this should involve a distrust of one's own preferences and dislikes (p. 398).

35 See Tschichold, 'New Typography' (1937) for his own comparison of New Typography and 'new traditionalism', a term that he introduced in this essay.

PAUL RENNER

'Handy' formats for the book

In Renner's consideration of the 'book for reading' [*Lesebuch*] after the Second World War, he stressed more strongly than ever before that he favoured small, thin books that were not too heavy. It seemed that he was proposing the handy pocket-format as his ideal form of the book for that time, as if an important aspect of post-war society would be the ability for everyone to have easily transportable and handleable books – to be able to carry a piece of literary culture around with them. A book that was 'reasoned and functional' was for him one that could be held in the hands for hours when sitting upright in the open air. The DIN A5 format was too wide for this purpose: 'The thin book formats of the old days were better and in this remain more modern.'[36] Books that were too voluminous were a nuisance to him: 'Even buckets and watering cans', he commented, 'are only made so big that one can carry them when full, not so that the greatest possible amount goes into them'.[37]

In Renner's view, the taste for large volumes, which equated weight with prestige, betrayed a potential flaw in the German character: 'the "fatal desire for greatness", by which Hitler was also notoriously motivated'.[38] Renner despised the tendency of luxurious editions towards monumentality, and his distaste grew when considering this tendency among the Nazis. He remarked thoughtfully: 'Where the needs of people are no longer the measure of things, there begins barbarism.'[39]

Renner took account of the futuristic arguments of the 1920s that had predicted the death of the book. He reported a conversation that he had in 1925 with a colleague at the Frankfurter Kunstschule, who believed that the 1000-page book would develop into a film strip that would be projected onto a ceiling, so that one could read it lying comfortably on a couch. Renner disagreed at that time, and, in 1947, reaffirmed his belief in the 'comfortably legible, handy and easily transportable book'.[40]

The place and time in which Renner wrote these words was Germany, just after 'year zero', the end of a war that had ravaged its people, landscape, tradition and culture. In some ways, this situation recalled the state of Germany after the First World War, when the initial burst of 'heroic modernism' had emanated from the new era of technological advance and economic rationalization in Weimar Germany. In those days, it was really a matter of constructing a new urban society for

36 *Das moderne Buch* (1947d) p. 30.
37 *Das moderne Buch* (1947d) p. 32.
38 *Das moderne Buch* (1947d) p. 33.
39 *Das moderne Buch* (1947d) p. 37. Renner was referring to the kind of decadent luxury evident in Nazi architecture. Speer, commenting in *Inside the Third Reich* on his and Hitler's plans for the Berlin Axis, realized that the projected buildings could not possibly be good in aesthetic terms because they had lost any sense of human scale.
40 *Das moderne Buch* (1947d) p. 33.

a rapidly industralizing nation; whereas in 1946, Germany needed *re*construction, in both its material and spiritual life. Consequently, Renner seized the moment to reiterate some of his most passionately-held ideas for reform in German typography, arguing that the rebirth of Germany after the Second World War was an ideal opportunity to put them into effect.

Reform of orthography

The matter of choosing between roman or gothic as the everyday style of type had effectively been made for the German people by the Nazi decree of 1941:

> Without this command from above, the Germans would have held even longer to the script that never became a German national script, rather a late form of gothic script, changed slightly, and not at all improved, by the south-German writing masters.[41]

It is ironic that the regime so deplored by Renner was able to effect a change that he had desired for many years.[42] Indeed, he called in 1947 for a far-sighted official to implement his suggestions for orthographic reform, because he knew that his lone voice could not achieve this. He feared that the traditional resistance of publishers and authors to reform could not be overcome except by 'an undemocratic decree' of the kind that the Nazis had used to get rid of fraktur.[43] In this sense, Renner's programme for German orthography was a modernist (or even a modernizing) initiative, in that he wanted to make it into a more logical system; systematization rarely grows from grass roots – it has to be imposed from above. Renner asserted that the cumbersome doubling of consonants in German was 'arbitrary and without sense', and he also repeated his support for Jakob Grimm's idea of restricting capitals to the beginning of sentences.[44] Renner berated his fellow Germans for being 'unteachable', because they had continually ignored the teaching of this 'great Germanist'. As in Grimm's earlier formulation of the argument, Renner stressed the internationalizing potential of a rationalized orthography, which would align Germany with the rest of the western world. This must have seemed especially important after the Second World War, when Germany was trying to re-establish benign relations with other countries.

Renner's sense of urgency about this issue, which he had often laboured, remained undiminished: he felt that the time had hardly ever been more favourable for a reform in spelling

41 *Das moderne Buch* (1947d) p. 11.

42 This reflects a central dilemma within twentieth-century modernism. Rationalization and technological progress, as the secular groundwork for social equality and spiritual emancipation, were central desires of some modernists; yet these processes required the backing of industrial capital or powerful governments. Furthermore, some regimes perceived the advantage in being associated with progressive cultural movements, and so the avant garde was occasionally aligned with extreme politics: for example, the approval of Futurism by the Italian Fascist regime, and the initial sponsorship of Constructivism by the Soviet State.

43 Renner, 'Interview mit Paul Renner', p. 7. Some progressive German authors, such as Günter Grass, began to 'write small' in their poems after the Second World War, but they were exceptions. (See Kinross, 'Large and small letters: authority and democracy', p. 4.) New rules for German spelling developed in 1996, which will be officially taught in schools, do not adopt any of Renner's principles; indeed the new rules seem to introduce some further complications.

44 *Das moderne Buch* (1947d) p. 21. In 'Interview mit Paul Renner', p. 7, Renner remarked that the programme advocated by the Bildungsverband der Deutschen Buchdrucker in 1931/2 could form the basis of a new reform. (See above: p. 119, note 125.) In contrast to Renner's idealism, Eric Gill stated that spelling was irrational and would always remain so: 'And all the games they get up to to rationalize it only make it worse'. (Gill, *Autobiography* [London: Jonathan Cape, 1940] p. 36.)

PAUL RENNER

than after the 'atrocious mass destruction of books' undertaken
by the Nazis, which meant that many texts had to be printed
anew. Renner felt that Germany should not let such an opportunity pass, because 'nobody would wish for this opportunity
to come a second time'.[45] He shrugged off the old objections
from publishers, who had feared that their stock of books
would become obsolete after spelling reform: there were
no great stocks of books anymore. And, of course, Renner
believed that people would easily read themselves into a new
way of spelling. He recognized the central problem of making
radical changes acceptable on a broad basis: a reformer like
himself was in danger of being seen as an eccentric who
'wants to differentiate himself from the crowd by a private
system of spelling'.[46] But Renner made clear that it was not
a question of spreading the avant-garde into the mainstream;
there was no hint of artistic vanity in his mission to reform
everyday spelling, because it was not a matter of superficial
style or taste. Renner's words were underpinned by a social
motive: he really felt that a simplified spelling would aid the
use of the language. As he saw it, he was carrying out his duty
as a 'citizen of time';[47] and I would add, on this issue, a citizen
of place. Although Renner's rationalism here accords with the
accepted view of modernism as an attempt to instil the values
of universally valid reason, the subjects of his reforming initiative were specific to his milieu of post-war Germany. David
Harvey has commented: 'While modernism always ostensibly
asserted the values of internationalism and universalism, it
could never properly settle its account with parochialism and
nationalism.'[48] Modernism has often been couched in the
rhetoric of universality and uniformity, but, at least in the
field of design and manufacture, it has most often satisfied
the immediate demands of local economies and cultures.

Renner had always resisted the epochal rhetoric of extreme
modernism, and had often spoken for the difficulties of the
mundane and the everyday (see pp. 115–19 above on orthographic reform in the 1920s). The kind of modernism that
he espoused after the Second World War can perhaps be
partly explained by material scarcity and poverty, which led
naturally to rationalization, and to design solutions that relied
on a necessary sparseness of form.[49] As in the first years of the
Weimar era, the immediate needs of a war-torn country inspired
the ambition for social amelioration, and this often resulted in

45 Renner, 'Interview mit Paul
Renner', p. 7.
46 *Das moderne Buch* (1947d) p. 23.
47 *Das moderne Buch* (1947d) p. 5.
48 Harvey, *The condition of post-
modernity*, pp. 275–6.
49 For example, in *Das moderne
Buch* (1947d) p. 27, he recommended
that running headings should be generally omitted from books, due to the
scarcity of paper at that time.

an appeal to what Renner had earlier called the 'communally human' and not the 'divisively folk-like [*Völkische*]'.[50] The situation in Germany after the Second World War provided a new impetus to ally design with a belief in human progress, and this alliance had conventionally found its most fitting environment in the reductionist aesthetic of modernism.

Towards a typographical philosophy

The formal aspects of a modern typography

Renner's late essays on typography, taken as a whole, outlined a mature and balanced approach to designing. He attempted to summarize a pragmatic view, underpinned by a philosophy of form, which, in comparison to the strictures of the New Typography, was both more modest and more widely applicable.

One of the central issues in the dispute between Bill and Tschichold had been the opposition of asymmetric and symmetrical layout. Bill advocated an unconditional use of asymmetric layout, including unjustified text (often termed ranged-left). This signified a departure from New Typography of the 1920s and 1930s: Tschichold himself never used this form for text in his 'modernist' period. The overall layout of elements in New Typography may have been asymmetric, but within blocks of text for lengthy reading, justified setting was always employed. In some publicity brochures designed in central Europe in the 1930s, some short passages of text were set unjustified, but even in this area, these were exceptions.[51] Ranged-left setting became more common for lengthy texts only after the Second World War in the work of certain isolated designers in various parts of Europe.[52] In discussing the work of these designers, Robin Kinross has observed the clear 'social overtones' of unjustified or 'free' typesetting, as it is sometimes called: '...the spaces between words are equal, so the right edge has to be ragged; lines find their own length. Free, informal, self-determining....'[53] Renner recognized certain social connotations of symmetrical typography:

> It is an established fact, and not the discovery of German or modern typographers, that symmetry is the expression of divine or imperial power, or at least a strong self-confidence or self-estimation. Where one needs representational qualities, symmetry can be the correct form. But, for most tasks, a free-ordering, streamline typography is to be preferred, because it places less force on the unique quality of the typeface and eases its functioning, its being read.[54]

50 *Mechanisierte Grafik* (1931d) p. 94.

51 See the examples of brochures designed by Xanti Schawinsky in Italy in 1936, illustrated in Hollis, *Graphic design*, p. 139. Eric Gill's *Essay on typography* (1931) was an exceptional early instance of unjustified setting.

52 See Kinross, 'Unjustified text and the zero hour' for a survey of the use of unjustified text after the Second World War.

53 Kinross, 'Unjustified text and the zero hour', p. 246.

54 'Die moderne Typografie wird funktionell sein' (1948e) p. 181. 'Streamline typography' [*Stromlinientypographie*] probably alludes to the way in which lines flow raggedly from the left-hand edge like a wind-blown flag from a flagpole.

PAUL RENNER

In his writings about typography after the Second World War Renner did recommend the general applicability of asymmetric layout to most printing tasks, while his erstwhile colleague Tschichold was stressing the more classical and symmetrical aspects of his own approach. Renner looked forward to a questioning of the 'tyranny' of the central axis. Furthermore, he stressed the importance of respecting the dynamism and movement inherent within letterforms, and, consequently, he still maintained that 'there is no better schooling for the prospective typographer than writing'.[55] He admitted that his ideal double-page opening of 'grey' text in a book might resemble the construction of a solid wall in some respects, but made a qualification to this comparison:[56]

> There can only be functional, modern typography where the type is always reckoned with as a specific stream of characters defined for reading, in other words, where the lines are not treated roughly, as one would treat inert building bricks. ...
>
> Our script, particularly in its small letters, is no ornament in which every movement from left to right is balanced by an opposing one; instead a rightward flow is inherent in it. The only letters that lack this movement are the capitals A, H, I, M, O, T, V, W, X & Y; in all others, particularly in the small letters and italics, a pressing to the right cannot be overlooked.[57]

Renner used this observation to argue that it was therefore more natural to range headings (or all 'short lines') to the left, instead of aligning them on a central axis. Yet, like most of his colleagues, he must have regarded the traditionally straight edges of lengthy, continuous text as an impenetrable edifice of convention. He recognized that ranged-left was the natural format for poetry (although he took comfort from the fact that show-through would define a ghostly, straight, right-hand edge); but, even in 1950, he still believed that to set prose like this was a senseless 'destruction of the geometric column outline'.[58] Renner's approach to the construction of typeset pages in a book did not begin with the words and expand to accommodate them in their appropriate area; instead he seemed to work from the outside inwards – from the uncut sheet, to the furniture in the printing forme, enclosing a block of type, which was ideally a neutral area of grey. The symmetrical disposition of mirror-image pages remained for him an inviolable principle: 'Let us return to our open book with two columns. If

55 'Die moderne Typografie wird funktionell sein' (1948e) p. 179.
56 This also recalls Renner's comparison in 1912 of words to bricks. (See p. 32 above.)
57 'Die moderne Typografie wird funktionell sein' (1948e) p. 180.
58 'Die künstlerische Leistung des Typografen' (1950) p. 406.

they are well and regularly set and stand correctly on the leaf, then, already, every artistic demand is fulfilled.'[59]

Before the advent of New Typography, he had been content to suggest that an indent for the purpose of indicating a new paragraph should be no more than one em in width. But, in *Die Kunst der Typographie*, he argued that it was preferable for the left-hand edge of text to remain regular, and for paragraphs to be marked by the extra space that occurs at the end of the last line of the previous paragraph (figure 113). The lack of an indent was a common stylistic attribute of text setting in New Typography: indention was an obvious trace of 'the old typography' that was ripe for rejection. Yet, setting paragraphs without indents does not cater for the instance when the last line of a paragraph reaches the end of the measure; the lack of a cue at the beginning of the next paragraph means that there is no distinction between them. Renner seems not to have considered putting extra line-space between paragraphs. He relied on compositors to exercise tricks of spacing so that the end of a full last-line in a paragraph was retracted or knocked over onto a new short line.

Renner refrained from stressing the social implications of asymmetry too strongly, although he realized that choosing asymmetric principles of layout was a conscious stylistic decision that created certain connotations: as opposed to the stiffness of symmetry, asymmetry implied a kind of 'extremely careful nonchalance'.[60] Consequently it required more care and refinement than symmetrical typography. Renner's advocacy of asymmetric layout was strongest in the programmatic days of the late 1920s; his views after the Second World War were more equivocal. He denied that there was an either/or choice to be made, recognizing that the principles of New Typography could be extended beyond a simple advocacy of asymmetric layout: 'Of course it is not so that symmetrical setting is unmodern and bad, and that asymmetric setting is modern and good.'[61] Ever since the discovery of printing, he observed, typography had oscillated between a style that sought to take account of 'a ranged-left "streamline typography", which occurs equally in parchment manuscripts and the most modern advertising', and 'a tectonic style that uses the type characters like building bricks, neutral in form, with which it prefers to erect strictly symmetrical structures'.[62]

59 'Die künstlerische Leistung des Typografen' (1950) p. 401.

60 'Gegen den Schematismus in der Typographie' (1933) p. 29.

61 'Die künstlerische Leistung des Typografen' (1950) p. 406.

62 *Die Kunst der Typographie* (1939c) pp. 62–3.

PAUL RENNER

134

135

Renner believed that it was a fallacy to think that symmetry played no part in asymmetric layout:

> If one understands by symmetry not mirror-image but equal mass, then so-called asymmetric setting should also not lack symmetry. It would therefore be better here to speak of exocentric balance. Because a feeling for balance also belongs to finding equality of mass without a central axis. The goal of all design is to make a whole from the variety, from the manifold a unity, and not to dissipate a whole into independent parts.[63]

This last sentence contains one of Renner's lasting principles of typographic design: that there was a higher goal of visual order to be attained.[64] Whereas Dadaists and Futurists had wanted to produce discord in their typographic compositions (of their mostly self-penned writings), Renner sought to smooth the channels of communication in the sphere of everyday printed items. To this end, he brought his judgements as a painter to the task of ordering the elements of typography into a cohesive composition. But he was not guided by aesthetic vanity; he did not want to create pretty pictures with type. He deplored the practice of contorting words into blocks, so, despite his stated belief that geometric

113 Pages from *Die Kunst der Typographie* (reprint). 1948. 220 × 145 mm. Shows the lack of indention at the beginning of paragraphs which Renner favoured in his later typography.

63 'Die moderne Typographie wird funktionell sein' (1948e) p. 312.

64 An example of this view can be found in Renner's description of how to lay out the pages of an illustrated periodical: 'On each page, then, one takes care to achieve the necessary correspondences: in other words, regular heights and widths, without a strict symmetry being required or necessary. Even seemingly asymmetric layouts can find their balance in a kind of symmetry of a higher order.' (*Die Kunst der Typographie* [1939c] p. 106.)

shapes were the most readily understood, he accepted that they did not always lend themselves to integration into a whole design:

> Undoubtedly, the geometrically simplest form is easiest assimilated; but when individual groupings that should grow together are formed geometrically, they shut themselves off against assimilation into the total form. Individual forms with less hard outlines resolved in a painterly way channel themselves more willingly into the composition.[65]

Renner stated that 'Each individual group must be formed in accordance with the demands of the whole'. Yet he realized that the individual typographic groupings had to be typeset before the whole composition could arise. Therefore he felt that it was imperative to visualize the whole beforehand, in order to define the form of the parts: 'In architecture and in applied art, before the execution of the design is begun, one seeks to gain an impression of the total effect in sketches and plans; this is also indispensable in typography.'[66]

Particularly in tasks of complex typesetting, like tables or publicity, Renner felt that 'the sectioning determined by purpose already provides movement and a lack of calm, so it is the object of artistic layout to calm the forms'.[67] In his view, the typographer's role was to attune all typographic variables in the interests of order: a disparate variety of typographic forms could be combined into an 'organic unity', if factors of type-size, typeface and spacing were balanced 'in clearly hierarchical effects of contrast'.[68]

He maintained a belief that geometric order was fundamental to human understanding of visual phenomena. In this he did not refer to a decorative application of primary geometric forms, but to underlying graphic structures of simple shapes. Pure geometry only existed in a vacuum – like an engine running in neutral – and was not valid unless moderated and modified in a practical application.[69] He accepted Immanuel Kant's suggestion that certain visible structures form an *a priori* basis for new experience, and he extended this to suggest that geometric structures are pre-programmed models in human consciousness, providing a basis on which to map new visual stimuli.[70] He believed in the possibility of reducing shapes to universally understood standards, and sought to apply this notion to the structure of typography. By subjugating the heterogeneous forms of individual typo-

65 'Die moderne Typographie wird funktionell sein' (1948e) p. 311.
66 'Moderne Typografie' (1946f) p.124.
67 *Die Kunst der Typographie* (1939c) p. 164.
68 'Moderne Typografie' (1946f) p.137.
69 'Moderne Typografie' (1946f) p.133.
70 'Moderne Typografie' (1946f) p.135.

PAUL RENNER

graphic elements to a harmonious, simple outline, he felt that he would make documents more approachable and easier to navigate. This is a modernist belief, signifying a desire to find visual common denominators. Yet, as with many incidences of modernism, it is also a very classical desire – to achieve a harmonic composition. Renner viewed typography as subject to formal laws that ran higher than a facile distinction between symmetry and asymmetry. Although he described the difference between classical and modern 'form-giving' as the requirement of the latter to give static components 'a dynamic total composition', it is clear that he subjected this dynamism to further standards of balance and harmony.[71]

The balance of form and function

Renner discussed seriously the formal, or 'artistic', task: not as an end in itself, but as one aim intertwined with many others. He denied the lasting value of most precepts, and his writing often contained pragmatic exceptions to principles that he had established himself. His pervasive wish to create harmonic compositions from the often messy parts of text in a document was overridden in some cases by an object's dominant characteristics of use. For example, reference books, in which certain elements must be emphasized, were for him an exercise in 'achieving the difference between elements in defiance of a total unified effect'.[72]

Renner was principally concerned to balance the formal and functional demands of typography, because these two demands had each attained sovereign status over all other aspects of designing in theories of the recent past. He regarded the Jugendstil movement as a triumph of formalism, and technocratic movements like Constructivism as the triumph of functionalism.[73] In his late essays he criticized formalism most strongly, and, as a consequence, he favoured a consideration of function:

> We could judge a thing, then, in two ways: we test its functioning, its usability, or we test its good appearance, its artistic quality. So someone who wants to buy a car, sits in the car and drives it. What he 'learns' from this in terms of practical and technical advantages and disadvantages will decide the purchase. If he wants to test the good appearance of the car, he gets out and looks at the bodywork from the outside. And equally, it is best to read a book if we want to test its legibility and handleability.[74]

71 'Moderne Typografie' (1946f) p. 139.
72 'Moderne Typografie' (1946f) p. 145.
73 'Kunststil und Kunst-ismen' (1943) pp. [1–2].
74 'Die moderne Typographie wird funktionell sein' (1948e) p. 310.

Renner believed that typographic form must derive from the meaning of the text: 'In other words we should never begin with form, if form is our goal, instead we must begin with the task.'[75] Yet he was conscious of potential extremism here and was careful not to elevate functionalism above formalism:

> Functionalism favours the derivation of form solely from practical demands; in other words, from the service it has to render to the client. Formalism sees in creative work only a formation [*Bildung*] for the eye; it prejudges all consideration of material and work-process as materialistic and hardly concerns itself with the practical usability of the work, which lies so much at the heart of functionalism. ... Where differences are perceived, people always initially see irreconcilable oppositions, an either/or. ... The step from either/or to as-well-as already brings us nearer to the truth, for there is actually no artistic achievement in which the static and the dynamic, the Apollonian and the Dionysian, clarity of form and expressiveness, are not mixed together in a strange love-hate relationship.[76]

Renner was clearly not blinded by the rhetoric of his day. Despite the worthy practical achievements of functional designing, he recognized in it the potential for dogma: 'Even the suiting of form to purpose has, in the strict sense of the word, nothing more to do with materialism; it is a postulate of another art-ism, functionalism.'[77] He criticised all '-isms' as attempts to prioritize certain ideas over all others. He had never trusted manifestos, because they obscured deeds: in particular he disliked the Futurist manifesto of Marinetti, whom Renner dubbed a 'Radikalinski'. Renner felt that he had been vindicated when Marinetti, who had earlier called for the contents of museums to be emptied into the river, was appointed to a post in Mussolini's regime that gave him responsibility for those very museums.[78] Renner's denial of the general validity of any '-ism' provides a further reason not to call his views 'modernist': he was really pursuing a middle-way of modernity (although he had remarked that such a way was not comfortable; see p.181 above).[79]

Yet Renner realized that the complex and compromised nature of practice excluded the tidy implementation of any theoretical position, whether extreme or moderate. In 'the treadmill of business', where one has many jobs to do in a short time, he admitted that it was tempting to adhere to certain formal models in typography; but he felt that 'it is harder

75 'Moderne Typografie' (1946f) p.128.
76 'Zur Kunst der Typographie' (1949b) pp.193–4.
77 'Kunststil und Kunst-ismen' (1943) pp.[1–2].
78 *Kulturbolschewismus?* (1932b) p.49.
79 The resolution of a reasoned middle way was a consistent feature of Renner's writing on design. Indeed Renner had made explicit reference to Eastern philosophy in a passage of *Mechanisierte Grafik* (1931d, p.89) that could reasonably be subtitled 'Zen and the art of typography': 'Confucianism and Buddhism demand equilibrium and symmetry. But the dynamic expression of Taoistic Zenism lays primary stress on the process by which perfection is achieved and it therefore avoids symmetrical form, calm within itself, which acts as an expression of perfection, or at least the demand for perfection.'

to follow models in typography than it is in any other art. For here every new job brings a new text'.[80]

Renner stressed that, although spiritual aspirations may be higher, the first level of technique and materials is the most important, because, without it, no higher level could exist. Craft always maintained its place at the heart of his approach to design. But, for him, the highest goal was the striving for 'reasonable, rational simplicity and clarity of form', which he believed to be a prerequisite of objects that were pleasurable to use. His advocacy of simplicity and an economical use of typographic resources had a moral dimension. He declared: 'The fewer artistic means needed in order to reach one's goal, the nobler and more natural is the effect of the typographic achievement';[81] and '...every disproportion, every excess is barbaric'.[82] Ornament seemed to him a superfluous addition: a 'colourful patch one applies when a structural error is to be found'.[83] This somewhat ascetic view of typography must also have been rooted in the place and period in which Renner first developed his views on the Modern in typography: Germany in the 1920s, in which the drive for economic rationalization was a pervasive aspect of everyday life.

Renner attempted to balance the aesthetic and practical aspects of typography even when discussing specific examples in great detail. This balance, expressed in general terms, was an aspect of designing he felt safe in calling 'timelessly valid'. His pragmatic view can best be summarized by some of the more straightforward definitions he gave of a typographer's task:

> ...[Modern typography] must be purpose-serving to the highest degree, so much so that one should call it functional typography; secondly, and at the same time, it must satisfy all demands we make of artistic forms, those which are logically designed [durchgeformte]. From modern typographers we expect accordingly a feeling for the usability of the printed thing, for comfortable legibility and, in general, for the comfort of the reader....[84]

And in sharp summary, Renner said: 'A typographic solution should not only be usable, but should also look good.'[85]

Renner's last typeface

Steile Futura
Steile Futura only shares part of its name with Futura, although it had a direct predecessor in Futura Schlagzeile (headline),

80 'Moderne Typografie' (1946f) p. 119.
81 'Die künstlerische Leistung des Typografen' (1950) p. 403.
82 'Zur Kunst der Typographie' (1949b) p. 192.
83 'Die künstlerische Leistung des Typografen' (1950) p. 402.
84 'Die moderne Typographie wird funktionell sein' (1948e) p. 310.
85 'Moderne Typografie' (1946f) p. 118.

Tiefdruck Gutenberg KUNST UND

114 Futura Schlagzeile. Bauer, 1932.

which appeared in 1932 (figure 114). Steile Futura seems to have evolved over many years from Renner's attempt to design what he called a grotesk: in other words, a letterform more akin to nineteenth-century sanserifs than to Futura. (Renner consistently maintained that Futura was not a grotesk, due to its geometric basis.) *Steile* literally means upright, or steep, and there is a distinct vertical stress in Steile Futura's narrow letters. Renner also introduced a trace of handwriting into Steile Futura, which contributed further to making it a strange kind of gothic sanserif.

A typeface actually called 'Renner-Grotesk' appeared in trial type castings by the Stempel typefoundry in May 1936. The Stempel Renner-Grotesk was very condensed in its regular weight, with a consequent stress on the modular squareness of the letters (figure 115). This design seems to have been taken over by the Bauer typefoundry in 1938, and in 1939 the grotesk changed shape to some extent, becoming less modular and incorporating references to pen-made forms. The italic accompaniment to this grotesk, simply called Renner-Kursiv, was actually a true cursive, marking a decided difference between this typeface and Futura. Work on the Grotesk and Kursiv continued through the late 1930s and early 1940s. However, progress on these typefaces seems to have been very slow, perhaps due to Renner's failing health: he had a serious heart attack in 1948 (at 70 years of age) which restricted his activity. By 1951, Renner had begun to work again, and his Grotesk began to appear in 1952 from the Bauer typefoundry under the name of Steile Futura (figure 116). Perhaps the typeface was renamed merely in order to link it to the successful Futura family.

Sketches for unproduced typefaces among Renner's papers exhibit many unresolved attempts at novel genres of typeface, mixing styles and rationalizing letterforms. This is not uncommon for type designers, who are obviously anxious to make an innovation, but usually have to accept that they can only pro-

115 Proof of Renner-Grotesk in production at Stempel, 29 July 1936. Note that two forms of small g were being assessed.

Hamburg kann Horn hohl klug und arm lang darum

PAUL RENNER

Porcelanas y Cerámicas
EL PARQUE DEL RETIRO
La carta de enhorabuena
MERCADO DE ORENSE
Adventure in Canada
MADISON SQUARE
Reminiscent of Italy
AN AGRICULTURIST

116 Steile Futura as finally released in 1952/3. Regular and bold weights, and their italics, in 24 point size. Note that the small e and g follow the logic of pen-written letters, in contrast to the modular geometry of the main body of the Futura family.

duce modifications of existing genres. In an interview in 1947, Renner, aged 69, said that he saw no need for any new typefaces:

> The last typeface produced in Germany that the world adopted was Futura. That was no accident: next to the classic old-face form and the modern-face roman in the style of Bodoni and Didot, the serifless roman with classical proportions is the third and presumably the last *Typus* of eternally usable and timeless roman forms. I personally, at least, do not see the need for a fourth *Typus*. ...
>
> German printers – and not only those who must reconstruct their business – should be thinking more along the lines that, in order to do good typography, they don't need many typefaces, only a single one, but in all sizes and also with italic and small capitals. Instead of original artist-typefaces, a clear, impersonal, but thoroughly legible old-face roman. Plus perhaps an unfussy modern-face roman. Then, as a third typeface, particularly for jobbing setting, Futura.[86]

Renner's pride in Futura was evident, and he still maintained that it was a 'serifless roman', and not a grotesk.[87] Significantly, he implied that its principal role was in ephemeral printing, and that seriffed typefaces were best for text.

86 Renner, 'Interview mit Paul Renner', p. 7. Renner had expressed almost the same view on the typefaces necessary for good typography in 1922, in *Typografie als Kunst* (1922a) p. 55. Stanley Morison once asserted that no German understood roman typography because they did not use small capitals: here, Renner proved him wrong. See Nicolas Barker, *Stanley Morison* (London: Macmillan, 1972) p. 335.

87 Renner made the same point in 'Fraktur und Antiqua' (1948b) p. 347. Hermann Zapf also used the term 'serifless roman' for his Optima typeface.

He commented in a post-war article that gothic was no longer forbidden and might be useful for its nostalgia value:

> Just as now and again one likes to forget the unpleasantness of time's arrow and to revive youthful memories with a good drop of wine behind the bull's-eye window of an old German, wooden-tabled *Weinstube*; so, after some years, one will also occasionally like to read a book set in fraktur.[88]

But it was clear that, for general use, he now regarded gothic typefaces as a thing of the past: 'It is however an almost unde-served fortune that now finally roman has become the stan-dard script here too.'[89] Despite the bizarre circumstances surrounding the disappearance of gothic, Renner, then living in the French-occupied zone of Germany, considered it inevit-able and proper that roman should be used in a Germany that had finally been dragged from the self-imposed cultural isola-tion of the Nazi era, and now had to reconstruct itself under the watchful eye of the rest of the world.

Final years

In 1946 Renner was preparing a book entitled *Die neue Zeit und ihr Stil* (The new era and its style), which was to consist largely of material from his earlier books, with some new essays and lectures.[90] It was retitled by Renner *Der Künstler in der mechanisierten Welt* (The artist in the mechanized world), but was never published in his lifetime. The project was finally realized in 1977 as a posthumous publication by the Akademie für das Graphische Gewerbe, the successor to the Munich trade school that Renner had led.

In 1947, Renner completed a book on colour, *Ordnung und Harmonie der Farben* (Order and harmony of colour), published by Otto Maier Verlag of Ravensburg. Colour theory and perception was a recurrent subject in his writings, and had formed a large section of his book *Mechanisierte Grafik* (1931). He rejected most established theories of colour, includ-ing those of Wilhelm Ostwald and even Goethe, in favour of his customary view that appearance was the only true yard-stick. So far, this has been the only book of his to have been translated into English.

Renner's post-war views on the Third Reich showed con-siderable grace in refraining from a simplistic criticism of the regime. He had certainly held no affection for Hitler; Renner

88 'Schrift und Rechtschreibung' (1946g) p. 36.
89 Renner, 'Interview mit Paul Renner', p. 7.
90 Letter to Heinz Haushofer, 30 March 1946 (Nachlaß Renner).

PAUL RENNER

was once overheard to say: 'We shall all end up in the grave if there is a drunkard at the wheel.'[91] Yet in an unpublished manuscript concerning the post-war situation Renner wrote:

> Nothing would be more stupid today, when National Socialism has become entirely harmless, than to join in an anti-Nazi war cry that would bring us into a front with the Communists, who are seeking to usurp the parts of Germany not already occupied by the Russians and are unfortunately enjoying the willing aid of many Allied military leaderships.[92]

He commented that those people who had lived during the Third Reich in Germany knew that many NSDAP members became disillusioned with the Party, and that one could confide in them without fear of denunciation. Similarly, those people who joined up for fear of losing their job did not 'follow' the Party. Renner felt that: 'A persecution of the "Nazis", as will now be instigated, is in many ways only the Nazi methods with an exchange of the word Nazi for Jew.' In his view, a change of direction by 180 degrees was of no use: 'All -isms and anti-isms are no more different from each other than the north-south direction is from the south-north.'[93]

Renner's health never properly recovered from the heart attack that he suffered in 1948. His wife, Annie, died in 1949, and in the last few years of his life Renner moved to live in the Bayerischer Hof, a large hotel in Munich. He died on 25 April 1956.

91 Haushofer, 'Paul Renner – ein Eindruck' in Luidl & Lange (ed.), *Paul Renner*, p. 22.

92 Untitled (Nachlaß Renner) p.3. Renner praised the British Labour Party and recommended that a German equivalent be set up, as the Social Democrats in Germany were, in his view, very similar to the Communists at that time. 'The English Labour Party is now making a tremendous attempt to realize all that is realistic and reasonable in socialist thought ... socialism *without* a totalitarian state.' (Untitled, pp. 1–2; Nachlaß Renner.)

93 Untitled (Nachlaß Renner) p. 4.

8 Conclusion

There may be a conformity with Renner's strict Protestant upbringing in his choice not to pursue the life of a fine artist, but instead to devote his time to designing. He was drawn to a field of activity in which he could put his aesthetic skills to a utilitarian purpose. He lamented in later years that he only ever wanted to be a painter, and longed to rid himself of his typographic and educational responsibilities so that he could return to this occupation. Yet he does not seem to have tried very hard to extricate himself from the world of typography and printing, and he was constantly and easily enticed back into it. He felt a responsibility to those institutions – schools, publishing houses – who sought his collaboration, and was always concerned to set a good example in his work for the younger generation of typographers. Consequently he took his role as a figurehead of the Munich Meisterschule seriously. He had a very German notion of leadership: he considered himself a *Fuhrer*, a strong figure, leading by example.

He stated on more than one occasion that the individual had to fulfil a duty as a 'citizen of time' – to meet 'the demand of the day'.[1] Renner credited this idea to both Goethe and Schiller, signalling his attachment to the classical German tradition. Educated in the conservative institutions of the nineteenth century, Renner felt himself to be an intellectual equipped (and compelled by this status) to steer German culture. He considered himself part of the German *bürgerliche* tradition; not a *Bürger* in the sense of a capitalist business-man, but a leading, responsible citizen – a kind of aristocrat of the intellect. Understanding this view today is complicated by the term *Bürger*, with its nuances specific to German culture.[2] *Bürger* is sometimes translated as 'citizen', and it has more positive connotations of responsible citizenship than *bourgeois*. Certainly Renner sought to reclaim the word's pre-Renaissance German meaning, a sense unsullied by the class divisions of capitalist society. He interpreted the traditional 'sense of being a Bürger' [*Bürgersinn*] as follows:[3]

> Having *Bürgersinn* has not always meant insisting on one's rights and privileges, instead it meant a feeling of being bound to the whole, the 'collective' of citizens [*Bürgerschaft*]. One only becomes a leader by feeling more duty-bound to the whole than others, by feeling more responsible than others for a larger circle of people and things.[4]

1 *Das moderne Buch* (1947d) p. 5; and 'Die erste Diplomverteilung an unserer Meisterschule' (1932a) p. 38.

2 See the entry 'Bourgeois' in Williams, *Keywords*.

3 In modern German-English dictionaries, 'Bürgersinn' is variously translated as 'public-spiritedness' and 'middle-class mentality', demonstrating the kind of ambiguity reflected in Renner's argument.

4 *Kulturbolschewismus?* (1932b) pp. 33.

He claimed that New Architecture was an expression of true *bürgerliche* culture: egalitarian and socially responsible.

Renner proposed the German tradition of craft guilds, which predated the development of big industry, as a model for social order; but his romantic vision of this tradition was idealized from the murky depths of the past, stripped of any social divisions. A notion of happy workers united in a common goal formed the basis of the kind of German socialism which he proffered in his writings as an alternative to Marxism soon after Germany's revolutions in 1918 and 1919. Renner's vision shared with Marxism a desire for a purer society beyond the shackles of capitalism, but to be attained by an undefined spiritual regeneration (linked to the Werkbund idea of 'quality'), not by revolutionary or merely economic methods.

The rapidity of Germany's industrial development in the decades around the turn of the twentieth century really pulled the rug from under the feet of those intellectuals attached to the culture of the old order. Renner expressed his scepticism about modernization:

> We have rationalized up to the twentieth century, without always examining the Ratio. The old *Bürger*-spirit, which placed individual work in the service of the whole *Bürgerschaft*, the whole people, has been exchanged for the fanaticism of specialists, who do not see beyond their own subjects. And therefore we believe in this mechanized era like sorcerer's apprentices who have forgotten the magic word that is able to put the brooms back in the corner.[5]

He disliked the modern forms of culture which were becoming popular in Germany in the late 1920s, bemoaning the fact that both rich and poor 'only have money and interest for sport, cinema, dancing and jazz-music';[6] he preferred the literary culture of the humanist tradition. Whereas some young European Moderns of the 1920s were excited by America and its commercialized culture, Renner wanted people instead to fill their time with pure kinds of thought and activity which flew free of capitalist structures, enriching some corner of their spirit unreachable by material concerns. Renner's ascetic rejection of frivolous, modern leisure pursuits concurs with the functionalist strain of modernism, which sought to deny what Pierre Bourdieu has called the 'symbolic capital' of objects – their value as commodities indicating the taste and status of the user.[7] The maxim 'form follows function', which

5 *Kulturbolschewismus?* (1932b) pp. 40.
6 'Bildungskrise' (1926b) p. 130.
7 See Harvey, *The condition of post-modernity*, p. 80.

PAUL RENNER

Renner accepted only as a starting point for design, restricted the intended value of an object to its operational success, and professed to exclude any conscious consideration of pleasure or style. Renner was not an uncomplicated functionalist: he demanded, in addition, that design should be attuned to the 'style of the era'. He desired a certain uniformity and correctness of contemporary taste in form: in his view, form had to aspire to a spiritual expression of modernity. Renner felt it imperative to find a levelling style to suit a society becoming aware of the need for equality. He never succumbed to a romantic modernist belief in 'the machine' as a mythical symbol of all that was rational and good in the modern age; although, in Futura, he did use forms which were expressive of technological progress in order to represent modern times. Yet, unlike the unrefined, geometrically-constructed Bauhaus alphabets, Futura's appearance of impersonality was effected by subtle visual judgements and compromises.

Renner's idealism was mixed with a pragmatic concern for material constraints and possibilities. He consistently recommended an unprejudiced attitude to new tasks – indeed this characterized the approach which underpinned his principal book on typography, *Die Kunst der Typographie* (1939). The message in this book was: adopt some established principles, try them out, see how that looks, and then progress from there using your own visual judgement.

117 *Zeit im Bild.* 1911.

Renner worked with those technologies which would become central motifs in modernist theories of graphic design. Integrating type with photographic illustrations was a principal tenet of the New Typography, and some designers developed innovative ways of combining the two elements, breaking the tyranny of letterpress printing's mechanical constraints. In 1911 Renner had worked on the illustrated reportage magazine, *Zeit im Bild*, which integrated type and photographs, but in a centred layout, using gothic type, with rules around halftone photographs (figure 117). The modernist 'Typofoto' style of the 1920s, which dispensed with symmetry, and the clutter of gothic type and box rules, was an aesthetic development indicating the self-confidence of designers in adapting technology, and hinting at the visual possibilities of future developments (the freedom soon to be given by offset lithography, for example). Renner later became more concerned with developing a 'modernist' style in his work on Futura, and in his advertising booklets for the Swiss Tourist Board; but even in these booklets, printed by photogravure, his visual sense was bound by tradition. He was no revolutionary stylist – his typography was always staid and static. Does this make him less of a modernist? He was working in modern media – the illustrated press and advertising brochures; but perhaps there is a distinction to be made between the modernity of the medium and the modernism of the graphic style employed in it.

Serious books, despite the fact that they too were commodities, were excluded from Renner's scorn as cultural artefacts. Designing books remained for him the principal and most important kind of typographic work. He expressed the view early in his career that typography was a '*bürgerliche* affair', by which he meant that it should be restrained, polite and self-effacing in the interests of serving the sense of the given words (see p. 33 above). Shorn of its class overtones (if that is possible), this is an honourable and perhaps widely adaptable principle. Renner was not one of those book-artists who applied original ornament to a book in order to make it a saleable item; in his early years working for publishers he developed a sober, almost ornament-free style of traditional book design, providing anonymous typographic guidance for the production of thousands of books. Renner's approach to designing was driven by a concept of service, to both the writer of a text and its potential readers. This concept formed the heart of his own, modern approach to typography, which changed little from his earliest years of practice. For Renner, a certain kind of design work, which was really unbound artistic self-expression masquerading as design, was the height of irresponsibility. In the same way that he was suspicious of abstract art and non-representational painting (he considered Cézanne's work to be a pinnacle of achievement), he disapproved of designing which neglected a consideration of utility.

Renner can be seen as a bridge between design in the nineteenth and twentieth centuries, not only due to the span of his life, but in terms of his outlook on the life around him. He was an almost exact contemporary of Thomas Mann, with whom he was acquainted between the wars in Munich. Mann's books and essays reflect an attempt to reconcile the modern world with the nineteenth-century German ideal of spirituality. The same theme can be traced in Renner's work and writings: he consistently, and conservatively, attempted to anchor his sense of a new modern sensibility by establishing a firmly German, historical example in the idea of the *Bürger*. He observed that the 'collectivist' sensibility, which he considered integral to being modern, was very close to the traditional Prussian 'will-to-order'.[8] He was caught between the old world and the new; between what he called 'humanism', an elitist notion of high culture, and 'materialism', an egalitarian approach to modern life. This dialectic informs his design work – in, for example, the delicate balance of historical proportions and innovative letterforms in Futura. He consistently attempted to tread the ridge between tradition and innovation. His belief in 'timeless' solutions to certain tasks of design was not an unthinking acceptance of certain traditional forms or a denial of the principle of ever-renewing modernity; on the contrary it indicates a very modern belief in the potential of perfectibility. In any case, he admitted that each generation had a different opinion about what is timeless.

8 *Kulturbolschewismus?* (1932b) pp. 44.

Published writings of Paul Renner

The titles of self-contained books and booklets are in bold.

1908

Paul Renner über Buchausstattung
[Paul Renner on book design]
*1903–1908: Georg Müller Verlag München,
Katalog.*

1910

a Privat- und Verlegereinband
[Private and publisher's binding]
Der Zwiebelfisch, Jhg 3, Heft 2, 1910, pp. 52–3.

b Zur Kultur des Buches: I
[On the culture of the book]
Allgemeine Buchhändlerzeitung, Jhg 17, Nr 19,
12 May 1910, pp. 242–4.

c Zur Kultur des Buches: II
Allgemeine Buchhändlerzeitung, Jhg 17, Nr 23,
9 June 1910, pp. 290–2.

d Zur Kultur des Buches: III
Allgemeine Buchhändlerzeitung, Jhg 17, Nr 28,
14 July 1910, pp. 345–8.

e Zur Kultur des Buches: IV
Allgemeine Buchhändlerzeitung, Jhg 17, Nr 32,
11 August 1910, pp. 405–8.

1911

Vom Zwiebelfisch und vom Ziegenleder
[On wrong fonts and kid leather]
Allgemeine Buchhändlerzeitung, Jhg 18, Nr 6,
9 February 1911, pp. 62–4.

1912

Die Kunst im Buchgewerbe
[Art in book production]
Kunst und Künstler, Jhg 11, 1912/13, p. 158.

1913

Buchgewerbe und bildende Kunst
[Book production and the fine arts]
*Deutscher Bibliophilen-Kalender: Jahrbuch für
Bücherfreunde und Büchersammler*, Jhg 1, 1913,
pp. 65–75.

Content overlaps with 1912.

1917

Typographische Regeln [Typographic rules]
Börsenblatt für den deutschen Buchhandel, Jhg 84,
Nr 65, 19 March 1917, pp. 265–6.

Renner's rules were reprinted as the text for a type speci-
men produced by the printers Brügel & Sohn, Ansbach,
*Typographische Regeln und Beispiele nach Angaben
Paul Renners* (undated).

1920

a Der Künstler zur Rechtschreibungsreform
[Artists on the reform of spelling – contribution
to questionnaire]
Archiv für Buchgewerbe und Gebrauchsgraphik,
Band 57, Heft 5/6, 1920, p. 102.

b Münchener Typographie [Munich typography]
Archiv für Buchgewerbe und Gebrauchsgraphik,
Band 57, Heft 5/6, 1920, pp. 112–20.

c **Zwanzig Jahre Münchener Typographie**
[Twenty years of Munich typography]
Munich: Paul Renner, 1920. 196 × 133 mm.
24 pages.

Special booklet edition of 1920b (without illustrations),
published by Renner and printed in an edition of 100 by
Knorr & Hirth, Munich.

1921

Künstler und Gewerbe [The artist and the trade]
Deutscher Werkbund Mitteilungen, Februar/März
1921.

This also appeared in *Typographische Mitteilungen*,
Jhg 18, Heft 2, February 1921, pp. 15–17. It also constituted
the first chapter in *Typografie als Kunst* (1922a), and was
partly reprinted in Deutscher Werkbund, *Zwischen Kunst
und Industrie* (1982).

1922

a **Typografie als Kunst** [Typography as art]
Munich: Georg Müller Verlag, 1922. 205 × 128 mm.
176 pages [including 10 pages plates at end].

Typeset in 'the so-called "Original-Ungerfraktur" of the
Klinkhardt foundry in Leipzig'. The book is dedicated
'with admiration and gratitude' to Hans Cornelius. A Russian translation was issued in 1925 by the Soviet state publishing house Gosizdat, which had a Berlin office (where
El Lissitzky worked in the early 1920s). In a lecture of 1947
Renner amusedly remarked that the Soviet state issued
his book, which contained the critical words about socialism quoted on p. 36 above. This passage may well have
been cut from the Russian translation.

b Über den Verlegereinband
  [On the publisher's binding]
  Börsenblatt für den deutschen Buchhandel, Jhg 89,
  Nr 105, 6 May 1922, pp. 645–7.

1924

a Aufruf zur Gründung einer Arbeitsgemeinschaft
  für buchgewerbliche Fortbildung
  [Call for the establishment of a working community for further training in the book trade]
  Die Bücherstube, Jhg 3, 1924, pp. 415–23.

b Die beiden Ziele [The two goals]
  'Das schöne Buch' special issue of *Kunst und
  Künstler*, Jhg 22, Nr 12, 1923/4, pp. 372–3.

c Der Buchtitel auf dem Einband
  [The book-title on the cover]
  Die Bücherstube, Jhg 3, 1924, pp. 27–30.

d Das moderne Holzschnittbuch
  [The modern woodcut book]
  Die Bücherstube, Jhg 3, 1924, pp. 218–69.

e [Editor with Günther Hildebrandt]
  Die Bücherstube, Jhg 3, 1924.

  Book and exhibition reviews by Renner on pp. 174–5;
  p. 299; pp. 301–2. These were credited to 'rr', a contraction
  of 'Renner'. Not to be confused with the Munich writer
  Alexander Roda Roda.

1925

a Das Ende des Historismus [The end of historicism]
  Gebrauchsgraphik, Jhg 1, Heft 9, 1925, pp. 45–8.

  Slightly expanded version of 1925g.

b Entbehrliche Künste, notwendige Kunst
  [Disposable arts, necessary art]
  Die Bücherstube, Jhg 4, 1925, pp. 236–46.

c Neue Ziele des Schriftschaffens
  [New goals in type design]
  Die Bücherstube, Jhg 4, 1925, pp. 18–28.

d [Editor with Günther Hildebrandt]
  Die Bücherstube, Jhg 4, 1925.

  Renner contributed a feature: '[Emil] Preetorius, Exlibris
  und Signete', pp. 29–33. Credited to 'rr'.

e Revolution der Buchschrift
  [Revolution in book script]
  Gutenberg Festschrift 1925, pp. 279–82.

f Vom Handwerk zur Großindustrie
  [From handcraft to large-scale industry]
  Hübel & Denck *Festschrift* 1875–1925. Leipzig:
  1925, pp. 13–33.

  This article is contained in a jubilee publication for the
  Leipzig binding firm of Hübel & Denck, printed in an edi-

tion of 1000. Renner quoted from this article at length in
Mechanisierte Grafik (1931d).

g Die Zukunft unserer Druckschrift
  [The future of our printing type]
  Typographische Mitteilungen, Jhg 22, Heft 5, 1925,
  pp. 86–7.

1926

a [Brief contribution to questionnaire about the
  character of Munich]
  Der Zwiebelfisch, Jhg 20, Heft 1, 1926/7, p. 38.

b Bildungskrise [Crisis in education]
  Typographische Mitteilungen, Jhg 23, Heft 5, 1926,
  pp. 130–1.

c **Denkschrift über die Errichtung eines Buch-
  druckertechnikums in München**
  [Memorandum about the setting up of a techni-
  cal college of printing in Munich]
  Undated & uncredited [Munich: Graphische
  Berufsschule, 1926?].

d Kampf um München als Kulturzentrum
  [Struggle for Munich as a cultural centre –
  contributed speech]
  Kampf um München als Kulturzentrum. Munich:
  Richard Pflaum, 1926, pp. 49–56.

1927

a Die alte und neue Buchkunst
  [The old and new book art]
  Die Literarische Welt, Jhg 3, Nr 24, Friday 17 June
  1927, p. 3.

  Slight overlap with articles 1927g, 1925c and 1924b.

b Andere Meinung als Paul Renner
  [A different opinion to that of Paul Renner]
  Die Form, Jhg 2, Heft 6, 1927, p. 192.

  Renner's brief response to a comment by typeface
  designer Georg Mendelssohn (also here on pp. 191–2)
  prompted by Renner's 1927g.

c Der Aufbau unserer Kunst- und Gewerbeschulen
  [The organization of our art and trade schools]
  Die Form, Jhg 2, Heft 4, 1927, pp. 170–4.

d Die Druckprobe [The printing specimen]
  Offset: Buch- und Werbekunst, Jhg 4, Heft 4, 1927.
  pp. 168–70.

e Paul Renner über seine Schrift „Futura"
  [Paul Renner on his typeface Futura]
  Börsenblatt für den deutschen Buchhandel, Jhg 95,
  Nr 220, 20 September 1927, pp. 1134–5.

  Same as 1928a.

f Rede des Oberstudiendirektors Paul Renner bei
der Eröffnung der Meisterschule für Deutschlands
Buchdrucker in München
[Speech by Principal Paul Renner at the opening
of the Master School for Germany's Printers in
Munich]
Börsenblatt für den deutschen Buchhandel, Jhg 95,
Nr 36, 12 February 1927, pp.179–80.

g Die Schrift unserer Zeit [The script of our time]
Die Form, Jhg 2, Heft 3, 1927, pp.109–10.

h Schulbuch und Kunst [The schoolbook and art]
Offset: Buch- und Werbekunst, Jhg 4, Heft 10, 1927.
pp.445–7.

i Vom Stammbaum der Schrift
[On the family tree of script]
Das Neue Frankfurt, Jhg 1, Nr 4, 1927, pp.85–7.

> Slight overlap with 1927a and 1931d, pp.38–9.

j Zu den Arbeiten von Ferdinand Kramer
[On the work of Ferdinand Kramer]
Die Form, Jhg 2, Heft 10, 1927, pp.320–3.

> Reprinted in Deutscher Werkbund, *Die Zwanziger Jahre...*
> pp.218–220.

1928

a Futura: die Schrift unsrer Zeit
[Futura: the typeface of our time]
in type specimen *Futura: die Schrift unserer Zeit*.
Frankfurt am Main: Bauer'sche Gießerei, 1927/8,
pp.1–5.

> Text the same as 1927e. This version has been placed
> under 1928 because it is likely that the undated type speci-
> men was produced in this year, and in order to distinguish
> it from 1927g, which has a slightly different spelling of
> 'unserer' in its title. There is also a discrepancy in the
> spelling of this word between the title of this article and
> the title of the type specimen.

b Gegen den Dogmatismus in der Kunst
[Against dogmatism in art]
Die Form, Jhg 3, Heft 11, 1928, pp.313–24.

c Kunst, Natur, Technik [Art, nature, technology]
*Münchner Mitteilungen für künstlerische und
geistige Interessen*, Jhg 2, Heft 49, 8 December
1928, pp.745–7.

d Mensch und Maschine [Man and machine]
Graphische Berufsschule, Jhg 14, Heft 1, March
1928, pp.1–2.

> Excerpt from 1925f.

e Rundfrage zum Problem des ewigen Handwerks
[Survey on the problem of eternal craftwork –
contribution to questionnaire]
Handwerkskunst im Zeitalter der Maschine.

[Exhibition catalogue] Staedtische Kunsthalle
Mannheim, 1928, pp.45–6.

f Type und Typographie [Type and typography]
Archiv für Buchgewerbe und Gebrauchsgraphik,
Band 65, Heft 6, 1928, pp.453–67.

> Number 2 in the Winter 1928 lecture series 'Kunst und
> Technik im Buchgewerbe' (Art and technology in the book
> trade) run by the Deutsche Buchgewerbeverein. Also pub-
> lished in small format as a supplement to *Typographische
> Mitteilungen*. Text overlaps with 1931d.

g Über die Schrift der Zukunft
[On the script of the future]
Typographische Mitteilungen, Jhg 25, Heft 8, 1928.
pp.189–92.

> Almost exactly the same as 1925c.

1929

a Das Deutsche Buchgewerbe
[The German book trade]
Typographische Mitteilungen, Jhg 26, Heft 1, 1929.
supplement: pp.1–16.

> Second edition of a glossary of printing terms compiled
> for the Deutsche Sprachverein. Updated with a brief fore-
> word by Renner. Also published as a special number of
> *Graphische Berufsschule*, Jhg 15, Heft 2, July 1929.

b Die fünf Bedeutungen des Wortes Farbe
[The five meanings of the word colour]
Die Form, Jhg 4, Heft 4, 1929, pp.90–2.

c Johanna von Orléans in film
[Joan of Orléans on film]
Die Form, Jhg 4, Heft 4, 1929, pp.88–90.

> An essay on the Danish director Carl Dreyer's silent film
> about Joan of Arc, filmed in Paris. For particular praise,
> Renner singled out the lead actress Marie Falconetti, 'who
> one cannot help but love'. He expressed the hope that she
> would make further films in Russia, not in Hollywood.

d Kritische Anmerkungen zum Farben-Unterricht
[Critical observations on the teaching of colour]
Die Form, Jhg 4, Heft 11, 1929, pp.284–8.

e Konstruktive und Konstruierte Form
[Constructivist and constructed form]
Die Form, Jhg 4, Heft 21, 1929, pp.563–6.

f Praktische Vorschläge zum Farben-Unterricht
[Practical suggestions for the teaching of colour]
Die Form, Jhg 4, Heft 14, 1929, pp.396–8.

> Along with 1929b and 1929d, this is a speech from the
> fourth colour conference in Munich, 18 & 19 February, 1929.
> These texts later formed the section on colour in 1931d.

g Warum geben wir an Kunstschulen immer noch
Schreibunterricht?
[Why do we still give instruction in formal
writing at art schools?]
Die Form, Jhg 4, Heft 3, 1929, pp.49–52.

h Zur Farbenlehre [On colour theory]
Graphische Berufsschule, Jhg 14, Heft 4, April
1929, pp. 53–5; & Jhg 15, Heft 2, July 1929,
pp. 17–29.

Also appears in *Klimschs Jahrbuch*, Band 12, pp. 37–43.

1930

a Asymmetrie im Buchdruck und in der modernen
Gestaltung überhaupt
[Asymmetry in printing and in modern design
in general]
Die Form, Jhg 5, Heft 3, 1930, pp. 57–9.

Text reappears in 1931d, pp. 83–92.

b Drei Jahre Futura [Three years of Futura]
in type specimen *Futura: die Ergänzungs-
Garnituren*. Frankfurt am Main: Bauer'sche
Gießerei, 1930/1.

c Das Formproblem der Druckschrift
[The problem of form in printing type]
Imprimatur: ein Jahrbuch für Bücherfreunde, Jhg 1,
1930, pp. 27–33.

Also appears in *Graphische Berufsschule*, Jhg 15, Heft 4,
March 1930, pp. 50–2.

d Das Lichtbild: Rede zur Eröffnung der interna-
tionalen Ausstellung „Das Lichtbild" München
1930, am 5 Juni, gehalten von Paul Renner
[The photograph: speech given by Paul Renner
for the opening of the international exhibition
'The photograph' in Munich on 5 June 1930]
Die Form, Jhg 5, Heft 14, 1930, pp. 377–8.

Reprinted in *Graphische Berufsschule*, Jhg 16, Heft 1/2,
January 1931, pp. 30–2.

e Phonetische oder etymologische Rechtschreibung
– oder?
[Phonetic or etymological spelling – or?]
Gutenberg Jahrbuch 1930, pp. 338–42.

Largely the same as 1931d, pp. 58–63.

f Wie müssen die Arbeitskräfte des Buchdruck-
gewerbes ausgebildet werden
[How should the work force in the printing
trade be educated]
Zeitschrift für Deutschlands Buchdrucker
(Festausgabe zur Deutscher Buchdrucker-Verein
Hauptversammlung 1930: Bad Harzburg)
pp. 753–5.

1931

a Begrüßung des dritten Jahrganges der Meisterschule für Deutschlands Buchdrucker
[Welcome for the third year of the Master School
for Germany's Printers – speech]

Graphische Berufsschule, Jhg 14, Heft 4, April
1929, pp. 53–5.

b [Introduction to issue dealing with modern style
in design]
Graphische Berufsschule, Jhg 16, Heft 1/2, January
1931, p. 1.

c Leder- und Buntpapier
[Leather and coloured paper]
G. F. Hartlaub [Herausgeber] *Das ewige Handwerk
im Kunstgewerbe der Gegenwart: Beispiele modernen kunsthandwerklichen Gestaltens*. Werkbund-
Buch. Berlin: Verlag Hermann Reckendorf, 1931,
p. 79.

d **Mechanisierte Grafik: Schrift · Typo · Foto ·
Film · Farbe**
[Mechanized graphic design: script · typo · photo ·
film · colour]
Berlin: Verlag Hermann Reckendorf, 1931. 210 ×
155 mm. 208 pages of text + xxxx pages plates.

'Dedicated in friendship to Fritz Wichert'.

e Schrift und Druck [Type and printing]
in same book as 1931c, pp. 85–6.

f Das Schöne Buch [The beautiful book]
Literaturblatt der Frankfurter Zeitung, Sonntag
13 December 1931, p. 4.

1932

a Die erste Diplomverteilung an unserer
Meisterschule
[The first award of diplomas at our
Meisterschule – speech]
Graphische Berufsschule, Jhg 1931–32, Heft 4,
April 1932, pp. 37–9.

Reprinted in *Zeitschrift für Deutschlands Buchdrucker*,
Jhg 44, Nr 12, 9 February 1932, pp. 102–4.

b **Kulturbolschewismus?** [Cultural Bolshevism?]
Zurich: Eugen Rentsch Verlag, 1932. 220 × 145 mm.
64 pages.

c Das Luxus-Buch und unsre Zeit
[The luxury book and our time]
Zeitschrift für Bücherfreunde, Jhg 36 [Dritte Folge 1],
Heft 3, 1932, pp. 57–9.

Partial overlap with 1931c.

d Modern, traditionell, modisch
[Modern, traditional, modish]
Imprimatur: ein Jahrbuch für Bücherfreunde, Jhg 3,
1932, pp. 65–85.

e Verkehrswerbung, deutsche Lebensform und
   Kulturpropaganda
   [Tourist publicity, the German form of life,
   and cultural propaganda]
   Die Form, Jhg 7, Heft 8, 1932, pp. 233–47.

f Werkbund und Erziehung
   [Werkbund and education]
   Die Form, Jhg 7, Heft 11, 1932, pp.332–5.

1933

a Gegen den Schematismus in der Typographie
   [Against schematism in typography]
   Klimschs Jahrbuch, Band 26, 1933, pp. 25–31.

b Im Kampf um neue Gestaltungsfragen: Paul Renner
   [In the struggle for new questions of design –
   response to questionnaire]
   Typographische Mitteilungen, Jhg 30, Heft 1,
   January 1933, pp. 5–6.

c Paul Renner
   [contribution to a feature in which designers
   were requested to comment on the current state
   of graphic design]
   Gebrauchsgraphik, Jhg 10, Heft 1, January 1933,
   pp. 34–5.

1939

a Aus meinem Leben [From my life]
   Privately published.

   Part of Renner's memoirs of his career, which dealt with
   his arrest and must have been judged too controversial for
   publication alongside 1939b & 1939d by Renner and *Imprimatur*'s publisher Siegfried Buchenau. (A copy of this
   essay is among Georg Trump's papers; Klingspor.)

b Erinnerungen aus meiner Georg-Müller-Zeit
   [Recollections from my Georg-Müller period]
   Imprimatur: ein Jahrbuch für Bücherfreunde, Jhg 9,
   1939/40. unpaginated supplement: pp.[1–4], after
   p.184.

   Reprinted on the occasion of Renner's 65th birthday in
   Gebrauchsgraphik, Jhg 20, Heft 5, 1943/4.

c **Die Kunst der Typographie**
   [The art of typography]
   Berlin: Frenzel & Engelbrecher 'Gebrauchsgraphik'
   Verlag, 1939. 244 × 160 mm. 316 pages, including
   16 pages plates; many illustrations within text,
   some in 2 colours [black and red]. 130 typefaces
   illustrated and categorized. Jacket designed by
   Albrecht Heubner.

   Marked 'Copyright 1939'. But the permission to publish
   the book was given by the Nazi régime in December 1939,
   so it was not printed until 1940.

Zweite Auflage. Berlin: Verlag des Druckhauses
Tempelhof, 1948. 220 × 145 mm. 312 pages,
including 16 pages plates. Reprint with some
changes to illustrations.

Dritte Auflage. Berlin: Deutsche Verlag, 1953.
220 × 145 mm. 312 pages, including 16 pages
plates. Reprint with some changes to illustrations.

   'Neue bearbeitet von Georg Schautz' (updated by Georg
   Schautz). Many of the illustrations taken from Schautz's
   teaching.

d Vom Georg-Müller-Buch bis zur Futura und
   Meisterschule: Erinnerungen Paul Renners aus
   dem Jahrzehnt von 1918 bis 1927
   [From Georg-Müller book to Futura and the
   Meisterschule: recollections by Paul Renner
   from the decade 1918 to 1927]
   Imprimatur: ein Jahrbuch für Bücherfreunde, Jhg 9,
   1939/40. unpaginated supplement: pp.1–12, after
   p.192.

   Reprinted in slightly truncated form in *Gebrauchsgraphik*, Jhg 20, Heft 5, 1943/4. The republication of this
   essay in *Gebrauchsgraphik* in 1943 shows that Renner
   was no longer entirely *persona non grata* with the Nazis,
   as this periodical had become the official organ of the
   Fachgruppe Gebrauchsgraphiker (Graphic Design Division) of the Reichskammer für bildende Künste.

e [Review of an edition of Cézanne's letters]
   Die Literatur, June 1939.

1941

Antiqua und Fraktur
Frankfurt, 1941. 263 × 184 mm. 8 pages.

   A special printing of an article Renner wrote for the
   Frankfurter Zeitung. Printed as a practice exercise for the
   apprentices at the Frankfurter Societäts-Druckerei, Frankfurt am Main. Also appears in *Blätter aus der Mathilde-
   Zimmer-Stiftung*, Jhg 35, Nr 10, October 1941.

1942

a Die Farbe der Wand [The colour of the wall]
   Literaturblatt der Frankfurter Zeitung, Jhg 75, Nr 9,
   Monday 30 March 1942, p. 4.

   About choosing what colour to paint a wall.

b Nach der Entscheidung [After the decision]
   Archiv für Buchgewerbe und Gebrauchsgraphik,
   Band 79, Heft 6, Juni 1942, pp. 201–5.

1943

Kunststil und Kunst-ismen [Art-style and art-isms]
Gebrauchsgraphik, Jhg 20, Heft 5, 1943/4.
unpaginated supplement.

   Reappears in 1977.

1946

a Aforismen [Aphorisms]
   Der Künstler in der mechanisierten Welt (1977)
   pp.165–89.

b Das Geheimnis der Darstellung in der bildenden
   Kunst
   [The secret of representation in fine art]
   Der Künstler in der mechanisierten Welt (1977)
   pp.189–223.
   > See 1955.

c Der Hersteller [The producer]
   Der Künstler in der mechanisierten Welt (1977)
   pp.150–3.

d Die moderne Buchform [The modern book-form]
   Mitteilungen für den Buchhandel in der französischen Zone, Jhg 1, Nr 7, 1 September 1946,
   pp.101–3.
   > Reappears as section in 1947d.

e Das moderne Künstlerplakat
   [The modern artist's poster]
   Der Künstler in der mechanisierten Welt (1977)
   pp. 223–30.

f Moderne Typografie [Modern typography]
   Der Künstler in der mechanisierten Welt (1977)
   pp.118–49.

g Schrift und Rechtschreibung [Script and spelling]
   Pandora, Nr 4, 1946, pp.31–7.
   > Same as 1942b.

1947

a Die Bedeutung Europas [The meaning of Europe]
   Nouvelles de France, 16 July 1947, p. 4.
   > Renner quotes statistics from the Isotype publication
   > *Gesellschaft und Wirtschaft* (1930). This article is credited
   > to 'r–r'.

b Diktatur oder Demokratie in der öffentlichen
   Kunstpflege
   [Dictatorship or democracy in public art policy]
   Die Pforte, Jhg 1, Heft 2, 1947, pp.160–81.

c Das Großschreiben der Hauptwörter
   [The capitalization of nouns]
   Nouvelles de France, 16 April 1947.

d **Das Moderne Buch** [The modern book]
   Lindau: Jan Thorbecke Verlag, 1947. 200 × 125 mm.
   40 pages.

e **Ordnung und Harmonie der Farben:
   eine Farbenlehre für Künstler und Handwerker**
   [Order and harmony of colour: a colour theory
   for artists and craftsmen]

Ravensburg: Otto Maier Verlag, 1947. 275 × 190 mm.
80 pages. 8 colour plates; 8 diagrams in text.

> In discussing the prospective publication of this book,
> Renner commented that it would have a large print run,
> but would be quite expensive (7 Marks), due to the necessary four-colour illustrations. 'I would prefer that it cost
> 30 pfennigs and was read in the senior class of all schools.'
> (Letter to Heinz Haushofer, 30 March 1946; Nachlaß
> Renner.) This book allowed Renner to make many abstract
> points about form, and even to stray into philosophy.

Zweite Auflage [reprint]. Ravensburg: Otto Maier
Verlag, 1964.

f **Typografische Regeln** [Typographic rules]
   Lindau: Jan Thorbecke Verlag, 1947. 200 × 124 mm.
   16 pages.
   > Reprint of Renner's typographic rules as they appeared in
   > *Typografie als Kunst* (1922a). This booklet is described in
   > the colophon as a preview of a chapter from the forthcoming book *Der Künstler in der mechanisierten Welt* (1977).
   > This book, as posthumously published, did contain sections from *Typografie als Kunst*, but not the typographic
   > rules. Typeset in Renner-Antiqua & Kursiv.

g [Review of cheap editions published by Rowohlt]
   Nouvelles de France, 20 June 1947.
   > Credited to 'rr'.

1948

a Deutsche Hauptwörter – groß oder klein?
   [German nouns – big or small?]
   Nouvelles de France, 2 March 1948.

b Die Farbe als Kunstmittel der Formgebung
   [Colour as a creative resource in form-giving]
   Schweizer Graphische Mitteilungen, Jhg 67, Heft 11,
   November 1948, pp. 451–6.
   > Reprint from 1939c, pp. 203–21.

c Fraktur und Antiqua
   Schweizer Graphische Mitteilungen, Jhg 67, Heft 8,
   August 1948, pp.345–7.
   > Slightly truncated form of 1942b.

d Kleine Farbenlehre [Brief colour theory]
   Schweizer Graphische Mitteilungen, Jhg 67, Heft 12,
   December 1948, pp. 486–8.
   > Text overlaps with 1947e.

e Die moderne Typographie wird funktionell sein
   [Modern typography shall be functional]
   Schweizer Graphische Mitteilungen, Jhg 67, Heft 7,
   July 1948, pp.310–12.
   > Reprinted in slightly rewritten form in *Gutenberg
   > Jahrbuch* 1951, pp.178–181.

f Über moderne Typographie
   [On modern typography]
   Schweizer Graphische Mitteilungen, Jhg 67, Heft 3,
   March 1948, pp.119–120.

g Vom Hand- und Verleger-Einband
[On hand-bindings and publisher's bindings]
Lindau: Jan Thorbecke Verlag, 1948. 200 × 124 mm.
16 pages.

> Reprint of a chapter from *Typografie als Kunst* (1922a).
> Typeset in Renner-Antiqua & Kursiv.

h Werbedrucksachen [Publicity documents]
Schweizer Graphische Mitteilungen, Jhg 67, Heft 2,
February 1948, pp. 70–3.

> Reprint from 1939c, pp. 193–203.

1949

a Paul Renner [contributed paragraph]
*Der Geist weht wo er will: Kalender für das Jahr
1949.* Ulmer Volkshochschule.

> A short note in praise of the Volkshochschule in Ulm
> founded in 1946 by Inge Scholl, Otl Aicher, and others
> associated with the war-time resistance group, Die weiße
> Rose. Reprinted in Barbara Schüler, *Von der weißen Rose
> zur Eule der Weisheit: die Anfänge der Ulmer Volkshoch-
> schule* (Ulm: Süddeutsche Verlagsgesellschaft, 1996) p.86.

b Zur Kunst der Typographie
[On the art of typography]
Gutenberg Jahrbuch 1944/9, pp. 190–4.

> Slight overlap with 1946f.

1950

Die künstlerische Leistung des Typografen:
ein Versuch über das Zeitlos-Gültige
[The artistic achievement of the typographer:
an essay on the timelessly valid]
Gutenberg Jahrbuch 1950, pp. 397–409.

1953

Funktionelle Typografie: ein Kapitel aus dem
Buche „Mechanisierte Grafik"
[Functional typography: a chapter from the book
'Mechanisierte Grafik']
Frankfurt am Main: Deutscher Typokreis e.V.,
1953. A5. 32 pages.

> Typography by Georg Schautz. The Deutscher Typokreis
> e.V. is described on the title page as 'Society for the
> improvement of the arts of composing and printing'.

1955

Vom Geheimnis der Darstellung
[On the mystery of representation]
Frankfurt am Main: Deutscher Typokreis e.V.,
1955. 199 × 135 mm. 40 pages.

> Essay first published privately by Renner in 1938. Re-
> appears in re-written form, under a slightly different title,
> in 1977 (see 1946b).

1964

Color: order and harmony. A color theory for
artists and craftsmen
Translated by Alexander Nesbitt. London: Studio
Vista, 1964. 270 × 190 mm. 80 pages. 8 colour
plates; 8 diagrams in text.

> Translation of 1947e.

1977

Der Künstler in der mechanisierten Welt
[The artist in the mechanized world]
Munich: Akademie für das Grafische Gewerbe,
1977. 204 × 127 mm. 232 pages.

> Produced according to Renner's design specification,
> except for binding and title pages, which he did not spec-
> ify. Renner mentioned the imminent publication of this
> book in correspondence in 1946, although at that time he
> called it *Die neue Zeit und ihr Stil* (The new era and its
> style; letter to Heinz Haushofer, 30 March 1946; Nachlaß
> Renner). The colophon in 1948g stated erroneously that
> *Der Künstler in der mechanisierten Welt* was already
> available. As posthumously published, the book contains
> chapters from *Typografie als Kunst* (1922a), *Mechanis-
> ierte Grafik* (1931d) and several previously unpublished
> essays, which are listed here under 1946, when they were
> originally ready for publication. The essay 'Kunststil und
> Kunst-ismen' (1943) had already appeared elsewhere.

[n.d. – c.1947?]

a Der Buchausstatter und Hersteller
[The book designer and producer]

> Newspaper clipping (Nachlaß Renner). Likely to be
> from *Nouvelles de France*, the bi-lingual newspaper
> of Germany's French zone.

b Münchner Kunstbrief [Munich art bulletin]
Nouvelles de France.

> Newspaper clipping (Nachlaß Renner).

c Von der Bildniszeichnung [On portrait drawing]

> Undated offprint (Nachlaß Renner).

d Was ist der Werkbund? [What is the Werkbund?]

> Newspaper clipping (Nachlaß Renner). Likely to be from
> *Nouvelles de France.*

e Wiederaufbau oder Neuaufbau
[Reconstruction or starting anew]

> Newspaper clipping (Nachlaß Renner). Likely to be from
> *Nouvelles de France.*

Archive sources

BASK

Bayerische Akademie der Schönen Künste, 80539 München, Max-Joseph-Platz 3, Residenz, Postfach 100141, 80075 München.

Houses the papers of Walter Riezler, Renner's colleague in the Werkbund. Contains interesting Werkbund material in general, and copies of the memoranda Renner distributed to committee members in 1932.

Bay HStA

Bayerisches Hauptstaatsarchiv, Postfach 221152, 80501 München.

Files on the formation of the Munich Meisterschule and on Renner's dismissal from his post there.

Getty

Getty Center for the History of Art and the Humanities, 1200 Getty Center Drive, Los Angeles, CA 90049-1681.

The Special Collection houses the papers of Piet Zwart and Franz Roh. Includes some correspondence from Renner to Roh.

GNM

Germanisches National Museum, Postfach 9580, 90105 Nürnberg.

Houses the papers of Richard Riemerschmid, Renner's colleague in the Münchner Bund. Contains interesting Werkbund material from the *Gleichschaltung* period, including letters relating to Renner's work on the Milan Triennale exhibition.

Klingspor

Klingspor-Museum, Herrnstraße 80, 63012 Offenbach am Main.

A collection of material concerning Futura and an abortive roman typeface. It was inherited from the Bauer typefoundry, and includes proofs and type specimens.

Also Georg Trump's papers, where I found a copy of Renner's privately published memoir 'Aus meinem Leben' (1939a).

Nachlaß Renner

Paul Renner's papers. Private family archive.

Mostly private letters, typescripts of articles and lectures. Some offprints and news clippings of rare articles written by Renner. One folder of typeface material – mostly rough sketches dating from after 1933, most of which are reproduced in Luidl & Lange (ed.), *Paul Renner*. (Nothing on Futura.)

NAL

Jobbing Printing Collection, National Art Library, Victoria & Albert Museum, London SW7 2RL.

Contains a collection of material from 1920s and 1930s mostly given by Jan Tschichold: Swiss and German graphic design, including the work of Herbert Bayer, Moholy-Nagy, Max Burchartz. Among examples of Tschichold's work there is publicity material and student work from the Munich Meisterschule.

Stadtarchiv FFM

Institut für Stadtgeschichte (Stadtarchiv), Karmelitergasse 5 (Karmeliterkloster), 60311 Frankfurt am Main.

Records of the Frankfurter Kunstschule, including documents relating to Renner's employment there.

Stempel

Stempel-Archiv, Lehrdruckerei, El-Lissitzky-Straße 1, 64287 Darmstadt.

Several files of material on Renner's typeface designs, including Renner-Antiqua, and some which remained unfinished. Drawings, proofs, and documents, including a report by Stempel pertaining to a lawsuit concerning Futura.

Bibliography

Ades, Dawn *et al* (ed.), *Art and power: Europe under the dictators 1930–45*. London: Hayward Gallery, 1995.

Arnold, Susanne, *Entstehung und Werdegang der Futura*. Unpublished MA thesis. Mainz: Johannes-Gutenberg-Universität, 1985.

Aynsley, Jeremy, 'Gebrauchsgraphik as an early graphic design journal, 1924–1938' in *Journal of design history*, vol. 5, no. 1, 1992, pp. 53–72.

Banham, Reyner, *Theory and design in the first machine age*. London: Architectural Press, 1960.

Barron, Stephanie, & Sabine Eckmann *et al*, *Exiles + emigrés: the flight of European artists from Hitler*. Los Angeles County Museum of Art / New York: Harry N. Abrams, 1997.

Bauer'sche Gießerei, *Wie ein Druck-Buchstabe entsteht*. Frankfurt am Main: Bauer'sche Gießerei, 1930.

Bauer, Konrad F., 'Der Schöpfer der Futura' in *Linotype Post*, Nr 21, 1954, pp. 3–7.

—. *Wie eine Buchdruckschrift entsteht*. Frankfurt am Main: Bauer'sche Gießerei, 1958 [?].

[Bayer, Herbert] *Herbert Bayer; painter designer architect*. New York: Reinhold; London: Studio Vista, 1967.

Bayer, Herbert, 'Versuch einer neuen Schrift' in *Offset: Buch- und Werbekunst*, Heft 7, 1926. Reprint; Munich: Kraus-Thomson, 1980, pp. 398–400.

Beaucamp, Eduard *et al* (ed.), *Städelschule Frankfurt am Main: aus der Geschichte einer deutschen Kunsthochschule*. Frankfurt am Main: Waldemar Kramer, 1982.

Beck, Heinrich, 'Paul Renner' in *Berufen und Bewährt: vier verdienstvolle Typographen und Berufspädagogen*. Rechenschaftsbericht der Graphischen Bildungsarbeit, Bezirk Bielefeld· Bielefeld, 1967, pp. 21–4.

Benton, Tim & Charlotte, and Dennis Sharp (ed.), *Form and function: a source book for the history of architecture and design 1890–1939*. London: Crosby Lockwood Staples, 1975.

—. *History of architecture and design 1890–1939*. Arts: a third level course (units 5, 6, 11–16, and 'Documents'). Milton Keynes: Open University Press, 1975.

Berghahn, V. R., *Modern Germany*. Cambridge: Cambridge University Press, 1987.

Berman, Marshall, *All that is solid melts into air: the experience of modernity*. London / New York: Verso, 1983.

Bertheau, Philipp, Eva Hanebutt-Benz & Hans Reichardt, *Buchdruckschriften im 20. Jahrhundert: Atlas zur Geschichte der Schrift*. Darmstadt: Technische Hochschule Darmstadt, 1995.

Bill, Max, 'Über Typografie' in *Schweizer Graphische Mitteilungen*, Jhg 65, Heft 5, 1946, pp. 193–200.

Brüning, Ute (ed.), *Das A und O des Bauhauses*. Berlin: Bauhaus-Archiv; Edition Leipzig, 1995.

Bühnemann, Michael & Thomas Friedrich, 'Zur Geschichte der Buchgemeinschaften der Arbeiterbewegung in der Weimarer Republik' in Neue Gesellschaft für Bildende Kunst, *Wem gehört die Welt: Kunst und Gesellschaft in der Weimarer Republik*. Berlin: NGBK, 1977, pp. 363–97.

[Bugra] *Internationale Ausstellung für Buchgewerbe und Graphik Leipzig 1914*. Amtlicher Katalog.

Burke, Christopher, 'The authorship of Futura' in *Baseline*, no. 23, 1997, pp. 33–40.

Caflisch, Max, *Die Schriften von Renner, Tschichold und Trump*. Munich: Typographische Gesellschaft München, 1991.

Campbell, Joan, *The German Werkbund: the politics of reform in the applied arts*. Princeton: Princeton University Press, 1978.

Carter, Harry, 'Sanserif types' in *Curwen Miscellany*. London: Curwen Press, 1931.

Cobden-Sanderson, T. J., *Ecce Mundus; industrial ideals and the book beautiful*. London: Hammersmith Publishing Society, 1902.

Craig, Gordon, *Germany 1866–1945*. Oxford: Clarendon Press, 1978.

—. *The Germans*. Harmondsworth: Penguin Books, 1984.

Day, Kenneth (ed.), *Book typography 1815–1965: in Europe and the United States of America*. London: Ernest Benn, 1966.

De Zurko, Edward Robert, *Origins of functionalist theory*. New York: Columbia University Press, 1957.

Deutscher Werkbund, *Die Zwanziger Jahre des Deutschen Werkbunds*. Berlin: Deutscher Werkbund und Werkbund-Archiv, 1982.

—. *Zwischen Kunst und Industrie: der Deutsche Werkbund*. Munich: Die Neue Sammlung, 1975.

Dilnot, Clive, 'The state of design history' in Victor Margolin (ed.), *Design discourse: history / theory / criticism*. Chicago: University of Chicago Press, 1989, pp. 213–50.

Dreyfus, John, 'A reconstruction of the lecture given by Emery Walker on 15 November 1888' in *Matrix*, no.11, Winter 1991, pp. 27–52.

Ehmcke, F.H., *Drei Jahrzehnte Deutscher Buchkunst 1890–1920*. Berlin: Euphorion Verlag, 1922.

—. *Geordnetes und Gültiges: gesammelte Aufsätze und Arbeiten aus den letzten fünfundzwanzig Jahren*. Munich: C.H. Beck'sche Verlagsbuchhandlung, 1955.

—. *Persönliches und Sachliches: gesammelte Aufsätze und Arbeiten aus fünfundzwanzig Jahren*. Berlin: Verlag Hermann Reckendorf, 1928.

—. *Schrift: ihre Gestaltung und Entwicklung in neuerer Zeit*. Hannover: Günther Wagner, 1925.

—. 'Wandlung des Schriftgefühls' in *Buch und Schrift*, Heft IV, 1930, p.101.

Ehrlich, Frederic, *The new typography and modern layouts*. London: Chapman & Hall, 1934.

Evans, Bertram, 'A note on modern typography' in John C. Tarr, *Printing to-day*. Oxford: Oxford University Press, 1945.

—. *Modern typography on the continent*. London: Royal Society of Arts; Cantor Lectures, 1938.

—. 'Typography in England' in *Penrose's annual*, vol. 36, 1934, pp. 57–61.

Eyssen, Jürgen, *Buchkunst in Deutschland: vom Jugendstil zum Malerbuch*. Hannover: Schlütersche Verlagsanstalt, 1980.

Fleischmann, Gerd (ed.), *Bauhaus: Drucksachen Typografie Reklame*. Düsseldorf: Marzona, 1984.

Flood, John L., '"Es verstand sich fast von selbst, dasz die ungestalte und häszliche schrift... beseitigt bleiben muste.": Jacob Grimm's advocacy of roman type' in *Das Unsichtbare Band der Sprache: studies in German language and linguistic history in memory of Leslie Seiffert*. Stuttgart: Verlag Hans-Dieter Heinz, Akademischer Verlag Stuttgart, 1993, pp. 279–312.

Franklin, Colin, *The private presses*. London: Studio Vista, 1969.

Garland, Ken, 'Structure and substance' in *The Penrose Annual*, vol. 54, 1960, pp. 1–10.

Gay, Peter, *Art and act: on causes in history – Manet, Gropius, Mondrian*. New York: Harper & Row, 1976.

—. *Weimar culture: the outsider as insider* (1969). Harmondsworth: Penguin Books, 1974.

Gerhardt, Claus, 'Die Entstehung der funktionellen Typographie in den zwanziger Jahren in Deutschland' in *Gutenberg Jahrbuch*, 1982, pp. 282–95.

Giedion, Siegfried, *Mechanization takes command: a contribution to anonymous history*. New York: Oxford University Press, 1948.

Gill, Eric, *An essay on typography*. 2nd edn. London: Dent, 1936.

Grimm, Jakob and Wilhelm, *Deutsches Wörterbuch*. Leipzig: S. Hirzel, 1854.

Grisebach, August, 'Paul Renner' in *Zeitschrift für Bücherfreunde*. Neue Folge: 3, 1911/12, pp. 345–58.

Gropius, Walter, *The new architecture and the Bauhaus*. London: Faber & Faber, 1936.

—. 'Theory and organization of the Bauhaus' (1923) in Herbert Bayer, Walter Gropius and Ise Gropius (ed.), *Bauhaus 1919–1928*. London: Secker & Warburg, 1975, p. 21.

Habermas, Jürgen, 'Modernity – an incomplete project' in Hal Foster (ed.) *The anti-aesthetic*. Washington: Bay Press, 1983, pp. 3–15.

Handover, P.M., 'Grotesque letters' in *Monotype Newsletter*, no. 69, March 1963.

Harvey, David, *The condition of postmodernity*. Oxford: Blackwell, 1989.

Heiderhoff, Horst, *Antiqua oder Fraktur: zur Problemgeschichte eines Streits*. Frankfurt am Main: Polygraph Verlag, 1971.

Hemken, Kai-Uwe, 'El Lissitzky zwischen Revolution und Reklame: zur elementaren Typografie und Buchgestaltung von 1922–1934' in Victor Malsy (ed.), *El Lissitzky: Konstrukteur, Denker, Pfeifenraucher, Kommunist*. Mainz: Verlag Hermann Schmidt, 1990, pp.14–37.

Herf, Jeffrey, *Reactionary modernism: technology, culture and politics in Weimar and the Third Reich*. Cambridge: Cambridge University Press, 1984.

Heskett, John, *German design 1870–1918*. London: Trefoil, 1986.

—. 'Modernism and archaism in design in the Third Reich' in *Block*, no. 3, 1980, pp.13–24.

Hochuli, Jost, *Book design in Switzerland*. Zurich: Pro Helvetia, 1993.

Hochuli, Jost & Robin Kinross, *Designing books: practice and theory*. London: Hyphen Press. 1996.

Holborn, Hajo, *A history of modern Germany 1840–1945*. London: Eyre & Spottiswoode, 1969.

Hollis, Richard, *Graphic design: a concise history*. London: Thames & Hudson, 1994.

Huygen, Frederike (ed.), *1928: Schoonheid en transparantie, logica en vernunft*. Rotterdam: Museum Boymans-van Beuningen, 1993.

Jackman, Jarrell C. and Carla M. Borden (ed.), *The muses flee Hitler: cultural transfer and adaptation*. Washington D.C.: Smithsonian Institution, 1983.
Johnson, A.F., 'Sans serifs: the present-day revival' in *Printing Review*, vol.1, no.1, Summer 1931, pp.5–6.
—. *Type designs: their history and development*. 3rd edn. London: Andre Deutsch, 1966.
Johnston, Edward, *Writing & illuminating, & lettering*. London: John Hogg, 1906.
Jost, Heinrich, 'Paul Renner: siebzig Jahre' in *Der Druckspiegel*, Nr 9, 1948, p.9.

Kaes, Anton, Martin Jay and Edward Dimendberg [ed.], *The Weimar Republic sourcebook*. Berkeley: University of California Press, 1994.
Kapr, Albert, *Fraktur: Form und Geschichte der gebrochenen Schriften*. Mainz: Verlag Hermann Schmidt, 1993.
Kautzsch, Rudolf, *Die neue Buchkunst*. Weimar: Gesellschaft der Bibliophilen, 1902.
Kershaw, Ian, *Popular opinion and political dissent in the Third Reich: Bavaria 1933–1945*. Oxford: Clarendon Press, 1983.
Kinross, Robin, 'Large and small letters: authority and democracy', in *Octavo*, no.5, 1988, pp.2–5.
—. *Modern typography: an essay in critical history*. London: Hyphen Press, 1992.
—. introduction to Jan Tschichold, *The new typography*. Berkeley: University of California Press, 1995.
—. 'Relics of the modern' in *Eye*, vol.3, no.11, 1993, p.66.
—. 'The rhetoric of neutrality' (1985) in Victor Margolin (ed.), *Design discourse: history / theory / criticism*. Chicago: University of Chicago Press, 1989, pp.131–43.
—. 'Universal faces, ideal characters' in *Baseline*, no.6, 1985, pp.18–21.
—. 'Unjustified text and the zero hour' in *Information design journal*. vol.7, no.3, 1994, pp.243–52.
—. 'What is a typeface' in *Baseline*, no.7, 1986, pp.14–18.
Kirschmann, August, *Antiqua oder Fraktur (lateinische oder deutsche Schrift)*. 3rd edn. Leipzig: Verlag des Deutschen Buchgewerbevereins, 1930 [?].
Klemperer, Klemens von, *Germany's new conservatism*. Princeton: Princeton University Press, 1957.

Kostelanetz, Richard (ed.), *Moholy-Nagy*. London: Allen Lane, 1971.
[Kramer, Ferdinand] *Ferdinand Kramer Werkkatalog 1923–1974*. Frankfurt: Schriftenreihe 3 der Architektenkammer Hesse, 1974 [?].

Lane, Barbara Miller, *Architecture and politics in Germany, 1918–45*. Cambridge, Mass: Harvard University Press, 1968.
Lane, John A., 'Futura' in *26 Letters*. Munich: Typostudio Schumacher-Gebler, 1989.
—. 'Twentieth-century punchcutters' in *Matrix*, no.11, Winter 1991, pp.7–23.
Lang, Lothar, *Konstruktivismus in Buchkunst*. Leipzig: Edition Leipzig, 1990.
Le Corbusier, *Towards a new architecture* (1923). 2nd English edn; London: The Architectural Press, 1946.
Lehmann-Haupt, Hellmut, *Art under a dictatorship*. Oxford University Press: New York, 1954.
Leitmeier, Hans, 'Das deutsche illustrierte Buch unserer Zeit' in *Gutenberg Jahrbuch*, 1927, pp.131–39.
Loubier, Hans, *Die neue deutsche Buchkunst*. Stuttgart: Felix Krais, 1921.
Luidl, Philipp, *Meisterschule für Deutschlands Buchdrucker, 1927 / Akademie für das Grafische Gewerbe, 1977 / München*. Supplement 6 to *Der Druckspiegel*, June 1977.
—. 'München – Mekka der schwarzen Kunst' in Christoph Stölzl (ed.), *Die Zwanziger Jahre in München*. Munich: Schriften des Stadtmuseums 8, 1979, pp.195–209.
—. (ed.), *J.T.* Munich: Typographische Gesellschaft München, 1976.
Luidl, Philipp, and Günter Gerhard Lange (ed.), *Paul Renner*. Munich: Typographische Gesellschaft München, 1978.

McLean, Ruari, *Jan Tschichold: typographer*. London: Lund Humphries, 1975.
—. (ed.), *Typographers on type*. London: Lund Humphries, 1995.
McMurtrie, Douglas C., *Modern typography and layout*. Chicago: Eyncourt Press, 1930.
Megaw, Denis, '20th century sans serif types' in *Typography*, no.7, Winter 1938, pp.27–35.
Meggs, Philip, *A history of graphic design*. London: Allen Lane, 1983.
Meiner, Annemarie, 'Die Münchener Renaissance' in *Gutenberg Jahrbuch*, 1935, pp.313–25.
[Meisterschule] *Fünfundzwanzig Jahre Meisterschule für Deutschlands Buchdrucker München 1927/52*. Munich, 1952.

Moholy-Nagy, László, *The new vision* (1928). 4th revised edn. New York: George Wittenborn Inc, 1947.

Monguzzi, Bruno, 'Piet Zwart: the typographical work 1923/1933' in *Rassegna*, no. 30, 1987.

Morris, William, and Emery Walker, 'Printing' in *Arts and crafts essays by members of the Arts and Crafts Exhibition Society* (1893). London and Bombay: Longmans Green and Co, 1899.

Morris, William, *News from nowhere and selected writings and designs*. Harmondsworth: Penguin Books, 1962.

Mosley, James, 'The nymph and the grot' in *Typographica*. New Series, no. 12, 1965, pp. 2–19.

Naylor, Gillian, *The Bauhaus reassessed*. London: Herbert Press, 1985.

Nerdinger, Winfried (ed.), *Bauhaus-Moderne im Nationalsozialismus: zwischen Anbiederung und Verfolgung*. Munich: Prestel, 1993.

Neumann, Eckhard, 'Frankfurter Typografie: Bemerkungen zur Futura und zur angeblichen Kramer-Grotesk' in Claude Lichtenstein (ed.), *Ferdinand Kramer: der Charme des Systematischen*. Gießen: Anabas Verlag, 1991, pp. 32–4.

—. *Functional graphic design in the 1920s*. New York: Reinhold, 1967.

Noordzij, Gerrit, 'Broken scripts and the classification of typefaces' in *Journal of typographic research*. vol. 4, no. 3, 1970, pp. 213–40.

Olsen, Mogens Greve, *Omkring en visit hos Paul Renner*. Nakskov: Rasmussen, 1953.

Oschilewski, Walter G., 'Paul Renner zum 70. Geburtstag' in *Das Druckgewerbe*. Jhg 1, Heft 25, 1948, p. 357.

Ovink, G. Willem, 'After all, what does "functional typography" mean?' in *Fine Print on type*. London, Lund Humphries, 1989, pp. 17–21.

—. *Legibility, atmosphere-value and forms of printing types*. Leiden: A.W. Sijthoff, 1938.

—. 'Jan Tschichold 1902–74: Versuch zu einer Bilanz seines Schaffens' in *Quaerendo*, vol. 7, no. 3, Summer 1978, pp. 187–220.

Passuth, Kristina, *Moholy-Nagy*. London: Thames & Hudson, 1985.

Peterson, William S., *The Kelmscott Press: a history of William Morris's typographical adventure*. Oxford: Clarendon Press, 1991.

Pevsner, Nikolaus, *Academies of art: past and present*. Cambridge: Cambridge University Press, 1940.

—. *Pioneers of modern design*. Harmondsworth: Penguin Books, 1960.

Piper, Ernst, and Bettina Raab, *90 Jahre Piper*. Munich: Piper, 1994.

Plata, Walter, 'The present status of Black Letter in German-speaking countries' in *Alphabet*, 1964, pp. 131–8.

—. *Schätze der Typographie: gebrochene Schriften*. Frankfurt: Polygraph Verlag, 1968.

Posener, Julius, *Anfänge des Funktionalismus: von Arts and Crafts zum Deutschen Werkbund*. Berlin: Verlag Ullstein, 1964.

Raabe, Paul (ed.), *Das Buch in den zwanziger Jahren*. Wolfenbütteler Schriften für Geschichte des Buchwesens, Band 2. Hamburg: Hauswedell, 1978.

[Renner] 'Interview mit Paul Renner' in *Der Druckspiegel*, Folge 5, May 1947, pp. 6–7.

Rodenberg, Julius, *Deutsche Pressen: eine Bibliographie*. Zurich: Amalthea-Verlag, 1925.

Schauer, Georg Kurt, *Deutsche Buchkunst 1890 bis 1960*. 2 vols. Hamburg: Maximilian Gesellschaft, 1963.

—. 'Die Herkunft von Linearschriften' in *Börsenblatt für den Deutschen Buchhandel*. Frankfurter Ausgabe; Nr 22a, 19 März 1959, pp. 294–8.

Schmidt-Künsemüller, Friedrich Adolf, *William Morris und die neuere Buchkunst*. Wiesbaden: Otto Harrassowitz, 1955.

Schuitema, Paul, 'New typographical design in 1930' in *Neue Grafik*, 11. Ausgabe, December 1961, pp. 16–19.

[Schwitters, Kurt] „*Typographie kann unter Umständen Kunst sein*". *Kurt Schwitters: Typographie und Werbegestaltung*. Wiesbaden: Landesmuseum, 1991.

Selle, Gert, *Die Geschichte des Designs in Deutschland von 1870 bis heute*. Cologne: DuMont Buchverlag, 1978.

Sharp, Dennis (ed.), *The rationalists: theory and design in the modern movement*. London: Architectural Press, 1978.

Sichowsky, Richard von, and Hermann Tiemann (ed.), *Typographie und Bibliophilie*. Hamburg: Maximilian-Gesellschaft, 1971.

[Soldans] *From sketch to type. 1930*. Translation of Bauer'sche Gießerei, *Wie ein Druck-Buchstabe entsteht*.

Speer, Albert, *Inside the Third Reich*. New York: Macmillan, 1970.

Spencer, Herbert, *Pioneers of modern typography*. London: Lund Humphries, 1969.

Spiekermann, Erik, 'Futura – a typeface of its time' in *Type & typographers*. London: Architecture Design and Technology Press, 1991, pp. 84–8.

Stark, Gary, *Entrepreneurs of ideology: neo-conservative publishers in Germany, 1890–1933*. Chapel Hill: University of North Carolina Press, 1981.

Steinberg, S. H. *Five hundred years of printing*. Harmondsworth: Penguin Books, 1955.

—. 'Secret decree reveals Hitler's real attitude to gothic type' in *Printing news*, 9 May 1957, pp. 9–11.

[Stempel] *Chronik der Schriftgießerei D. Stempel AG. Frankfurt A.M: sechzig Jahre im Dienste der Lettern, 1895–1955*.

Stern, Fritz, *The failure of illiberalism*. London: George Allen & Unwin, 1972.

—. *The politics of cultural despair*. Berkeley: University of California Press, 1963.

Stiff, Paul, 'Tschichold's stamp: specification and the modernization of typographic work' in *Printing Historical Society Bulletin*. no. 38, Winter 1994, pp. 18–24.

Stresow, Gustav, 'German typography today' in *The Penrose annual*, 1937, pp. 60–4.

—. 'Paul Renner' in Typographische Gesellschaft München, *Hundert Jahre Typographie*. Munich: TGM, 1990, pp. 67–71.

—. 'Paul Renner und die Konzeption der Futura' in *Buchhandelsgeschichte*, Nr 2, 1995; supplement to *Börsenblatt für den Deutschen Buchhandel*, Nr 51, 27 Juni 1995, pp. B41–51.

—. *Stil und Buch: ein Vortrag*. Munich: Typographische Gesellschaft München, 1989.

Timms, Edward, and Peter Collier (ed.), *Visions and blueprints: avant-garde culture and radical politics in early twentieth-century Europe*. Manchester: Manchester University Press, 1988.

Tracy, Walter, *Letters of credit*. London: Gordon Fraser, 1986.

[Trump, Georg] *Vita activa: Georg Trump; Bilder, Schriften & Schriftbilder*. Munich: Typographische Gesellschaft München, 1967.

Tschichold, Jan, *Asymmetric typography*. Translated by Ruari McLean from *Typographische Gestaltung* (1935). Toronto: Cooper & Beatty / London: Faber & Faber, 1967.

—. 'Elementare Typographie' in *Typographische Mitteilungen*, no. 10, 1925, pp. 191–214. Reprinted in facsimile by The Type Directors Club of New York, 1986.

—. *Leben und Werk des Typographen Jan Tschichold*. Dresden: VEB Verlag der Kunst, 1977.

—. 'New life in print' in *Commercial art*, July 1930, pp. 2–20.

—. 'New typography' in *Circle: international survey of constructive art*. London: Faber & Faber, 1937, pp. 249–50.

—. *The new typography: a handbook for modern designers*. Translated by Ruari McLean from *Die neue Typographie* (1928). Berkeley: University of California Press, 1995.

—. *Schriften 1923–1974*. 2 vols. Berlin: Brinkmann & Bose, 1991/2.

Turner, Henry A., 'Fascism and modernization' in Turner (ed.), *Reappraisals of Fascism*. New York: New Viewpoints, 1975.

Typographische Gesellschaft München, *Hundert Jahre Typographie; Hundert Jahre Typographische Gesellschaft München: eine Chronik*. Munich: TGM, 1990.

Volmer, Nordlunde G., 'Antikvaen har sejret i Tyskland: interessant Artikel af Paul Renner' in *De grafiske fag*, aargang 38, 1942, pp. 347–51.

Waller, Robert, 'Functional information design: research and practice' in *Information design journal*, vol. 1, no. 1, pp. 43–50.

Wetzig, Emil (ed.), *Handbuch der Schriftarten*. Leipzig: Seemann Verlag, 1925.

Whitford, Frank, *Bauhaus*. London: Thames & Hudson, 1984.

Wilkes, Walter, 'Twentieth-century fine printing in Germany' in *Fine print*, vol. 12, no. 2, April 1986, pp. 87–99.

Willberg, Hans Peter, *Schrift im Bauhaus/Die Futura von Paul Renner*. Neu Isenburg: Wolfgang Tiessen, 1969.

—. 'Schrift und Typographie im Dritten Reich' in Typographische Gesellschaft München, *Hundert Jahre Typographie*. Munich: TGM, 1990, pp. 87–103.

—. 'Vom falschen Image der Fraktur' in Kapr, *Fraktur*. Mainz: Verlag Hermann Schmidt, 1993, pp. 101–5.

Willett, John, *The new sobriety 1917–1933: art and politics in the Weimar period*. London: Thames & Hudson, 1978.

—. *The Weimar years: a culture cut short*. London, Thames & Hudson, 1984.

Williams, Raymond, *Keywords: a vocabulary of culture and society*. 2nd edn. London: Fontana, 1983.

Wingler, Hans M. (ed.), *The Bauhaus*. Cambridge, Mass: MIT Press, 1969.

—. (ed.), *Kunstschulreform 1900–1933*. Berlin: Gebr. Mann Verlag, 1977.

Zachrisson, Bror, *Studies in the legibility of printed text*. Stockholm: Almqvist & Wiksell, 1965.

Picture sources

Items illustrated come from libraries, archives, and private collections, including the author's. Thanks to Christian Scheffler, Walter Wilkes, Martin & Renate Haushofer, Eckehart SchumacherGebler, and David Knott for permission to reproduce items in their care. Thanks to Gustav Stresow, Philipp Luidl, Hans Dieter Reichert, Gerard Unger, Max Caflisch, Robin Kinross, and Mathieu Lommen for lending material.

Principal photography by Simon Chaffin Johnson

Index

March 29/07